Better Homes and Gardens®

Minutes to Mealtime

CHICKEN
and Turkey Recipes

BETTER HOMES AND GARDENS® BOOKS
Des Moines, Iowa

BETTER HOMES AND GARDENS® BOOKS
An Imprint of Meredith® Books
President, Book Group: Joseph J. Ward
Vice President and Editorial Director: Elizabeth P. Rice
Executive Editor: Nancy N. Green
Managing Editor: Christopher Cavanaugh
Art Director: Ernest Shelton
Test Kitchen Director: Sharon Stilwell

Minutes to Mealtime: Chicken and Turkey Recipes
Editors: Shelli McConnell and Lisa Mannes
Text and Recipe Writer: Marlene Brown
Associate Art Director: Tom Wegner
Graphic Designer: Linda Vermie
Electronic Production Coordinator: Paula Forest
Test Kitchen Product Supervisors: Diane Nolin and Colleen Weeden
Food Stylists: Lynn Blanchard, Jennifer Peterson, Janet Pittman
Photographers: Mike Dieter, Scott Little
Production Manager: Douglas Johnston

On the cover: Chicken with Polenta, page 285

Meredith Corporation Corporate Officers:
Chairman of the Executive Committee: E. T. Meredith III
Chairman of the Board, President and Chief Executive Officer: Jack D. Rehm
Group Presidents: Joseph J. Ward, Books; William T. Kerr, Magazines; Philip A. Jones, Broadcasting;
    Allen L. Sabbag, Real Estate
Vice Presidents: Leo R. Armatis, Corporate Relations; Thomas G. Fisher, General Counsel and Secretary;
    Larry D. Hartsook, Finance; Michael A. Sell, Treasurer; Kathleen J. Zehr, Controller and Assistant Secretary

WE CARE!

All of us at Better Homes and Gardens® Books are dedicated to providing you with the information
and ideas you need to create tasty foods. We welcome your comments and suggestions. Write us at:
Better Homes and Gardens® Books, Cookbook Editorial Department, RW-240, 1716 Locust Street,
Des Moines, IA 50309-3023

If you would like to order additional copies of any of our books,
call 1-800-678-2803 or check with your local bookstore.

Our seal assures you that every recipe in *Minutes to
Mealtime: Chicken and Turkey Recipes* has been tested in
the Better Homes and Gardens® Test Kitchen. This
means that each recipe is practical and reliable, and meets
our high standards of taste appeal. We guarantee your
satisfaction with this book for as long as you own it.

introduction

Poultry has a very special place on our everyday menus—whether it's being grilled for a family picnic, simmered into a soup, or brought out with fanfare on Thanksgiving Day. Its versatility, great flavor, and nutrient benefits are advantages that can't be equaled. You can buy the whole bird or just your favorite parts—and even have the deli cook it for you. The only challenge left is figuring out what to do with that favorite bird that's fast, different, and great-tasting.

That's where this cookbook comes in. It's a collection of more than 280 chicken and turkey main-dish recipes that are table-ready in 15 minutes, 30 minutes, 45 minutes, or 60 minutes—it's your choice. You'll also find a 60-plus minute chapter with recipes that call for a bit more time—but time well-spent!

We'll help you serve up chicken wings, turkey tenderloins, chicken breasts, or Cornish hens—everything from roasting a chicken to dressing up a sliced turkey breast from the deli. No matter what your taste in poultry, this book will show you where to go from there—deliciously. Throughout this book, you'll find plenty of tips, guidelines, and cooking techniques to let you enjoy what makes poultry so versatile—and so good for you. You'll also find some creative ideas on the new chicken- and turkey-based meat products such as turkey franks, sausage, and luncheon meats.

When time is of the essence, it's nice to know that poultry can be fast food as well as a big-deal-dinner entrée. So if you're staring at that chicken, wondering how to fix it and fix it fast, don't get ruffled—turn the page! A whole new repertoire of great ideas awaits.

contents

basic chicken and turkey information

Follow these simple guidelines for safe handling and storage of fresh poultry.

Refrigerating

Place poultry in the coldest part of your refrigerator. Poultry that is packaged in supermarket trays can be refrigerated in its original wrapping. Uncooked chicken should be refrigerated promptly after it is purchased and then used within 2 days. Cut-up cooked chicken can be stored in the refrigerator for up to 2 days, and whole cooked chicken for up to 3 days. If stuffing a whole bird, do not stuff the bird ahead of time and refrigerate it. Instead, add the stuffing just before cooking the bird.

Freezing

For longer storage, freeze fresh poultry at 0° or below. For individual poultry pieces or cubed poultry, spread the meat on a tray and freeze till firm. Then transfer to freezer bags. Press out air, and seal, label, and freeze. Keep frozen, uncooked whole turkeys or chickens no longer than a year, chicken pieces up to 9 months, and fresh or frozen uncooked turkey pieces up to 6 months. Never freeze stuffed chickens. The stuffing may not reheat to a high enough temperature to kill bacteria that can cause food poisoning.

Thawing

Refrigerator thawing is the best way to thaw poultry. Place poultry in freezer wrapping on a tray in your refrigerator. Allow 5 hours of thawing time for every pound of poultry.

Cold-water thawing is another safe way to thaw poultry. Place poultry in its freezer wrapping in a sink or large bowl of cold water. Allow about 30 minutes of thawing time for every pound of poultry, changing the water every 30 minutes.

Room-temperature thawing is not recommended for poultry or other meats because bacteria that can cause food poisoning thrive at these warm temperatures.

Tips from our Test Kitchen

• Always wash your hands, countertops, and utensils in hot soapy water between each step of food preparation. Bacteria on raw poultry, meat, or fish can contaminate other food that is exposed to the same surfaces.

• When cutting raw poultry, use a plastic cutting board because it is easier to clean than a wooden one. Improperly cleaned wooden cutting boards may retain harmful bacteria that can contaminate other foods and cause food poisoning.

• Never leave poultry out at room temperature for more than 2 hours. Cooked poultry that is not eaten immediately should be kept hot (140° to 165°) or chilled at 40° or less.

• Always thoroughly reheat leftover cooked poultry and gravy before eating (till bubbly, about 185°) for best taste and maximum food safety. Cover the food to retain as much moisture as possible and to thoroughly heat.

Talking Poultry

Get the answers to poultry questions by calling the U.S. Department of Agriculture's Meat and Poultry Hot Line. The toll-free number is 1-800-535-4555. Calls are taken from 10 a.m. to 4 p.m. eastern time Monday through Friday.

cutting up a whole chicken

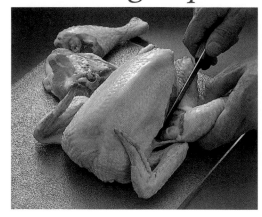

1. To cut up a bird, cut through the skin between the thigh and body. Bend thigh back until hip joint breaks. Cut through joint, separating the leg from the body. To separate the thigh and drumstick, slit the skin above the knee joint, break the joint, then cut apart. Repeat on the other side.

2. To remove a wing, pull it away from the body. Slit the skin between the wing and body. Bend the wing back until the joint breaks. Cut through the joint. Repeat on the other side.

3. With a sharp knife or kitchen shears, cut along the breast end of ribs on one side, cutting toward the neck to separate the breast from the back. Repeat on the other side. Bend front and back halves apart. Cut through neck joints that connect halves.

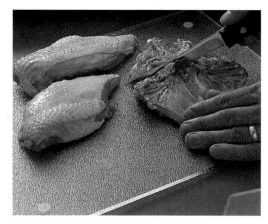

4. To divide the back in half, hold the piece at each end. Bend the ends toward the skin side until the bones break. Cut the back in half where the bones are broken. Cut off the tail.

5. To divide the breast in half, cut lengthwise along breastbone. Or, to divide breast in half crosswise, grasp breast at each end and bend breast toward the skin side to break bones. Cut between the wishbone and the breastbone, as shown.

skinning and boning chicken breasts

1. To skin chicken breasts, place the whole breast, skin side up, on a cutting board. Starting on one side of the breast, use your hand to pull the skin away from the meat. Discard the skin.

2. To bone chicken breasts, cut the meat away from one side of the breastbone, using a thin, sharp knife. Then move the knife over the rib bones, pulling away the meat. Repeat on the other side.

3. To remove the long white tendon from each breast half, hold one end of the tendon with your fingers. Use the tip of the knife to scrape the meat away from the tendon as you pull it out.

testing for doneness

To test chicken for doneness, grasp the end of a drumstick with a paper towel. It should twist easily in the socket. Or, pierce the thigh meat with a fork. The juices should be clear, not pink.

buying guide to chicken parts

Poultry, whether it's chicken, turkey, Cornish game hens, duck, or goose, is one of the best convenience foods around. It comes in all shapes, sizes, and forms, as well as ready-to-cook or ready-to-eat. Whatever bird or form you buy, look for plump, meaty birds or parts with clean, smooth skin in unbroken packages with no off-odors.

Your market deli may offer cooked whole chickens or chicken parts, such as the breast, thigh with drumstick attached, wings, or a sliced cooked chicken or turkey breast. Some stores offer a variety of flavors, such as herbed or barbecued poultry.

Cut-up birds in a package may contain the thighs with the drumstick attached or the breast with the wing attached. To cut them apart, squeeze the thigh and drumstick together to find the knee joint; cut through the knee joint. To remove the wing, cut on the inside of the wing, down and around the joint.

The most popular chicken parts sold include the thigh (above left), the breast (above right) and the drumstick (above bottom). Often these parts are available without the skin, and skinned and boned.

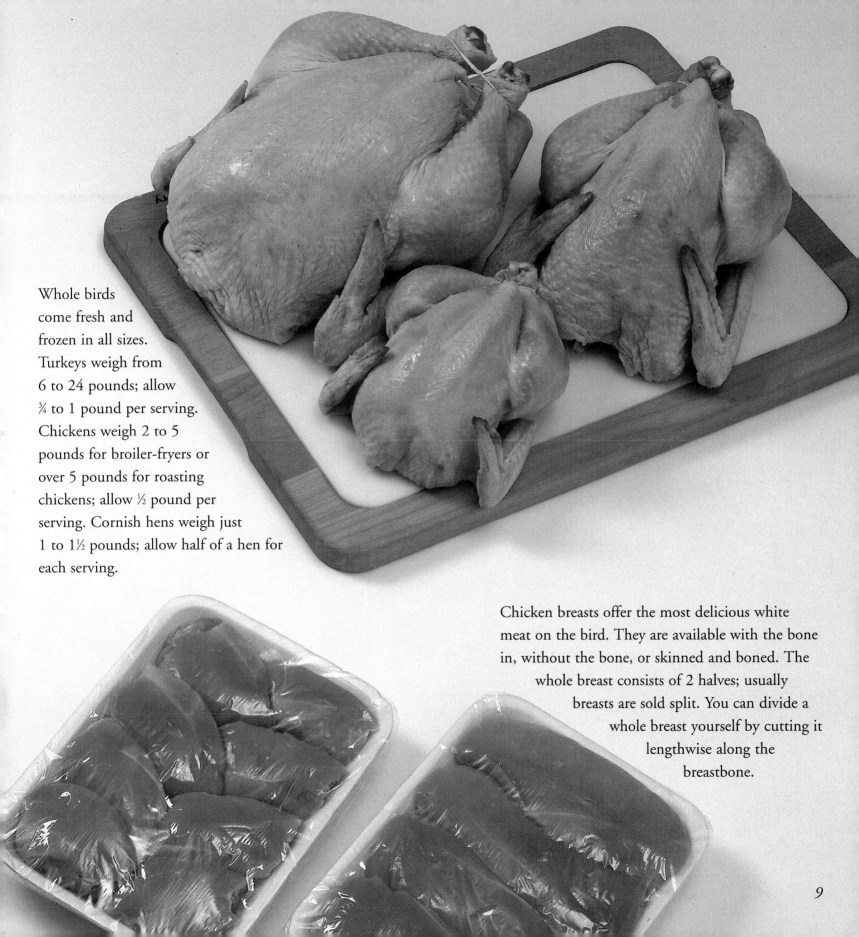

Whole birds
come fresh and
frozen in all sizes.
Turkeys weigh from
6 to 24 pounds; allow
¾ to 1 pound per serving.
Chickens weigh 2 to 5
pounds for broiler-fryers or
over 5 pounds for roasting
chickens; allow ½ pound per
serving. Cornish hens weigh just
1 to 1½ pounds; allow half of a hen for
each serving.

Chicken breasts offer the most delicious white
meat on the bird. They are available with the bone
in, without the bone, or skinned and boned. The
whole breast consists of 2 halves; usually
breasts are sold split. You can divide a
whole breast yourself by cutting it
lengthwise along the
breastbone.

buying guide to turkey parts

There's no need to buy a whole turkey; you can purchase just your favorite parts. There's no waste and you can cook these in a minimum of time just as you would the chicken counterparts. Shown below is the turkey breast tenderloin (top) and the turkey breast tenderloin steak (bottom).

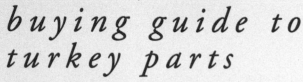

Lean ground turkey may be all dark or all light meat or a mixture with some skin. Ground turkey sausage, made from turkey processed to give it a sausage flavor, is available ground or in links.

You'll find prepackaged sliced turkey meat products in the luncheon meat section of the dairy counter or ready-to-slice at the deli counter. Look for sliced turkey, turkey pastrami, turkey bologna, turkey ham, or turkey salami.

Pre-cooked turkey breast is found at the grocery meat counter or the in-store deli. Available seasoned and unseasoned, salted and unsalted, or even barbecued or smoked, turkey can be bought whole, in pieces, or sliced.

Domestic, or farm-raised, turkeys are specially bred to be plump and juicy and are noted for having a large amount of white meat. Whole turkeys can be purchased fresh or frozen, unbasted or prebasted.

All dark meat turkey parts include the thighs, that, with the bone, weigh ½ pound to 1½ pounds each. Drumsticks with the bone weigh ½ pound to 1½ pounds each. Allow ½ pound per serving with bone or ¼ to ⅓ pound without the bone.

Both chicken and turkey franks in a variety of flavors are available in the luncheon meat section. Their appearance and special seasonings make them hard to distinguish from the all-beef products. Use them as you would standard franks.

broiled turkey with tropical fruit salsa

4 turkey breast tenderloin steaks (about ½-inch thick) or
    skinless, boneless chicken breast halves
    (about 1 pound total)
    Olive oil or cooking oil
    Salt
    Pepper
1 16-ounce can tropical fruit salad, drained and
    chopped
2 tablespoons lime juice
1 green onion, sliced
1 teaspoon finely chopped jalapeño or mild
    green chili peppers

Preheat broiler. Rinse turkey or chicken; pat dry. Place on the unheated rack of a broiler pan. Brush with oil. Broil 4 to 5 inches from the heat for 5 minutes. Turn and brush with oil; season with salt and pepper. Broil for 4 to 6 minutes more or till tender and no longer pink.

Meanwhile, for salsa, in a medium bowl stir together drained fruit, lime juice, onion, and chili peppers. Serve turkey slices topped with salsa. If desired, garnish with slices of kiwi fruit and carambola (star fruit) and serve with hot cooked rice. Makes 4 servings.

Preheat the broiler unit before cooking but don't preheat the broiler pan and rack. Often, preheating the pan and rack causes them to warp and poultry pieces will stick to the rack.

Per serving: 227 calories, 22 g protein, 22 g carbohydrate, 6 g total fat (1 g saturated), 50 mg cholesterol, 181 mg sodium, 359 mg potassium

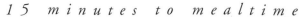

skillet chicken alfredo

1 10-ounce package frozen broccoli or asparagus spears
12 ounces skinless, boneless chicken breast halves or
    turkey breast tenderloins
1 tablespoon cooking oil
1 10- or 12-ounce container Alfredo pasta sauce
4 English muffins or bagels, split and toasted
¼ teaspoon coarsely ground pepper (optional)

Cook broccoli or asparagus according to package directions; drain and keep warm. Meanwhile, rinse chicken or turkey; pat dry. With a sharp knife cut chicken or turkey crosswise into ½-inch strips.

In a large skillet cook chicken in hot oil over medium-high heat for 3 to 4 minutes or till tender and no longer pink. Drain off fat. Stir in pasta sauce. Simmer 2 to 3 minutes or till sauce is heated through. Place toasted muffin or bagel halves on plates. Arrange broccoli spears atop. Spoon chicken and sauce over all. If desired, sprinkle with pepper. Makes 4 servings.

If you want to season poultry for pan-frying or broiled recipes, try rubbing the seasoning, such as salt or pepper, right into the chicken or turkey rather than sprinkling it on. Or, for a salt-free version, try garlic or lemon or lime juice.

Per serving: 520 calories, 27 g protein, 38 g carbohydrate, 29 g total fat (1 g saturated), 80 mg cholesterol, 730 mg sodium, 623 mg potassium

quick chicken oriental

12 ounces skinless, boneless chicken breast halves or
   turkey breast tenderloins

⅓ cup chicken broth or orange juice

2 tablespoons soy sauce

2 teaspoons cornstarch

1 teaspoon brown sugar

½ teaspoon ground ginger

1 tablespoon cooking oil

1 16-ounce package fresh cut-up Oriental stir-fry
   vegetables or one 16-ounce package frozen vegetable
   combination, thawed and drained

   Hot cooked rice

Rinse chicken or turkey; pat dry. Cut into ¼-inch
strips. In a small bowl stir together broth or juice, soy
sauce, cornstarch, brown sugar, and ginger; set aside.

Pour the cooking oil into wok or large skillet. (Add
more oil as necessary during cooking.) Preheat over
medium-high heat. Add fresh or thawed Oriental
vegetables; stir-fry for 2 to 3 minutes or till crisp-tender.
Remove vegetables. Add the chicken to the hot wok. Stir-
fry for 2 to 3 minutes till tender and no longer pink. Push
chicken from the center. Stir sauce. Add sauce to the
center. Cook and stir till thickened and bubbly.

Return the cooked vegetables to the wok. Stir all
ingredients together to coat with sauce. Cook and stir
about 1 minute more or till heated through. Serve
immediately with hot cooked rice. Makes 4 servings.

Per serving: 374 calories, 30 g protein, 39 g carbohydrate, 10 g total fat (2 g saturated),
76 mg cholesterol, 642 mg sodium, 512 mg potassium

hoisin-broiled chicken with cashews

4 skinless, boneless chicken breast halves or turkey breast
   tenderloin steaks (about 1 pound total)

3 tablespoons hoisin sauce

⅓ cup cashew halves and pieces

2 green onions, sliced

1 tablespoon sesame seed

1 tablespoon peanut oil or cooking oil
   Hot cooked rice (optional)

Preheat broiler. Rinse chicken or turkey; pat dry.
Arrange chicken or turkey on unheated rack of a broiler
pan. Brush with hoisin sauce. Broil 4 to 5 inches from the
heat for 5 minutes; turn and brush with sauce. Broil for
4 to 6 minutes more or till tender and no longer pink.

Meanwhile, in a small skillet cook cashews, onions,
and sesame seed in oil about 3 minutes, stirring
constantly, till nuts are golden brown. Remove from heat;
spoon mixture over chicken breasts just before serving. If
desired, serve over hot cooked rice. Makes 4 servings.

Hoisin, or Chinese catsup, is a wonderful Oriental condiment that lends a far-Eastern flavor to any type of poultry. Next time, mix it half and half with barbecue sauce for a flavor twist.

Per serving: 222 calories, 24 g protein, 3 g carbohydrate, 12 g total fat (3 g saturated),
59 mg cholesterol, 345 mg sodium, 247 mg potassium

mustard-puff chicken

4 skinless, boneless chicken breasts halves
    (about 1 pound total)
⅓ cup mayonnaise or salad dressing
1 tablespoon Dijon-style mustard
1 tablespoon sliced green onion
   Dash ground red pepper

Preheat broiler. Rinse chicken; pat dry. Place chicken on the unheated rack of a broiler pan. Broil 4 to 5 inches from the heat for 5 minutes. Meanwhile, in a small bowl stir together mayonnaise or salad dressing, mustard, green onion, and pepper. Turn chicken; brush liberally with mayonnaise mixture. Broil for 4 to 6 minutes more or till chicken is tender and no longer pink. If desired, serve with green beans. Makes 4 servings.

Want to conserve calories and fat? Use a small sharp knife to trim the thin rim of fat from the chicken breasts. Try the nonfat mayonnaise salad dressing instead of regular mayonnaise. Serve with your favorite steamed vegetable.

Per serving: 256 calories, 22 g protein, 1 g carbohydrate, 18 g total fat (3 g saturated), 70 mg cholesterol, 252 mg sodium, 187 mg potassium

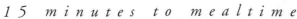

all-american chicken burgers

4 skinless, boneless chicken breast halves
    (about 1 pound total)
4 slices onion, cut ¼ inch thick
¼ cup barbecue sauce
4 onion rolls or mini hoagie buns, split
    Lettuce leaves
8 thin tomato slices

Preheat broiler. Rinse chicken; pat dry. Place chicken and onion slices on the unheated rack of a broiler pan. Brush with barbecue sauce. Broil 4 to 5 inches from the heat for 5 minutes; turn and brush again with barbecue sauce. Broil for 4 to 6 minutes more or till chicken is tender and no longer pink.

Place lettuce and tomato slices on bottoms of buns. Add chicken breast and an onion slice separated into rings; replace bun tops. If desired, serve with additional barbecue sauce. Makes 4 servings.

To halve a whole chicken breast, cut lengthwise along breastbone. Or, divide crosswise by grasping breast at each end, then bending breast toward the skin side to break bones. Cut between wishbone and breastbone.

Per serving: 438 calories, 31 g protein, 61 g carbohydrate, 7 g total fat (2 g saturated), 59 mg cholesterol, 756 mg sodium, 407 mg potassium

sautéed chicken in green peppercorn sauce

4 skinless, boneless chicken breast halves
    (about 1 pound total)
1 shallot, peeled and chopped, or 1 green onion, sliced
1 teaspoon bottled minced garlic
2 tablespoons cooking oil
⅓ cup dry white wine
⅔ cup whipping cream
2 teaspoons drained green peppercorns
1 teaspoon seasoned salt
¼ teaspoon pepper
    Hot cooked pasta (optional)

Rinse chicken; pat dry. Slice chicken breast halves in half horizontally to make 8 slices. In a 12-inch skillet cook and stir shallot and garlic in hot oil for 1 minute. Add chicken slices; cook over medium-high heat for 3 to 4 minutes or till tender and no longer pink, turning once. Remove chicken from pan; cover and keep warm. Stir wine into skillet, scraping up browned bits from pan. Bring to boiling; reduce heat and simmer 2 minutes. Slowly stir in cream; add peppercorns, seasoned salt, and pepper. Cook and stir over medium heat for 3 minutes more or till slightly thickened; pour over chicken and serve immediately. If desired, serve with hot cooked pasta. Makes 4 servings.

Green peppercorns come packed in brine or water, or may be dried. They have a milder flavor and less of a bite than does black pepper.

Per serving: 339 calories, 23 g protein, 3 g carbohydrate, 25 g total fat (11 g saturated), 114 mg cholesterol, 388 mg sodium, 249 mg potassium

brandied chicken breasts with mushrooms

4 skinless, boneless chicken breast halves
   (about 1 pound total)
1 teaspoon bottled minced garlic
2 tablespoons cooking oil
¼ cup chicken broth or water
2 4-ounce cans sliced mushrooms, drained
3 tablespoons brandy
¾ cup whipping cream
1 tablespoon all-purpose flour
   Hot cooked pasta

Rinse chicken; pat dry. In a 12-inch skillet cook chicken and garlic in hot oil over medium-high heat about 3 minutes per side till chicken is lightly browned and no longer pink.

Add broth or water; bring to boiling. Reduce heat; cover and simmer for 3 minutes. Remove chicken to warm platter. Add mushrooms and brandy to skillet; bring to boiling. Stir cream into flour; add to skillet. Cook and stir till mixture thickens; cook and stir 1 minute more. Pour sauce over chicken. Serve with pasta. If desired, garnish with snipped parsley. Makes 4 servings.

Vary the "taste" by using a flavored brand, such as blackberry, apricot, or apple brandy, sometimes called "applejack."

Per serving: 498 calories, 28 g protein, 29 g carbohydrate, 27 g total fat (12 g saturated), 121 mg cholesterol, 361 mg sodium, 325 mg potassium

broiled chicken with feta cheese

4 skinless, boneless chicken breast halves
(about 1 pound total)
2 tablespoons Italian salad dressing
½ cup crumbled feta cheese or blue cheese (2 ounces)
8 slices sourdough bread or 4 hamburger buns
(toasted, if desired)
Lettuce leaves
1 tablespoon snipped fresh parsley or 1 teaspoon dried
parsley, crushed

Preheat broiler. Rinse chicken; pat dry. Place chicken on the unheated rack of broiler pan. Brush with *half* of the Italian dressing. Broil 4 to 5 inches from the heat for 5 minutes; turn and brush with remaining Italian dressing. Broil 4 to 6 minutes more or till chicken is tender and no longer pink. Sprinkle cheese evenly over chicken; return to broiler just till cheese melts. Line bread slices or burger buns with lettuce; top with chicken. Sprinkle parsley over. Makes 4 servings.

Here's an easy broiling tip: when broiling chicken (or other meats as well), use some tongs for turning parts as they cook. Using a fork will pierce the meat and cause the succulent juice to flow out, taking flavor and moistness with it.

Per serving: 380 calories, 31 g protein, 29 g carbohydrate, 15 g total fat (6 g saturated), 88 mg cholesterol, 773 mg sodium, 286 mg potassium

quick chicken strips

6 ounces medium noodles

4 skinless, boneless chicken breast halves or turkey breast
   tenderloin steaks (about 1 pound total)

1 beaten egg

1 tablespoon Dijon-style mustard

1 tablespoon water

¼ cup all-purpose flour

½ cup fine dry seasoned bread crumbs

2 tablespoons cooking oil

4 tablespoons margarine or butter

2 tablespoons snipped fresh parsley

¼ teaspoon lemon-pepper seasoning
   Lemon wedges

Prepare noodles according to package directions.
Meanwhile, rinse chicken or turkey; pat dry. Halve
chicken breast halves lengthwise to form 8 strips. In a
shallow bowl stir together egg, mustard, and water. Place
flour in a second bowl and the bread crumbs in another
bowl. Coat chicken pieces in flour, then dip in egg
mixture, then in bread crumbs to coat well.

In a 12-inch skillet cook chicken in hot oil and
2 tablespoons of the margarine over medium-high heat
about 6 minutes, turning once, till tender and no longer
pink. Drain noodles; toss with remaining margarine,
parsley, and lemon-pepper seasoning. Serve noodles with
chicken; squeeze lemon wedges atop chicken. If desired,
garnish with parsley sprigs. Makes 4 servings.

Per serving: 454 calories, 32 g protein, 44 g carbohydrate, 16 g total fat (3 g saturated),
149 mg cholesterol, 679 mg sodium, 267 mg potassium

balsamic chicken with zucchini

2 tablespoons Italian salad dressing

1 tablespoon balsamic or red wine vinegar

⅛ to ¼ teaspoon crushed red pepper

4 skinless, boneless chicken breast halves
   (about 1 pound total)

2 tablespoons cooking oil

2 medium zucchini, sliced lengthwise into
   ¼-inch-thick slices

1 small tomato, chopped (optional)

In a small bowl stir together salad dressing, vinegar, and red pepper; set aside. Rinse chicken; pat dry. Slice chicken breast halves in half horizontally to make 8 slices.

In a 12-inch skillet cook chicken in hot oil over medium-high heat for 3 to 4 minutes or till tender and no longer pink, turning once. Remove from pan; cover and keep warm. Add zucchini to pan; cook about 3 minutes till crisp-tender. Transfer to serving platter. Stir dressing mixture and drizzle over chicken and zucchini. If desired, garnish with chopped tomato. Makes 4 servings.

To brown chicken, be sure the oil is hot before you add the chicken to the pan. Separate the pieces in your skillet so they're not touching; they'll brown instead of steaming.

Per serving: 227 calories, 22 g protein, 3 g carbohydrate, 14 g total fat (2 g saturated), 59 mg cholesterol, 114 mg sodium, 295 mg potassium

easy chicken and vegetable stir-fry

1 3-ounce can chow mein noodles or rice noodles
2 tablespoons soy sauce
1 tablespoon apricot or peach jam or preserves
1 tablespoon vinegar
1 teaspoon cornstarch
12 ounces skinless, boneless chicken thighs or skinless, boneless chicken breast halves
1 tablespoon cooking oil
3 cups loose-pack frozen broccoli, French green beans, onions, and red pepper

Preheat oven to 350°. Pour chow mein noodles or rice noodles onto an ungreased baking pan; heat in oven for 5 minutes. Meanwhile, for sauce, in a small bowl stir together soy sauce, jam, vinegar, and cornstarch; set aside.

Rinse chicken; pat dry. Cut into 1-inch pieces. Pour cooking oil into a wok or large skillet. (Add more oil as necessary during cooking.) Preheat over medium-high heat. Add frozen vegetables; stir-fry for 2 to 3 minutes or till crisp-tender. Remove vegetables. Add the chicken to the hot wok. Stir-fry for 3 to 4 minutes or till no longer pink. Push chicken from the center. Stir sauce. Add sauce to the center. Cook and stir till thickened and bubbly.

Return the cooked vegetables to the wok. Stir all ingredients together to coat with sauce. Cook and stir about 1 minute more or till heated through. Serve immediately over the noodles. Makes 4 servings.

Per serving: 394 calories, 19 g protein, 34 g carbohydrate, 20 g total fat (4 g saturated), 41 mg cholesterol, 842 mg sodium, 303 mg potassium

garlic chicken pasta

1 9-ounce package refrigerated fresh linguine

2 cups loose-pack frozen cut broccoli

8 cups boiling water

⅓ cup chopped walnuts

2 to 3 teaspoons bottled minced garlic

2 tablespoons margarine or butter

1 9-ounce package frozen chopped cooked chicken, thawed (2 cups) or two 5-ounce cans chunk-style chicken, drained and flaked

1 tablespoon chopped fresh basil or 1 teaspoon dried basil, crushed

¼ teaspoon lemon-pepper seasoning or pepper

⅓ cup grated Parmesan or Romano cheese

In a large saucepan cook linguine and broccoli in the boiling water for 3 minutes. Meanwhile, in a small skillet cook walnuts and garlic in margarine or butter over medium heat for 2 minutes, stirring constantly. Stir in chicken, basil, and lemon-pepper seasoning; heat through. Drain pasta and broccoli; turn into serving dish. Add chicken mixture and Parmesan cheese; toss well. Serve immediately. Makes 4 servings.

You can have pasta with vegetables quickly and easily, as shown here. Simply add vegetables to the boiling pasta so they'll be nearly tender when the pasta is done.

Per serving: 511 calories, 34 g protein, 47 g carbohydrate, 21 g total fat (5 g saturated), 119 mg cholesterol, 367 mg sodium, 360 mg potassium

easy six-ingredient salad

4 cups purchased torn mixed greens for salads

1 16-ounce can julienne beets, drained

1 15-ounce can garbanzo beans, kidney beans, or black beans, rinsed and drained

4 ounces cooked chicken breast

1 cup pre-shredded cheddar, Monterey Jack, or Swiss cheese (4 ounces)

1 8-ounce bottle creamy salad dressing (any flavor)

In a deep, narrow 2-quart salad bowl arrange in layers the greens, drained beets, and drained beans. Dice chicken breast; sprinkle evenly over beans. Top with a layer of cheese. Spoon salad dressing evenly over top of salad. Toss salad at the table just before serving. Makes 4 servings.

This recipe is a quick adaptation of the classic make-ahead "24-hour salad." Actually, you can cover and chill this salad to serve the next day because the dressing layer on the top helps keep the salad fresh.

Per serving: 513 calories, 21 g protein, 36 g carbohydrate, 33 g total fat (10 g saturated), 68 mg cholesterol, 1,309 mg sodium, 594 mg potassium

chicken and bean tacos

8 taco shells or 6-inch flour tortillas

1 3⅛-ounce can bean dip

6 ounces sliced fully cooked chicken breast or turkey breast

2 cups shredded lettuce or purchased torn mixed greens for salads

1 2¼-ounce can sliced pitted ripe olives, drained

1 cup pre-shredded cheddar or Monterey Jack cheese
Chunky salsa (optional)
Dairy sour cream (optional)

Preheat oven to 375°. Wrap taco shells or tortillas in foil; place on a baking sheet. Heat for 5 minutes. Heat bean dip according to directions on can. Meanwhile, stack chicken or turkey slices; roll up. Cut roll crosswise into 8 pieces; shred slightly with fingers.

To assemble tacos, spread 1 to 2 tablespoons bean dip in the bottom of taco shell; top with lettuce. Add chicken pieces, olives, and cheese. (If using tortillas, lay tortilla on a flat surface; sprinkle ingredients down center. Fold sides over filling.) If desired, serve tacos topped with salsa and sour cream. Makes 4 servings.

You can make these tacos ahead without the lettuce, and using soft tortillas. Wrap in foil and chill. Then at serving time, heat them in a 350° oven till warmed through.

Per serving: 340 calories, 24 g protein, 18 g carbohydrate, 20 g total fat (8 g saturated), 67 mg cholesterol, 478 mg sodium, 297 mg potassium

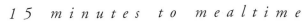

cream of chicken-vegetable soup

2 cups loose-pack frozen cut broccoli or cut asparagus
1 cup chicken broth
1¾ cups whipping cream, half-and-half, or light cream
1 teaspoon dried basil, crushed
⅛ teaspoon ground nutmeg
⅛ teaspoon pepper
6 ounces sliced fully cooked chicken breast
  Pimiento pieces (optional)

Run cold water over vegetables to thaw slightly. Drain well. In a blender container or food processor bowl blend or process broth with vegetables until pureed. Transfer mixture to a medium saucepan. Stir in cream, basil, nutmeg, and pepper. Bring mixture just to boiling. Meanwhile, cut up chicken breast. Add to soup; heat through. If desired, garnish with pieces of pimiento. Makes 4 servings.

If you have frozen loosepack vegetables and cooked or canned chicken handy, you have the basis for a quick and easy soup. Puree the vegetable, add a liquid such as broth or milk, and heat with the chicken. Season to taste and voilà—hot soup!

Per serving: 452 calories, 17 g protein, 7 g carbohydrate, 40 g total fat (24 g saturated), 176 mg cholesterol, 280 mg sodium, 344 mg potassium

open-face brie-pepper sandwiches

- 4 large slices sourdough bread
- 1 tablespoon olive oil
- 6 ounces sliced fully cooked smoked turkey or chicken breast
- 1 7-ounce jar roasted red sweet peppers, drained and cut into strips
- 4 ounces brie or creamy havarti cheese, thinly sliced
- ½ teaspoon dried basil, crushed

Preheat broiler. Place bread slices on unheated rack of a broiler pan. Brush the oil over bread slices to coat lightly. Broil 4 to 5 inches from heat for 1 to 2 minutes or till lightly toasted. Top with turkey or chicken slices, pepper pieces, then cheese slices. Sprinkle basil over sandwiches.

Broil 4 to 5 inches from the heat for 2 to 3 minutes or till cheese is melted. Halve sandwiches diagonally. Serve immediately. Makes 4 servings.

To save time, slice the cheese and peppers while the broiler preheats and the bread is toasting.

Per serving: 245 calories, 17 g protein, 16 g carbohydrate, 13 g total fat (6 g saturated), 46 mg cholesterol, 758 mg sodium, 267 mg potassium

chicken salad with black beans and corn

4 cups purchased torn mixed greens for salads

1 15-ounce can black beans, rinsed and drained

1 11-ounce can whole kernel corn with sweet peppers, drained

6 ounces sliced fully cooked smoked chicken or turkey breast, cut into strips (about 1 cup)

½ cup thinly sliced red onion

⅓ to ½ cup creamy garlic, Italian, or red wine vinegar and oil salad dressing

1 medium tomato, cut into thin wedges (optional)

In a large bowl combine greens, black beans, and corn. Add chicken or turkey to salad with onion. Pour dressing over salad as desired; toss. If desired, garnish with tomato wedges. Makes 4 servings.

Your supermarket salad bar is a wonderful source for conveniently pre-washed and pre-cut greens and vegetables as well as hard-cooked eggs, shrimp, and condiments. Grab your favorites for a super-quick homemade salad.

Per serving: 299 calories, 17 g protein, 35 g carbohydrate, 13 g total fat (3 g saturated), 31 mg cholesterol, 1,035 mg sodium, 600 mg potassium

turkey-mac dogs

4 frankfurter or hamburger buns, split
2 tablespoons margarine or butter
   Lettuce leaves
4 slices American cheese, halved (4 ounces)
6 ounces sliced fully cooked turkey breast and/or turkey
   bologna
1⅓ cups purchased macaroni salad

Spread frankfurter or hamburger buns with margarine
or butter. Line bottom halves of buns with lettuce leaves.
Layer cheese slices on top of lettuce. Fold turkey slices;
place on top of cheese. Top each sandwich with ⅓ *cup* of
the macaroni salad. Add bun tops. Cut sandwiches in half
crosswise; if desired, secure with wooden picks or party
picks. Makes 4 servings.

Ready-made deli salads are ideal for quick side dishes, condiments, or in this case, sandwich dressings. Try carrot-raisin salad, fruited coleslaw, red-skinned potato salad, and other varieties offered.

Per serving: 465 calories, 22 g protein, 37 g carbohydrate, 26 g total fat
(8 g saturated), 37 mg cholesterol, 1,455 mg sodium, 319 mg potassium

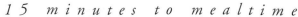

chicken antipasto salad

Lettuce leaves
8 ounces sliced fully cooked chicken or turkey breast
1 16-ounce can three-bean salad, drained
1 6-ounce jar marinated artichoke hearts
½ cup pitted ripe olives, drained
8 cherry tomatoes

Line four dinner plates with lettuce leaves. Roll each chicken or turkey slice; divide among the plates. Spoon three-bean salad on each plate. Drain artichoke hearts, reserving marinade (about ¼ *cup*); arrange artichokes, olives, and tomatoes on each plate. Drizzle reserved artichoke marinade over salads. (If desired, use 1 tablespoon *Italian salad dressing* per salad instead of the artichoke marinade.) Makes 4 servings.

With chicken in the fridge or freezer and a well-stocked pantry, you'll have the fixings for fast appetizers, salads, and main dishes like this one. Line a pretty platter with lettuce to show off this appealing creation.

Per serving: 258 calories, 21 g protein, 26 g carbohydrate, 10 g total fat (1 g saturated), 51 mg cholesterol, 654 mg sodium, 493 mg potassium

deli-melt sandwiches

4 slices sourdough or other bread, toasted

2 tablespoons mayonnaise or salad dressing

8 ounces sliced fully cooked turkey ham, chicken breast, or turkey breast

4 teaspoons prepared mustard

8 thin slices tomato

4 slices provolone, muenster, cheddar, Monterey Jack, or Swiss cheese (4 ounces)

Preheat broiler. Place bread slices on the unheated rack of a broiler pan; spread with mayonnaise or salad dressing. Layer turkey ham, chicken, or turkey slices over bread; spread with mustard. Top each sandwich with tomato slices; lay cheese slices over each sandwich to cover. Broil 4 to 5 inches from the heat for about 2 minutes or till cheese is melted. Serve immediately. Makes 4 servings.

You can freeze cooked chicken or turkey that is not in broth or gravy for up to one month. Wrap the meat in freezer wrap or freezer bags, pressing out as much air as possible. Then, label and date the packages before freezing.

Per serving: 302 calories, 21 g protein, 17 g carbohydrate, 16 g total fat (7 g saturated), 74 mg cholesterol, 1,153 mg sodium, 329 mg potassium

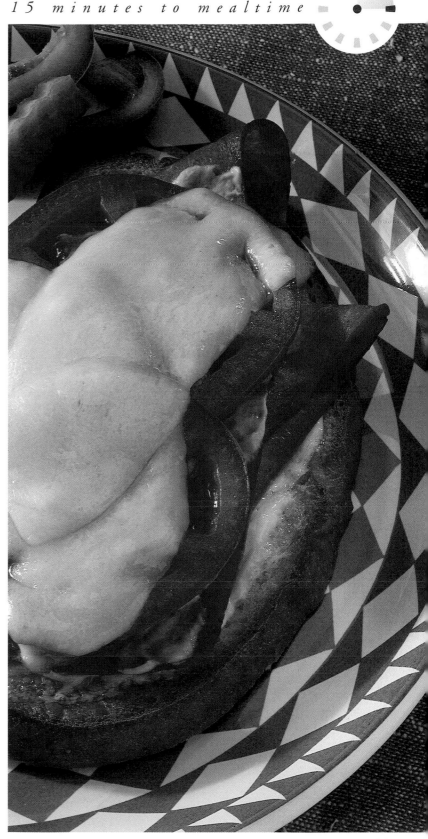

cajun-style chicken-egg scramble

1 14½-ounce can Cajun-style stewed tomatoes
4 eggs
¼ cup milk
⅛ teaspoon salt
⅛ teaspoon ground red or black pepper
½ cup chopped green or red sweet pepper
2 tablespoons margarine or butter
1 cup chopped cooked chicken
3 or 4 English muffins, split and toasted
    Bottled hot pepper sauce (optional)

In a small saucepan heat tomatoes to boiling, stirring occasionally; keep warm. Meanwhile, in a medium bowl beat eggs with milk, salt, and ground pepper. In a large skillet cook sweet pepper in margarine over medium heat for 3 minutes or till tender. Stir in chicken; pour egg mixture over all. Cook, without stirring, till mixture begins to set on the bottom and around the edge.

Using a large spoon or spatula, lift and fold partially cooked eggs so uncooked portion flows underneath. Continue cooking over medium heat for 2 to 3 minutes or till eggs are cooked throughout but are still glossy and moist. Remove skillet from heat immediately. Spoon mixture over toasted English muffins; top with stewed tomatoes. If desired, serve with bottled hot pepper sauce. Makes 3 or 4 servings.

Per serving: 472 calories, 30 g protein, 42 g carbohydrate, 20 g total fat (5 g saturated), 331 mg cholesterol, 1,208 mg sodium, 1,029 mg potassium

broccoli and chicken fettuccine alfredo

1 9-ounce package refrigerated fresh fettuccine pasta

1½ cups loose-pack frozen cut broccoli

8 cups boiling water

6 ounces boneless fully cooked smoked chicken or turkey breast

1 10- or 12-ounce container Alfredo pasta sauce

1 teaspoon dried basil, crushed
   Grated Parmesan or Romano cheese (optional)

In a large saucepan cook pasta and broccoli in the boiling water for 3 minutes. Meanwhile, chop chicken. In a medium saucepan heat together the Alfredo sauce, chicken, and basil just till heated through (do not boil). Drain pasta and broccoli; toss with sauce. If desired, serve with grated Parmesan or Romano cheese. Makes 4 servings.

With the fresh refrigerated pastas and pasta sauces available in your supermarket dairy section, you can concoct a number of variations of this easy dish. Substitute other colorful vegetables for the broccoli or use leftover cooked vegetables.

Per serving: 501 calories, 23 g protein, 49 g carbohydrate, 24 g total fat (0 g saturated), 126 mg cholesterol, 711 mg sodium, 215 mg potassium

fettuccine and chicken al pesto

1   9-ounce package refrigerated fresh fettuccine
2   purchased broiled or roasted chicken breast halves
1   7-ounce container refrigerated pesto
¼   cup chicken broth
2   plum-shaped tomatoes, chopped
    Freshly ground pepper

In a large saucepan cook pasta according to package directions. Meanwhile, remove bones from chicken pieces; cut meat into bite-size strips. Drain pasta; return to hot saucepan. Toss with chicken, pesto, and chicken broth. Heat through. Spoon onto serving plates; sprinkle with chopped tomatoes. Serve with freshly ground pepper. Makes 3 or 4 servings.

When buying deli-cooked chicken pieces, for safety's sake make certain that the pieces you buy are fully-chilled or very hot and sold in a "hot" or foil-lined food bag. Get them home and use immediately or refrigerate.

Per serving: 631 calories, 29 g protein, 45 g carbohydrate, 37 g total fat (1 g saturated), 55 mg cholesterol, 470 mg sodium, 285 mg potassium

chicken and avocado croissants

4 purchased broiled or roasted chicken breast halves

1 ripe medium avocado, halved, seeded, and peeled

2 teaspoons lemon juice

¼ teaspoon dried basil, crushed

4 croissants, split

2 teaspoons Dijon-style mustard

1 small tomato, thinly sliced

¼ to ½ teaspoon seasoned salt

Remove skin and bones from chicken breasts; slice meat. Mash avocado; stir in lemon juice and basil. Spread bottom halves of croissants with mustard, then avocado mixture. Top with chicken and tomato slices. Sprinkle with seasoned salt. Add croissant tops; if desired, halve sandwiches crosswise. Makes 4 servings.

Ripe avocadoes lend a nice flavor to this sandwich. To purchase an avocado that's ideal for mashing, look for fruit that is no longer firm but not yet mushy. Roll a ripe avocado between your palms; it should feel soft to the touch.

Per serving: 350 calories, 28 g protein, 13 g carbohydrate, 21 g total fat (5 g saturated), 105 mg cholesterol, 361 mg sodium, 631 mg potassium

chicken, spinach, and avocado toss

1 10-ounce package spinach, torn or torn mixed greens
   for salads
3 purchased broiled or roasted chicken breast halves
1 ripe medium avocado, halved, seeded, peeled,
   and cubed
⅓ cup cooked bacon pieces
⅔ cup Italian, Caesar, French, or Ranch salad dressing

Place spinach or mixed salad greens in a large bowl.
Remove bones from chicken breasts; cut meat into ¼-inch
strips. Add chicken, avocado cubes, and bacon pieces to
spinach or salad greens. Pour salad dressing over salad;
toss to coat well. Makes 4 servings.

For a wilted version of this salad, fry bacon in a skillet till crisp; remove from pan. Crumble the bacon, then toss the spinach in the hot pan drippings for 1 to 2 minutes till wilted. Add remaining ingredients with 1/3 cup of the dressing; toss.

Per serving: 418 calories, 26 g protein, 8 g carbohydrate, 33 g total fat (4 g saturated),
64 mg cholesterol, 663 mg sodium, 883 mg potassium

chicken and pasta with red pesto

½ of a 9-ounce package refrigerated fresh linguini

1 4-ounce jar roasted red sweet peppers, drained

½ cup mayonnaise or salad dressing

2 teaspoons lemon juice

1 teaspoon bottled minced garlic

⅛ teaspoon ground red pepper

3 purchased broiled or roasted chicken breast halves
Grated Parmesan or Romano cheese

In a large saucepan cook linguine according to package directions. Meanwhile, in blender container or food processor bowl process drained red peppers with mayonnaise, lemon juice, garlic, and ground red pepper till pureed. Remove bones from chicken breasts; cut meat into bite-size pieces. Drain pasta; toss with red pepper puree and chicken. Pass Parmesan or Romano cheese with pasta. If desired, garnish with parsley sprigs. Makes 3 or 4 servings.

For easy variations on the pesto sauce, puree cooked vegetables like zucchini, sweet peppers, or carrots with herbs, mayonnaise, lemon juice, garlic, and some Parmesan cheese. Fantastic!

Per serving: 601 calories, 33 g protein, 32 g carbohydrate, 38 g total fat (7 g saturated), 137 mg cholesterol, 368 mg sodium, 318 mg potassium

chicken poor-boys

4 French or poor-boy sandwich rolls, split
  Mayonnaise or salad dressing
  Shredded lettuce
3 purchased broiled or roasted chicken breast halves
8 slices green or red sweet pepper
4 slices red onion
4 slices American, Swiss, cheddar, or muenster cheese
  (4 ounces)

Spread rolls with mayonnaise. Line bottoms of rolls with lettuce. Remove bones from chicken pieces; slice chicken. Layer chicken slices over lettuce. Top each sandwich with *2 slices* sweet pepper, *1 slice* onion, and *1 slice* cheese. Add top of roll. Makes 4 servings.

Use this idea to make a crowd-sized sub sandwich. Simply purchase one, two, or three loaves of baguette-style French or sourdough bread, halve lengthwise, and layer with the same ingredients listed above. Slice crosswise to serve.

Per serving: 712 calories, 38 g protein, 79 g carbohydrate, 27 g total fat (9 g saturated), 82 mg cholesterol, 1,253 mg sodium, 395 mg potassium

chicken and pasta with salsa

1 9-ounce package refrigerated fresh angel-hair pasta or
    linguini
3 purchased broiled or roasted chicken breast halves
1 16-ounce jar chunky salsa
1 tablespoon lime juice
¼ cup pre-shredded Monterey Jack or mozzarella cheese
    (optional)
    Fresh cilantro or parsley sprigs
    Salsa

Prepare pasta according to package directions.
Meanwhile, remove skin and bones from chicken breasts;
cut meat into bite-size strips. In a large saucepan stir
together salsa, lime juice, and chicken strips. Heat
through. Drain pasta; toss with salsa mixture. If desired,
sprinkle with cheese. Garnish with cilantro or parsley
sprigs and pass additional salsa. Makes 4 servings.

*You might not think of salsa as instant-sauce
material, but it is! Available in saucy and chunk-
style versions, and from mild to hair-raising in
spiciness, this versatile, low-calorie, low-sodium
sauce is always ready when you are!*

Per serving: 391 calories, 29 g protein, 46 g carbohydrate, 9 g total fat (2 g saturated),
108 mg cholesterol, 1,047 mg sodium, 295 mg potassium

broiled chicken with tomato-pepper puree

4 purchased broiled or roasted chicken breasts halves
¼ cup oil-packed dried tomatoes
¼ cup roasted red sweet pepper
½ of a 2¼-ounce can sliced pitted ripe olives, drained
    (2 tablespoons)
½ teaspoon dried Italian seasoning, crushed
½ teaspoon bottled minced garlic
½ cup finely pre-shredded mozzarella cheese (2 ounces)
   Lettuce leaves (optional)
   Sliced tomatoes (optional)
   Sliced pitted ripe olives (optional)

Preheat broiler. Place cooked chicken breast halves, skin side up, on the unheated rack of a broiler pan.

For puree, drain tomatoes, reserving *1 tablespoon* of the oil. Halve tomatoes; combine in blender container with the reserved oil, red pepper, olives, Italian seasoning, and garlic. Cover and blend until almost pureed. Spread over chicken; broil about 5 inches from heat for 4 to 5 minutes or till heated through. Sprinkle with cheese and broil 1 to 2 minutes more. If desired, serve on lettuce leaves and garnish with tomatoes and olives. Serves 4.

Dried tomatoes, packed in oil, have a marvelous smoky flavor. If you are watching calories, purchase them dry-packed, without oil. Rehydrate in boiling water to use.

Per serving: 231 calories, 29 g protein, 3 g carbohydrate, 11 g total fat (3 g saturated), 84 mg cholesterol, 209 mg sodium, 356 mg potassium

chicken and tabbouleh salad

3 cups purchased torn mixed greens for salads
2 cups purchased tabbouleh salad
1 tablespoon finely snipped fresh mint or 1 teaspoon
   dried mint, crushed
2 purchased broiled or roasted chicken breast halves
½ cup oil and vinegar salad dressing

Arrange salad greens on a large platter. Toss together tabbouleh salad and mint. Spoon over greens. Remove bones from chicken breasts; cut meat into ¼-inch slices. Arrange chicken pieces over tabbouleh mixture. Shake dressing; drizzle over salad. Makes 3 servings.

If you can't find tabbouleh salad, substitute a seasoned rice salad.

Per serving: 426 calories, 20 g protein, 23 g carbohydrate, 31 g total fat (4 g saturated),
51 mg cholesterol, 797 mg sodium, 433 mg potassium

chicken pasta with gorgonzola and peas

1 9-ounce package refrigerated fresh angel hair pasta
4 purchased broiled or roasted chicken breast halves
1 teaspoon bottled minced garlic
1 tablespoon cooking oil
1 10-ounce package frozen peas
1 cup whipping cream
½ teaspoon salt
¼ teaspoon pepper
1 cup crumbled gorgonzola or blue cheese (4 ounces)

Cut or break pasta into shorter lengths (4 to 6 inches). In a large saucepan cook pasta according to package directions. Meanwhile, remove bones from chicken. If desired, remove skin; cut chicken into ¼-inch strips.

In a 12-inch skillet cook and stir garlic in hot oil over medium-high heat for 15 seconds. Add peas and cook for 3 minutes. Stir in cream, salt, and pepper; gently boil, stirring constantly, about 2 to 3 minutes, or till mixture thickens slightly. Drain pasta; toss with chicken, sauce, and cheese. Serve immediately. Makes 4 servings.

Gorgonzola cheese is just one of a family of "blues" available for the trying, such as Stilton, Roquefort, Saga, Maytag, or Danish blue.

Per serving: 774 calories, 44 g protein, 55 g carbohydrate, 42 g total fat (22 g saturated), 234 mg cholesterol, 830 mg sodium, 491 mg potassium

caesar salad with chicken

1 10-ounce package torn mixed greens for salads
½ cup Caesar or Italian salad dressing
4 purchased broiled or roasted chicken breast halves
1 cup garlic-seasoned croutons
1 2-ounce can anchovy fillets (optional)
2 tablespoons grated Parmesan or Romano cheese

In a large bowl toss together salad greens and dressing. Cut chicken into bite-size strips. On four dinner plates divide salad greens mixture; arrange chicken pieces on top. Sprinkle on croutons and add anchovies, if desired. Sprinkle with grated cheese. Makes 4 servings.

The classic Caesar salad was named for a chef in Tijuana, Mexico, who invented it during the 1920's. If you are using anchovies, rinse off the oil first, or pat them dry on paper towels before adding them to the salad.

Per serving: 383 calories, 28 g protein, 12 g carbohydrate, 24 g total fat (3 g saturated), 79 mg cholesterol, 259 mg sodium, 447 mg potassium

chicken, tomato, and mozzarella salad

Lettuce leaves

2 large tomatoes, halved and thinly sliced

½ of a 6-ounce package sliced mozzarella or Monterey Jack cheese, cut into triangles

3 purchased broiled or roasted chicken breast halves

½ cup oil and vinegar salad dressing

1 teaspoon dried Italian seasoning, crushed

⅛ teaspoon garlic powder

⅛ teaspoon pepper

1 green onion, sliced

Line 4 dinner plates with lettuce leaves. Arrange tomato slices and cheese triangles over lettuce. Remove bones from chicken; cut chicken into ½-inch strips. Arrange chicken over salad.

For dressing, in a screw-top jar combine oil and vinegar salad dressing, Italian seasoning, garlic powder, and pepper. Drizzle over salads. Sprinkle with green onion. Makes 4 servings.

This salad is easy picnic fare—simply pack the components in separate containers, and prepare the dressing ahead. Add some crusty rolls, a jug of iced tea, and fresh fruit.

Per serving: 339 calories, 25 g protein, 8 g carbohydrate, 24 g total fat (6 g saturated), 69 mg cholesterol, 584 mg sodium, 419 mg potassium

chicken and artichoke angel hair pasta

1 9-ounce package refrigerated fresh angel hair or spaghettini pasta

1 6-ounce jar marinated artichoke hearts

2 5-ounce cans chunk-style chicken

1 cup loose-pack frozen peas

1 2½-ounce jar sliced mushrooms, drained

⅛ teaspoon bottled hot pepper sauce

¾ cup crumbled feta cheese (3 ounces)

In a large saucepan cook pasta according to package directions; drain. In the same pan heat together *undrained* artichoke hearts, *undrained* chicken, peas, mushrooms, and hot pepper sauce for 2 minutes. Add pasta to pan; toss well. Sprinkle with feta cheese. Serve immediately. Makes 4 servings.

If you cook up a lot of pasta, it's nice to have some of the serving accouterments, such as a large pasta bowl (great for serving and tossing pasta with a sauce), a Parmesan cheese grater, and a pasta serving fork.

Per serving: 453 calories, 30 g protein, 52 g carbohydrate, 14 g total fat (5 g saturated), 113 mg cholesterol, 829 mg sodium, 311 mg potassium

chicken and asparagus with four cheeses

1 10-ounce package frozen cut asparagus or cut broccoli
4 English muffins, split
1 10- or 12-ounce container refrigerated four-cheese
   pasta sauce
2 5-ounce cans chunk-style chicken, drained and flaked
½ teaspoon dried fines herbes or basil, crushed
1 tablespoon dry white wine or milk

In a medium saucepan cook frozen asparagus or broccoli according to package directions; drain.

Meanwhile, toast English muffins; arrange 2 halves on each of 4 dinner plates. In a medium saucepan stir together pasta sauce, chicken, and fines herbes; cook over medium-high heat till heated through. Stir in drained asparagus or broccoli and wine. Spoon mixture over English muffins. Makes 4 servings.

Next time, try substituting frozen artichoke hearts that have been cooked and drained for the asparagus or broccoli, and split, warmed croissants for the toasted English muffins.

Per serving: 569 calories, 32 g protein, 39 g carbohydrate, 27 g total fat (2 g saturated), 114 mg cholesterol, 1,572 mg sodium, 301 mg potassium

chicken and egg salad bagelwiches

4 bagels, split
  Lettuce leaves (optional)
1½ cups purchased egg salad
1 5-ounce can chunk-style chicken, drained and flaked
1 2¼-ounce can sliced pitted ripe olives, drained
1 tablespoon diced pimiento, drained
  Dash bottled hot pepper sauce

Toast bagels, if desired. Line bottom halves of bagels with lettuce leaves, if desired. In a medium bowl stir together egg salad, chicken, olives, pimiento, and hot pepper sauce till combined. Divide mixture among lettuce-lined bagel halves, spreading salad evenly over lettuce. Add bagel tops. Halve each sandwich crosswise. Makes 4 servings.

Having spur-of-the-moment guests? This tasty salad mixture and variations of it can be made to spread on crackers or open-faced sandwiches, or to stuff into cherry tomatoes for quick appetizers. Or, use a dab to fill miniature cream puffs.

Per serving: 430 calories, 21 g protein, 34 g carbohydrate, 24 g total fat (5 g saturated), 241 mg cholesterol, 770 mg sodium, 207 mg potassium

chicken and shrimp-fried rice

3 tablespoons soy sauce
2 tablespoons dry sherry
   Few dashes bottled hot pepper sauce
2 tablespoons peanut oil or cooking oil
2 beaten eggs
4 cups purchased cooked brown or white rice with
   vegetables
1 5-ounce can chunk-style chicken, drained and flaked
1 4½-ounce can medium shrimp, rinsed and drained

   In a small bowl stir together soy sauce, sherry, and hot
pepper sauce; set aside. Pour *1 tablespoon* of the oil into a
wok or large skillet. (Add more oil as necessary during
cooking.) Preheat over medium heat. Add the eggs. Lift
and tilt the wok to form a thin sheet of egg. Cook,
without stirring, about 2 to 2½ minutes or just till set.
Invert the egg sheet onto a cutting board. Cut into
¼-inch strips. Set aside.
   Pour the remaining 1 tablespoon cooking oil into the
wok or skillet. Preheat over medium-high heat. Stir-fry
rice mixture for 1½ to 2½ minutes or till heated through.
Add the chicken, shrimp, and egg strips. Stir soy mixture;
add to wok. Stir-fry 1 minute or till heated through. Serve
immediately. Makes 4 servings.

*The Orientals invented fried rice as a wonderful
way to use leftover rice, vegetables, meats, and
seafood. You can do the same!*

Per serving: 436 calories, 25 g protein, 49 g carbohydrate, 14 g total fat (3 g saturated),
181 mg cholesterol, 966 mg sodium, 281 mg potassium

chicken and lentil soup with garlic-cheese toasts

1 19-ounce can ready-to-serve lentil soup
1 cup loose-pack frozen crinkle-cut carrots
¼ teaspoon dried thyme, crushed
8 slices French bread
2 tablespoons margarine or butter
¼ teaspoon garlic powder
¾ cup pre-shredded mozzarella or cheddar cheese
1 5½-ounce can tomato juice (about ⅔ cup)
1 cup cubed cooked chicken

Preheat broiler. In a medium saucepan stir together soup, carrots, and thyme. Bring mixture to boiling; reduce heat and simmer 8 to 9 minutes till carrots are tender.

Meanwhile, for garlic-cheese toasts, place bread slices on unheated rack of a broiler pan. Spread with margarine or butter; sprinkle with garlic powder. Broil 5-inches from heat for 1 minute or till golden brown. Top with cheese. Return to broiler; broil about 30 to 60 seconds till cheese melts slightly and edges are golden brown. Stir tomato juice and chicken into soup; heat through. Serve bread slices with soup. Makes 4 servings.

With a few imaginative touches, canned soups can be super starters for quick, tasty meals. Stock up on a variety of soups and jazz them up with cooked vegetables and poultry.

Per serving: 349 calories, 24 g protein, 32 g carbohydrate, 14 g total fat (6 g saturated), 49 mg cholesterol, 923 mg sodium, 451 mg potassium

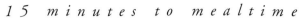

cheese tortellini primavera

1 9-ounce package refrigerated fresh cheese tortellini
2 cups loose-pack frozen zucchini, carrots, cauliflower, lima beans, and Italian beans
½ of an 8-ounce container soft-style cream cheese with chives and onion
¼ cup half-and-half, light cream, or milk
1 5-ounce can chunk-style chicken, drained and flaked
3 tablespoons grated Parmesan or Romano cheese
   Grated Parmesan cheese (optional)

In a large saucepan prepare tortellini according to package directions *except* stir in frozen vegetables along with tortellini. Drain pasta and vegetables. Return vegetables and pasta to saucepan.

Meanwhile, in a small saucepan heat cream cheese and cream or milk over medium-low heat till cheese melts and mixture is warm, stirring occasionally. Stir in chicken. Pour over vegetables and pasta in saucepan; toss well to coat. Stir in Parmesan or Romano cheese. If desired, pass additional grated Parmesan cheese. Makes 3 servings.

You'll find refrigerated fresh and dried tortellini available with a variety of fillings. Select cheese, chicken, or meat and tomato fillings in either egg or spinach pasta versions.

Per serving: 519 calories, 28 g protein, 42 g carbohydrate, 26 g total fat (10 g saturated), 77 mg cholesterol, 1,017 mg sodium, 355 mg potassium

fruited chicken salad

3   5-ounce cans chunk-style chicken, drained and flaked
1   6-ounce package mixed dried fruit bits
⅓   cup broken pecans, walnuts, or slivered almonds
⅓   cup mayonnaise or salad dressing
⅓   cup lemon or pineapple low-fat yogurt
    Lettuce leaves or lettuce cups

In a medium bowl stir together chicken, dried fruit, and nuts. In a small bowl stir together mayonnaise or salad dressing and yogurt till combined. Add dressing to salad mixture; toss. Serve on lettuce leaves or pile into lettuce cups. Makes 4 servings.

Variation: For fruited chicken salad croissants, split and butter 4 croissants and use mixture as a sandwich filling. (Or, put on raisin or sourdough toast.)

Tip: If chilling salad ahead of time, stir in 1 to 2 tablespoons milk, as necessary.

Per serving: 512 calories, 27 g protein, 39 g carbohydrate, 29 g total fat (5 g saturated), 70 mg cholesterol, 684 mg sodium, 666 mg potassium

curried chicken soup

1 cup loose-pack frozen crinkle-cut carrots

¼ cup sliced green onion

1 teaspoon curry powder

2 tablespoons cooking oil

3 cups chicken broth

1 14½-ounce can diced tomatoes

1 teaspoon dried basil, crushed

⅛ teaspoon ground red pepper

¾ cup instant mashed potato flakes

2 5-ounce cans or one 12½-ounce can chunk-style chicken, flaked

  Dairy sour cream (optional)

In a large saucepan cook carrots, onion, and curry powder in hot oil for 3 to 4 minutes, stirring frequently, till carrots are crisp-tender. Stir in broth, *undrained* tomatoes, basil, and ground red pepper. Bring to boiling; reduce heat. Stir in potato flakes and *undrained* chicken; heat 2 minutes more or till mixture is slightly thickened. If desired, dollop individual servings of soup with sour cream. Makes 3 or 4 servings.

In lieu of potato flakes, you can also puree half of the vegetables (before adding chicken) in a food processor or blender to thicken a hearty soup like this one.

Per serving: 270 calories, 21 g protein, 15 g carbohydrate, 14 g total fat (3 g saturated), 40mg cholesterol, 1,132 mg sodium, 641 mg potassium

gazpacho chicken salad

3 cups purchased torn mixed greens for salads

2 5-ounce cans or one 12½-ounce can chunk-style
   chicken, drained and flaked

½ cup pre-shredded carrots or pre-sliced mushrooms

½ cup sliced cucumber

½ cup sliced celery

6 cherry tomatoes, halved or 1 small tomato,
   cut into wedges

¼ cup hot-style vegetable juice cocktail or hot-style
   tomato juice

2 tablespoons cooking oil

1 tablespoon lemon juice

¼ teaspoon chili powder

⅛ teaspoon garlic powder

¼ teaspoon Worcestershire sauce
   Croutons

In a large bowl toss together mixed greens, chicken,
carrots, cucumber, celery, and tomatoes. In a screw-top jar
combine vegetable cocktail juice, cooking oil, lemon juice,
chili powder, garlic powder, and Worcestershire sauce.
Cover and shake well. Pour over salad; toss. Sprinkle with
croutons. Makes 3 servings.

For a special touch, place a few slices of medium-ripe avocado over each serving of salad.

Per serving: 296 calories, 24 g protein, 12 g carbohydrate, 17 g total fat (4 g saturated),
52 mg cholesterol, 636 mg sodium, 709 mg potassium

saffron chicken and rice

3 cups purchased cooked rice with vegetables

½ to ¾ cup chicken broth

⅛ teaspoon saffron or ¼ teaspoon ground turmeric

2 5-ounce cans or one 12½-ounce can chunk-style chicken, drained and flaked

8 cherry tomatoes, halved

In a large skillet stir together rice, *½ cup* of the broth, and saffron. Cook and stir over medium heat till heated through. Stir in chicken and cherry tomatoes; cook 2 minutes more. If desired, stir in additional broth to desired consistency. Makes 4 servings.

If you have more time, you can use this mixture to stuff sweet peppers, squash, or other vegetables. Simply cook the vegetable shells till nearly tender, stuff with the rice mixture, and bake till heated through.

Per serving: 351 calories, 26 g protein, 46 g carbohydrate, 6 g total fat (2 g saturated), 63 mg cholesterol, 301 mg sodium, 346 mg potassium

gingered-chicken wonton soup

2 10¾-ounce cans condensed chicken wonton soup .

1½ cups water

1 teaspoon freshly grated gingerroot

1 green onion, sliced

2 5-ounce cans or one 12½-ounce can chunk-style
    chicken, drained and flaked

1 cup loose-pack frozen peas and carrots or pea pods

1 cup cubed tofu (fresh bean curd), drained

In a medium saucepan combine soup, water, gingerroot, and green onion. Bring to boiling. Stir in chicken, peas and carrots, and tofu. Simmer 2 minutes more. Ladle into bowls. Makes 3 or 4 servings.

Variation: For an Italian soup, omit wonton soup, ginger, and tofu. Substitute canned tortellini soup, season with Italian seasoning or fresh basil, and use frozen green beans and carrots. Sprinkle with grated Parmesan cheese.

Per serving: 371 calories, 41 g protein, 17 g carbohydrate, 17 g total fat (3 g saturated), 65 mg cholesterol, 2,047 mg sodium, 404 mg potassium

monterey chicken-pesto pizza

1 16-ounce Italian bread shell (Boboli brand) or heat
and serve pizza shell

½ of a 7-ounce container refrigerated pesto

2 5-ounce cans or one 12½-ounce can chunk-style
chicken, drained and flaked

1 2-ounce jar sliced pimiento, drained

1 cup pre-shredded Monterey Jack or mozzarella cheese
(4 ounces)

Preheat oven to 450°. Place bread shell on baking
sheet or pizza pan. Spread pesto over pizza to within
1 inch of edges. Sprinkle on chicken and pimiento; top
with Monterey Jack or mozzarella cheese. Bake 5 to 8
minutes or till cheese melts. Makes 4 servings.

*The heat-and-serve pizza shells are naturals for
staples like canned chicken and ready-made sauces.
Keep the shells along with some sauces and toppings on hand for snacks, hors d'oeuvres, and
speedy suppers.*

Per serving: 653 calories, 38 g protein, 53 g carbohydrate, 33 g total fat (7 g saturated),
72 mg cholesterol, 1,265 mg sodium, 143 mg potassium

quick chicken and corn chowder

1 cup loose-pack frozen crinkle-cut carrots

½ cup frozen or fresh chopped onion

2 tablespoons margarine or butter

2 tablespoons all-purpose flour

1½ cups milk

1 16½-ounce can cream-style corn

1 14½-ounce can chicken broth

2 5-ounce cans or one 12½-ounce can chunk-style chicken

1 2-ounce jar diced pimiento, drained

⅛ to ¼ teaspoon pepper

In a large saucepan cook and stir carrots and onion in hot margarine for 2 minutes. Sprinkle flour over mixture; slowly stir in milk. Stir in creamed corn, broth, *undrained* chicken, pimiento, and pepper. Bring mixture to boiling; reduce heat. Simmer 3 minutes. Ladle into bowls. If desired, serve with breadsticks. Makes 4 servings.

Serve this soup to company by using 4 individual round sourdough bread loaves as soup bowls. Carefully slice off the tops, hollow out the centers (leaving a ½-inch shell), and use the crowns as whimsical covers!

Per serving: 353 calories, 24 g protein, 35 g carbohydrate, 14 g total fat (4 g saturated), 46 mg cholesterol, 1,158 mg sodium, 634 mg potassium

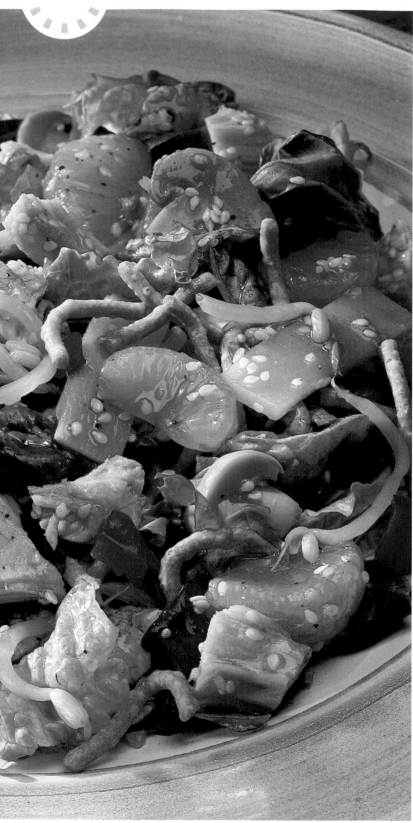

quick chinese chicken salad

1 10-ounce package torn mixed greens for salads
1 16-ounce can fancy Chinese mixed vegetables, drained
2 5-ounce cans or one 12½-ounce can chunk-style
     chicken, drained and flaked
1 11-ounce can mandarin oranges, drained
1 3-ounce can chow mein noodles or rice noodles
⅔ cup oil and vinegar salad dressing
1 tablespoon soy sauce or hoisin sauce
2 teaspoons sesame seed

In a large bowl toss together salad greens, mixed vegetables, chicken, mandarin oranges, and noodles. For dressing, in a screw-top jar combine dressing, soy or hoisin sauce, and sesame seed. Cover and shake well; pour over salad and toss to coat. Makes 4 to 6 servings.

Variation: For a hot entrée, omit the lettuce. Heat together the vegetables, chicken, and oranges; season with soy sauce and sesame seed. Stir in the Chinese noodles and serve the mixture on a bed of hot rice.

Per serving: 504 calories, 21 g protein, 31 g carbohydrate, 34 g total fat (6 g saturated), 39 mg cholesterol, 854 mg sodium, 494 mg potassium

scrambled eggs with chicken and dried tomatoes

4 eggs

2 tablespoons milk

1 tablespoon snipped fresh basil or 1 teaspoon dried
    basil, crushed

   Dash pepper

1 5-ounce can chunk-style chicken, drained and flaked

2 tablespoons sliced green onion

¼ cup oil-packed dried tomatoes, drained and cut into
    thin strips

1 tablespoon margarine or butter

1 tablespoon grated Parmesan or Romano cheese

In a medium bowl beat together eggs, milk, basil, and pepper till frothy. Stir in chicken, onion, and tomatoes.

In a large skillet melt margarine or butter over medium heat; pour in egg mixture. Cook, without stirring, till mixture begins to set on the bottom and around edge. Using a large spoon or spatula, lift and fold partially cooked eggs so uncooked portion flows underneath. Continue cooking over medium heat for 2 to 3 minutes or till eggs are cooked throughout but are still glossy and moist. Remove from heat. Sprinkle with Parmesan or Romano cheese and serve immediately. If desired, serve with fresh fruit. Makes 3 servings.

If you are watching your egg intake, substitute 1 8-ounce carton of a frozen egg product, thawed, for the eggs and milk.

Per serving: 239 calories, 21 g protein, 4 g carbohydrate, 15 g total fat (4 g saturated), 312 mg cholesterol, 504 mg sodium, 328 mg potassium

singapore frittata

1 10-ounce package frozen Chinese stir-fry vegetables
   with seasonings
6 eggs
1 tablespoon soy sauce
   Dash bottled hot pepper sauce
2 tablespoons margarine or butter
1 5-ounce can chunk-style chicken, drained and flaked
1 green onion, sliced

Preheat broiler. Remove seasoning packet from
vegetables; set vegetables aside. In a medium bowl beat
eggs with seasoning packet, soy sauce, and hot pepper
sauce till frothy; set aside.

In a large broiler-proof skillet cook vegetables in
margarine for about 3 minutes or till crisp-tender. Stir in
chicken. Pour egg mixture into skillet over vegetables and
chicken. Cook without stirring over medium heat. As
mixture sets, run a spatula around edge of skillet, lifting
egg mixture to allow uncooked portions to flow
underneath. Continue cooking and lifting edges till egg
mixture is almost set (surface will be moist).

Place skillet under broiler 4 to 5 inches from the heat.
Broil for 1 to 2 minutes or till top is just set. Cut into
wedges. Sprinkle with sliced green onion. If desired,
garnish with green onion brushes. Makes 3 or 4 servings.

*To broiler-proof your skillet, choose a heavy pan
and cover the handle with aluminum foil to protect it from the heating unit.*

Per serving: 335 calories, 25 g protein, 9 g carbohydrate, 21 g total fat (6 g saturated),
452 mg cholesterol, 1,036 mg sodium, 205 mg potassium

tortellini chicken salad with lemon dressing

1 6-ounce package refrigerated fresh cheese tortellini
2 5-ounce cans or one 12½-ounce can chunk-style
     chicken, drained and flaked
1 cup seedless grapes, halved
½ cup chopped walnuts
⅓ cup lemon or orange low-fat yogurt
⅓ cup mayonnaise or salad dressing
     Lettuce leaves
     Fresh ground pepper (optional)

In a large saucepan cook tortellini according to package directions. Meanwhile, in a large bowl toss together chicken, grapes, and walnuts. In a small bowl stir together yogurt and mayonnaise. Drain tortellini; rinse in cold water for 2 minutes. Drain again. Toss tortellini with chicken mixture and dressing till well coated. Serve on lettuce-lined plates and top with fresh ground pepper, if desired. Makes 4 servings.

Note: If using dry tortellini, allow 25 minutes for the cooking time.

Per serving: 522 calories, 26 g protein, 35 g carbohydrate, 32 g total fat (5 g saturated), 74 mg cholesterol, 665 mg sodium, 363 mg potassium

chicken-cannellini chili

1 cup frozen chopped onion

1 teaspoon bottled minced garlic

2 tablespoons cooking oil

1 19-ounce can white kidney beans (cannellini)

1 14½-ounce can chili-style chunky tomatoes

2 5-ounce cans or one 12½-ounce can chunk-style chicken, drained and flaked

1 10-ounce package frozen peas and carrots

1 6-ounce can tomato juice

1 tablespoon chili powder

½ teaspoon seasoned salt

¼ teaspoon ground cumin

1 cup pre-shredded cheddar or Monterey Jack cheese (4 ounces)

In a large saucepan cook onion and garlic in hot oil for 3 minutes, stirring frequently. Stir in *undrained* kidney beans, *undrained* tomatoes, chicken, peas and carrots, tomato juice, chili powder, seasoned salt, and cumin. Cook and stir till mixture comes to a boil; reduce heat and simmer, covered for 5 minutes. Sprinkle each serving with some of the cheese. Makes 4 or 5 servings.

You'll find bottled minced and pureed garlic in the garlic and onion section of your supermarket produce department.

Per serving: 461 calories, 35 g protein, 39 g carbohydrate, 23 g total fat (9 g saturated), 69 mg cholesterol, 1,489 mg sodium, 894 mg potassium

chicken, mushroom, and caper-stuffed rolls

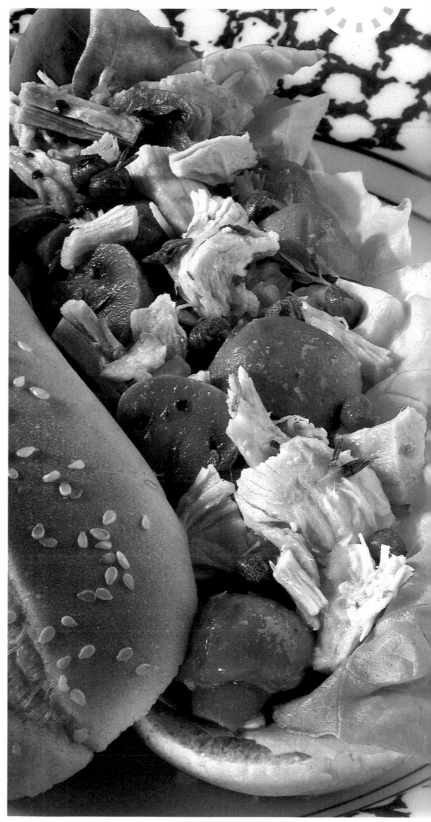

4 individual sourdough sandwich rolls

1 8-ounce jar pickled mushrooms

1 12½-ounce can or three 5-ounce cans chunk-style
   chicken, drained and flaked

1 tablespoon capers, drained

1 teaspoon snipped fresh thyme or ⅛ teaspoon dried
   thyme, crushed

   Lettuce leaves

Slice rolls in half lengthwise; remove centers, leaving a
½-inch shell. (Reserve bread crumbs for another use).
Drain mushrooms, reserving *2 tablespoons* liquid. Halve
mushrooms. In a medium bowl combine chicken,
mushrooms, the reserved mushroom liquid, capers, and
thyme. Line bottom halves of the sandwich rolls with
lettuce leaves; fill with chicken mixture. Top each with
roll tops. Makes 4 servings.

*You can also use this sandwich filling to stuff crois-
sants or pita bread rounds. Or, serve the chicken
mixture as a salad and stuff into hollowed-out
tomatoes, avocado halves, or a pretty lettuce leaf.*

Per serving: 434 calories, 27 g protein, 50 g carbohydrate, 13 g total fat (3 g saturated),
47 mg cholesterol, 1,231 mg sodium, 286 mg potassium

greek chicken soup with lemon

2 14½-ounce cans chicken broth
½ cup quick-cooking rice
2 tablespoons lemon juice
2 beaten eggs
1 12½-ounce can or two 5-ounce cans chunk-style
   chicken
1 teaspoon dried parsley, crushed
¼ teaspoon pepper
   Lemon slices (optional)

In a medium saucepan bring chicken broth to boiling. Stir in rice. Simmer, covered, for 2 minutes. Stir in lemon juice. Pour beaten egg into the soup in a steady stream while stirring 2 or 3 times to create shreds. Stir in *undrained* chicken, parsley, and pepper. Heat through, but do not simmer. If desired, garnish with lemon slices and serve with breadsticks. Makes 3 or 4 servings.

If you like to stew or poach chicken, be sure to refrigerate or freeze the broth to use for soups like these. You can also use the leftover stock as part or all of the cooking liquid to prepare vegetables, rice, or pasta.

Per serving: 323 calories, 35 g protein, 11 g carbohydrate, 14 g total fat (4 g saturated), 205 mg cholesterol, 1,487 mg sodium, 448 mg potassium

tropical fruit-chicken salad with melon

1 cantaloupe or honeydew melon

1 15¼-ounce can tropical fruit salad

1 12½-ounce can or two 5-ounce cans chunk-style
   chicken, drained and flaked

½ cup vanilla yogurt

⅓ cup peanuts or chopped pecans

Halve melons; remove seeds. Cut each half into
8 wedges. If desired, remove rind. Arrange melon wedges
on 4 salad plates. Drain fruit salad, reserving *1 tablespoon*
juice. Cut up any large pieces of fruit. In a medium bowl
toss together fruit and chicken. Spoon mixture onto
melon wedges. Stir together yogurt and reserved juice.
Spoon over chicken mixture. Sprinkle with peanuts or
pecans. Makes 4 servings

*If desired, chill the fruit and chicken the day
before you plan to prepare this salad.*

Per serving: 430 calories, 26 g protein, 56 g carbohydrate, 14 g total fat
(3 g saturated), 48 mg cholesterol, 564 mg sodium, 1,141 mg potassium

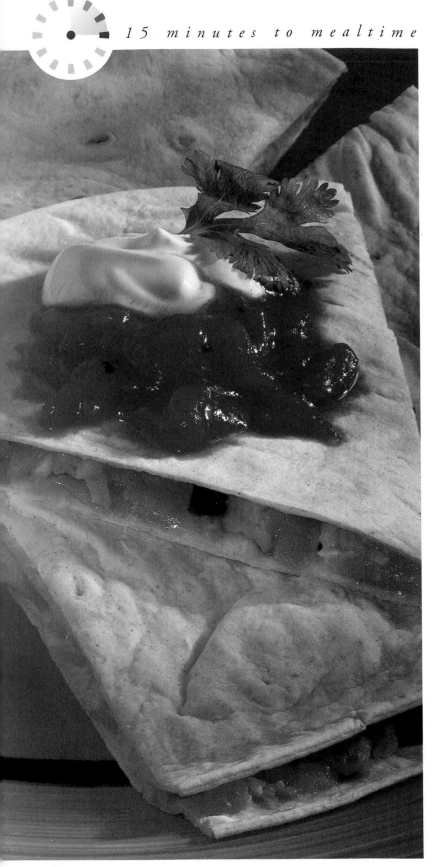

baja chicken quesadilla

8   8- or 10-inch flour tortillas
1   12½-ounce can or two 5-ounce cans chunk-style
      chicken, drained and flaked
1   4-ounce can diced green chili peppers, drained
1   2¼-ounce can sliced pitted ripe olives, drained
1   cup pre-shredded cheddar or Monterey Jack cheese
      (4 ounces)
      Salsa
      Dairy sour cream
      Fresh cilantro sprigs (optional)

Preheat oven to 375°. On two large baking sheets
arrange *half* of the tortillas. Sprinkle chicken, then
peppers and olives over tortillas to within ½ inch of edges.
Sprinkle cheese over; top each with a second tortilla. Press
down on second tortilla to flatten slightly. Bake for 5 to 7
minutes or till cheese is melted. Transfer each quesadilla
to a dinner plate; cut into six wedges. Top with salsa, sour
cream, and cilantro, if desired. Serve immediately. Makes
4 servings.

*Think of the quesadilla as a delightful Mexican
variation on a grilled cheese sandwich that's made
with tortillas. This hearty version features chicken,
chilies, and olives.*

Per serving: 515 calories, 33 g protein, 38 g carbohydrate, 27 g total fat
(11 g saturated), 85 mg cholesterol, 1,143 mg sodium, 298 mg potassium

chicken and feta salad-stuffed pitas

2 5-ounce cans or one 12½-ounce can chunk-style
    chicken, drained and flaked

½ cup crumbled feta cheese (2 ounces)

½ cup loose-pack frozen peas

1 medium tomato, chopped

1 green onion, sliced

⅓ cup mayonnaise or salad dressing

1 teaspoon dried dillweed

4 white or wheat pita bread rounds, halved crosswise
    Lettuce leaves

In a medium bowl place chicken and feta cheese.
Rinse peas in cold water until thawed; drain and pat dry
with paper towels. Add to chicken mixture with tomato
and green onion. Stir in mayonnaise or salad dressing and
dillweed; toss to combine. Line pita bread halves with
lettuce. Spoon chicken salad into pitas, dividing evenly.
Serve immediately. Makes 4 servings.

*This chicken salad is an easy make-ahead. Prepare
the salad up to 24 hours ahead to serve as a sandwich filling or on its own over a bed of lettuce
leaves. If using pitas, stuff just before serving to
prevent the pockets from becoming soggy.*

Per serving: 462 calories, 26 g protein, 27 g carbohydrate, 28 g total fat (9 g saturated),
78 mg cholesterol, 1,052 mg sodium, 314 mg potassium

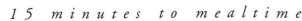

chicken crepes primavera

1 16-ounce package loose-pack frozen cauliflower, broccoli, and carrots

1 12- or 10-ounce container Alfredo pasta sauce

1 12½-ounce can or two 5-ounce cans chunk-style chicken, drained and flaked

4 packaged 9- or 10-inch crepes

2 tablespoons slivered almonds

¼ cup grated Parmesan or Romano cheese

In a large saucepan cook frozen vegetables according to package directions till crisp-tender; drain. In same saucepan combine cooked vegetables, Alfredo pasta sauce, and chicken; heat through, stirring frequently, but *do not boil.* Spoon *one-fourth* of mixture onto center of *each* crepe; sprinkle filling with some slivered almonds. Fold crepe over filling; transfer to dinner plates. Sprinkle Parmesan or Romano over crepes. Makes 4 servings.

Choose from the wide variety of frozen loose-pack vegetable mixtures to vary the content of this colorful crepe filling. You can also use the four-cheese sauce, the marinara sauce, or a garden-style sauce for the filling.

Per serving: 500 calories, 28 g protein, 14 g carbohydrate, 37 g total fat (3 g saturated), 98 mg cholesterol, 919 mg sodium, 384 mg potassium

peppercorn chicken with cognac

4 skinless, boneless chicken breast halves or turkey
    breast tenderloin steaks (about 1 pound total)
1 teaspoon coarsely cracked pepper
¼ teaspoon salt
1 tablespoon cooking oil
⅓ cup chicken broth
⅓ cup cognac or brandy
⅓ cup whipping cream
    Watercress sprigs (optional)
    Chopped tomato (optional)

Rinse chicken; pat dry. Place chicken breasts between
sheets of plastic wrap. With the flat side of a meat mallet,
pound to ¼-inch thickness. Season both sides with pepper
and salt.

In a 12-inch skillet cook chicken in hot oil over
medium-high heat for 3 to 4 minutes or till tender and no
longer pink, turning once. Remove from pan; cover and
keep warm. Stir chicken broth and cognac into skillet;
scrape up crusty bits in bottom of pan. Bring to boiling;
reduce heat and simmer 2 minutes. Stir in cream; simmer
2 minutes or till reduced to ⅓ cup. Pour sauce over
chicken. If desired, garnish with watercress and chopped
tomato. Serve immediately. Makes 4 servings.

Steamed baby vegetables along with tiny new potatoes would be an easy but elegant accompaniment to this dish.

Per serving: 266 calories, 22 g protein, 1g carbohydrate, 14 g total fat (6 g saturated),
86 mg cholesterol, 259 mg sodium, 211 mg potassium

chicken nicoise-style salad

4 to 5 cups purchased torn mixed greens for salads
1 16-ounce can sliced potatoes, drained
1½ cups loose-pack frozen French-style green beans
1 12½-ounce can or two 5-ounce cans chunk-style chicken, drained and flaked
½ cup oil and vinegar or Italian salad dressing
8 pitted ripe olives
1 tomato, cut into thin wedges

In a large bowl toss together salad greens and potatoes. Rinse green beans under cold running water for 1 minute; drain well. Add beans to salad with chicken, dressing, and olives. Toss. Serve with tomato wedges. Makes 4 servings.

The French word "nicoise" refers to a style of cooking that includes tomatoes, and often garlic, among the ingredients. Experiment with the different types of green, black, pickled, and Greek olives available at specialty delis.

Per serving: 355 calories, 22 g protein, 15 g carbohydrate, 25 g total fat (4 g saturated), 49 mg cholesterol, 1,053 mg sodium, 504 mg potassium

italian-style chicken soup

1 15-ounce container refrigerated marinara sauce

1 cup water

1 12½-ounce can or two 5-ounce cans chunk-style chicken

½ teaspoon dried sage, crushed

½ cup cheese and garlic croutons

In a medium saucepan stir together marinara sauce and water. Bring to boiling; reduce heat. Stir in the *undrained* chicken and sage. Simmer 5 to 8 minutes or till heated through. Garnish each serving with croutons. Makes 4 servings.

A slice of bread is common atop a bowl of French onion soup. The Italians also have a wonderful way of "stretching" their soups by placing bread cubes or a slice of stale bread at the bottom of the bowl and ladling the soup over it.

Per serving: 222 calories, 22 g protein, 9 g carbohydrate, 10 g total fat (2 g saturated), 49 mg cholesterol, 864 mg sodium, 123 mg potassium

tortilla chicken soup

1 cup tortilla chips

½ cup frozen chopped onion

1 teaspoon bottled minced garlic

1 tablespoon cooking oil

3 cups chicken broth

1 10½-ounce can tomato puree

1 tablespoon snipped fresh cilantro or parsley

1 teaspoon dried oregano, crushed

¼ teaspoon ground cumin

¼ teaspoon pepper

1 12½-ounce can or two 5-ounce cans chunk-style
   chicken, flaked

1 cup pre-shredded cheddar or Monterey Jack cheese
   (4 ounces)

   Additional tortilla chips

Place the 1 cup chips in a plastic bag; crush by
pressing with a rolling pin. Set aside. In a large saucepan
cook onion and garlic in hot oil about 2 minutes or till
tender but not brown. Stir in broth, tomato puree,
cilantro, oregano, cumin, and pepper. Bring to boiling;
reduce heat. Stir in crushed tortillas, *undrained* chicken,
and cheese; heat through. Serve with tortilla chips. Makes
4 servings.

*Mexicans know more than one way to thicken a
soup. This version calls for crushed tortillas to add
hearty character.*

Per serving: 415 calories, 33 g protein, 18 g carbohydrate, 24 g total fat (9 g saturated),
79 mg cholesterol, 1,568 mg sodium, 686 mg potassium

1-2-3 gourmet pizza

1 16-ounce Italian bread shell (Boboli brand) or heat and serve pizza shell

1 cup pizza sauce or marinara sauce

2 5-ounce cans or one 12½-ounce can chunk-style chicken, drained and flaked

⅔ cup oil-packed dried tomatoes, drained and chopped

½ cup crumbled blue cheese or feta cheese or semi-soft goat cheese (chèvre) (2 ounces)

½ cup pre-shredded mozzarella or Monterey Jack cheese (2 ounces)

Preheat oven to 450°. Place bread shell on a baking sheet or pizza pan. Spread pizza sauce or marinara sauce over crust to within ½-inch of edges. Sprinkle on chicken, dried tomatoes, and cheeses. Bake for 5 to 7 minutes or till cheese melts and ingredients are heated through. Cut into wedges. Makes 4 or 5 servings.

If your family eats dinner in shifts, this recipe can bridge the time gaps. Simply prepare the pizza shell with toppings ahead, then bake individual wedges of the pizza as they are needed. Serve with a crisp side salad.

Per serving: 589 calories, 40 g protein, 59 g carbohydrate, 23 g total fat (6 g saturated), 74 mg cholesterol, 1,667 mg sodium, 652 mg potassium

turkey sauté with tomato and feta

4 turkey breast tenderloin steaks (about 1 pound total)
½ teaspoon bottled minced garlic
1 tablespoon cooking oil
1 15-ounce container tomato alfresco or tomato-basil
   sauce
½ cup crumbled feta cheese or pre-shredded mozzarella
   cheese (2 ounces)
   Salt
   Pepper

Rinse turkey; pat dry. In a large skillet cook turkey steaks and garlic in hot oil over medium heat for 2 to 3 minutes on each side till lightly browned. Drain off fat. Add tomato sauce; bring to boiling. Reduce heat; simmer, uncovered, over low heat for 5 minutes or till turkey is tender and no longer pink. Sprinkle cheese over mixture; heat 1 minute more. Season to taste with salt and pepper. If desired, serve with cooked carrots. Makes 4 servings.

Some meat counters of larger supermarkets offer various cuts of turkey breast, including the whole tenderloins, thin turkey breast slices or cutlets, and turkey breast tenderloin steaks which are the thinner slices of whole tenderloins.

Per serving: 232 calories, 26 g protein, 7 g carbohydrate, 11 g total fat (3 g saturated), 63 mg cholesterol, 591 mg sodium, 230 mg potassium

turkey and vegetable soup

1 pound ground raw turkey
1 teaspoon bottled minced garlic
1 teaspoon chili powder
2 cups tomato juice
1 cup chicken broth
1 16-ounce package frozen mixed vegetables
  Shredded cheddar cheese* (optional)
  Corn chips

In a large skillet brown ground turkey and garlic; drain off excess fat. Stir in chili powder; cook and stir 1 minute. Add tomato juice, broth, and vegetables. Bring to boiling; reduce heat. Simmer 5 minutes or till vegetables are tender. If desired, top with cheese. Serve with corn chips. Makes 4 servings.

* Use pre-shredded cheese or shred while the mixture cooks.

Per serving: 275 calories, 21 g protein, 25 g carbohydrate, 11 g total fat (3 g saturated), 42 mg cholesterol, 754 mg sodium, 696 mg potassium

grilled turkey and muenster sandwiches

2 tablespoons Dijon-style mustard
2 teaspoons prepared horseradish
6 slices light or dark rye bread
6 ounces very thinly sliced fully cooked smoked turkey
   or chicken breast
4 ounces sliced muenster or Swiss cheese
3 tablespoons margarine or butter

In a small bowl stir together mustard and horseradish; spread on *half* of the rye bread slices. Arrange turkey slices over mustard-covered bread slices; top with cheese and a second slice of bread. Halve each sandwich.

In a 12-inch skillet melt *2 tablespoons* of the margarine or butter; cook sandwiches over medium heat for 3 to 4 minutes till golden brown and cheese is melted, turning once and adding the additional tablespoon of margarine or butter. If desired, serve with fruit. Makes 3 servings.

Variations: Add 2 slices crisp-cooked bacon and/or a slice of tomato to each sandwich before adding cheese; continue as directed.

Per serving: 441 calories, 26 g protein, 26 g carbohydrate, 26 g total fat
(10 g saturated), 60 mg cholesterol, 1,543 mg sodium, 348 mg potassium

russian-style turkey salad

12 ounces sliced fully cooked turkey breast, cut up
1 16-ounce jar julienne beets, drained
⅓ cup mayonnaise or salad dressing
¼ cup chopped onion
2 teaspoons lemon juice
⅛ teaspoon pepper
   Lettuce leaves or lettuce-lined pita bread halves

In a medium bowl stir together turkey and drained beets. In a small bowl stir together mayonnaise or salad dressing, onion, lemon juice, and pepper. Add to turkey mixture; toss well to coat with dressing. Spoon mixture into lettuce-lined bowl or pita bread halves. Makes 4 servings.

No need to wait for holiday leftovers to enjoy salads like these. To have sliced cooked turkey on hand, you can buy deli-sliced turkey breast or cook a boneless turkey breast, bone-in turkey breast, or turkey breast steaks or slices.

Per serving: 262 calories, 22 g protein, 10 g carbohydrate, 16 g total fat (3 g saturated), 26 mg cholesterol, 1,054 mg sodium, 432 mg potassium

chicago-style turkey sandwiches

8   slices pumpernickel or light rye bread
½   of an 8-ounce container soft-style cream cheese with
      chives and onion
      Shredded lettuce
6   ounces sliced fully cooked turkey or chicken breast
4   slices Canadian-style bacon or sliced fully cooked
      smoked turkey
4   teaspoons brown mustard or Dijon-style mustard

Spread bread with cream cheese. Line *half* of the bread slices with lettuce. Top each sandwich with *one-fourth* of the turkey slices and *one* slice of Canadian-style bacon. Spread *1 teaspoon* mustard over each sandwich; top with a second bread slice, cream cheese side down. If desired, cut sandwiches diagonally in half; cut each in half again. Makes 4 servings.

Variation: Instead of standard turkey breast, substitute one of the turkey pastrami, turkey ham, turkey salami, or turkey bologna products. Use soft cheeses such as goat cheese or boursin-style cheese in place of the cream cheese.

Per serving: 360 calories, 23 g protein, 35 g carbohydrate, 14 g total fat (7 g saturated), 76 mg cholesterol, 1,383 mg sodium, 577 mg potassium

turkey and orange salad with honey-orange dressing

4 cups purchased torn mixed greens for salads

1 11-ounce can mandarin oranges, drained

8 ounces sliced fully cooked turkey or chicken breast

⅓ cup sliced almonds or pine nuts

¼ cup orange juice

2 tablespoons olive oil or vegetable oil

1 tablespoon cider vinegar or white wine vinegar

1 to 2 teaspoons honey

Dash pepper

In a large bowl toss together salad greens and mandarin oranges. Stack turkey slices; roll up from the long side. Cut roll crosswise into ¼-inch strips. Add turkey strips to salad with almonds. For dressing, in a screw-top jar combine orange juice, oil, vinegar, honey to taste, and pepper. Cover and shake well. Pour over salad and toss gently to coat. Makes 4 servings.

If you have extra time, toast the nuts for the salad on a shallow baking pan in a 350° toaster oven or conventional oven. Toast for 10 to 15 minutes, stirring occasionally.

Per serving: 243 calories, 15 g protein, 19 g carbohydrate, 13 g total fat (3 g saturated), 43 mg cholesterol, 690 mg sodium, 420 mg potassium

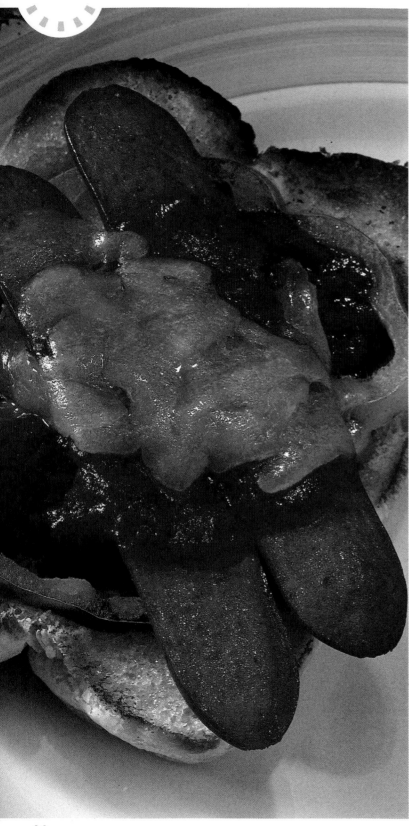

turkey franks mario

4 fully cooked turkey franks, split lengthwise
4 frankfurter buns or hamburger buns
   Margarine or butter
1 small green sweet pepper
¼ cup pizza sauce
½ cup pre-shredded cheddar or American cheese
   (2 ounces)

Preheat broiler. Arrange turkey franks on unheated rack of broiler pan. Broil 4 inches from the heat for 3 to 4 minutes; turn and broil 3 to 4 minutes more or till sizzling. Meanwhile, split frankfurter buns by cutting almost to, but not through, so they are open-faced. (If using hamburger buns, split completely.) Spread buns with margarine or butter. Cut green pepper into 8 slices. Place 2 slices on each bun. Top with broiled turkey franks; spread with pizza or spaghetti sauce. Sprinkle on cheese. Return to broiler just till cheese melts, about 1 minute. Serve immediately. Makes 4 servings.

Turkey franks are a versatile ingredient with more flavor than hotdogs—they're better for you, too. Try them sliced on a pizza or chopped into scrambled eggs.

Per serving: 325 calories, 12 g protein, 29 g carbohydrate, 17 g total fat (6 g saturated), 63 mg cholesterol, 1,180 mg sodium, 264 mg potassium

turkey and vegetables à la grecque

Lettuce leaves
1½ cups loose-pack frozen French-style green beans
6 ounces sliced fully cooked turkey or chicken breast, cut into strips
1 8¼-ounce can diced beets, drained, or 1 cup loose-pack frozen peas, or ½ of a 6-ounce package frozen pea pods
1 medium yellow summer squash or zucchini, halved lengthwise and thinly sliced
1 medium tomato, cut into wedges
⅓ cup Russian salad dressing
⅓ cup dairy sour cream

Arrange lettuce leaves on three or four individual salad plates or a platter. Rinse green beans under cold running water for 1 minute; drain well. (Rinse peas or pea pods, if using.) Arrange turkey, beans, beets or peas, summer squash or zucchini, and tomato wedges atop lettuce. In a bowl stir together salad dressing and sour cream. Spoon over salad. Makes 3 or 4 servings.

To cut turkey strips quickly, stack the turkey slices and roll them up the long way. Thinly slice the roll crosswise and pull the strips apart to use.

Per serving: 294 calories, 16 g protein, 14 g carbohydrate, 20 g total fat (6 g saturated), 21 mg cholesterol, 839 mg sodium, 511 mg potassium

italian-style open-face sandwiches

8 French or Italian bread slices, cut 1 inch thick
   Mayonnaise or salad dressing
8 ounces sliced fully cooked smoked turkey or chicken
   breast (8 slices)
4 ounces thinly sliced prosciutto or fully cooked ham
8 slices provolone or mozzarella cheese (4 ounces)
1 2¼-ounce can sliced pitted ripe olives, drained
8 large or 16 small fresh basil leaves

Preheat broiler. Place bread slices on unheated rack of a broiler pan or on baking sheet. Broil bread slices about 3 inches from the heat about 1 minute per side or till toasted; remove from oven.

Spread bread with mayonnaise or salad dressing; arrange turkey slices over. Top with prosciutto or ham.

Lay a cheese slice over the top of each sandwich, folding in half if necessary. Garnish with a few olive slices and the basil leaves. Broil 1 to 2 minutes more or till cheese melts. Arrange 2 sandwiches on each plate. Serve immediately. Makes 4 servings.

Variation: For an island version of this sandwich, substitute regular lettuce leaves for the basil, Canadian bacon for the prosciuitto, and add pineapple rings in place of the olives.

Per serving: 421 calories, 32 g protein, 29 g carbohydrate, 20 g total fat (6 g saturated), 44 mg cholesterol, 1,743 mg sodium, 290 mg potassium

turkey and black bean soup

2 14½-ounce cans chicken broth

1 15-ounce can black beans, rinsed and drained

1 14½-ounce can Mexican-style stewed tomatoes

1 cup loose-pack frozen whole kernel corn

½ cup dry red or white wine

1 teaspoon dried oregano, crushed

1 teaspoon bottled minced garlic

½ teaspoon seasoned salt

¼ teaspoon ground cumin

6 ounces sliced fully cooked smoked turkey or turkey
   breast, cut into squares

In a 3-quart saucepan combine broth, beans, *undrained* tomatoes, corn, wine, oregano, garlic, seasoned salt, and cumin. Bring to boiling; reduce heat and simmer, uncovered, 3 minutes. Stir in turkey; ladle into bowls. Makes 4 or 5 servings.

Black beans, as well as a variety of other beans such as garbanzos, great northerns, pintos, and red kidney beans, no longer need to be cooked from scratch. Keep the canned versions on hand to add to easy soups like this one.

Per serving: 226 calories, 22 g protein, 31 g carbohydrate, 2 g total fat (0 g saturated), 19 mg cholesterol, 1,874 mg sodium, 884 mg potassium

warm dilled chicken and potato salad

1 pound whole tiny new potatoes, quartered

12 ounces skinless, boneless chicken breast halves or skinless, boneless chicken thighs

1 tablespoon olive oil or cooking oil

1 cup sliced celery

1 cup chopped green pepper

½ cup Italian salad dressing

2 tablespoons snipped fresh dill

1 tablespoon Dijon-style mustard

2 large tomatoes, halved and sliced

Cook potatoes, covered, in boiling salted water for 6 to 8 minutes or till tender; drain.

Meanwhile, rinse chicken; pat dry. Cut into bite-size strips. In a large skillet cook chicken in hot oil over medium-high heat for 3 to 4 minutes till tender and no longer pink; remove from skillet.

In a large bowl place potatoes, cooked chicken, celery, and green pepper. Toss gently. In a small bowl stir together salad dressing, dill, and mustard; drizzle over salad and toss gently to coat with dressing.

Arrange sliced tomatoes on 4 dinner plates. Spoon salad over tomatoes. If desired, garnish with fresh dill and serve with breadsticks. Makes 4 servings.

Variation: Substitute sliced red onion for the celery, and a peppercorn dressing for the Italian dressing.

Per serving: 408 calories, 20 g protein, 36 g carbohydrate, 21 g total fat (3 g saturated), 45 mg cholesterol, 409 mg sodium, 987 mg potassium

sautéed chicken with pears

4 pound skinless, boneless chicken breast halves
1 teaspoon bottled minced garlic
1 tablespoon cooking oil
2 tablespoons margarine or butter
2 firm-ripe pears, peeled and sliced
½ cup chopped red onion
¼ cup apple jelly
¼ teaspoon salt
¼ teaspoon ground cinnamon
¼ teaspoon ground nutmeg
2 tablespoons snipped fresh parsley

Rinse chicken; pat dry. Place chicken breasts between sheets of plastic wrap; using a meat mallet pound lightly to ¼-inch thickness.

In a 12-inch skillet cook chicken and garlic in hot oil over medium-high heat for 3 to 4 minutes or till chicken is tender and no longer pink, turning chicken once. Remove to warm platter; cover and keep warm. In same skillet melt margarine; cook pears and onion for 3 to 4 minutes or till pears are nearly tender. Stir in apple jelly, salt, cinnamon, and nutmeg. Cook and stir 2 minutes more. Return chicken to skillet; cook 2 minutes or till heated through. Sprinkle parsley over. Makes 4 servings.

Complement the subtle flavors in this elegant dish with a side serving of herbed wild rice or a pilaf made with couscous.

Per serving: 314 calories, 22 g protein, 28 g carbohydrate, 13 g total fat (3 g saturated), 59 mg cholesterol, 259 mg sodium, 343 mg potassium

canadian bacon and chicken baguette

4 skinless, boneless chicken breast halves
    (about 1 pound total)
2 tablespoons olive oil or cooking oil
¼ teaspoon fines herbes
1 loaf French bread (baguette), split horizontally
    Margarine or butter
    Lettuce leaves
4 ounces sliced Canadian-style bacon
4 ounces Swiss or Monterey Jack cheese
4 to 6 tomato slices
3 to 4 tablespoons bacon and tomato, Caesar, or
    creamy ranch salad dressing

Preheat broiler. Rinse chicken; pat dry. Combine oil and fines herbes. Place chicken on the unheated rack of a broiler pan; brush with *half* of the oil and fines herbes mixture. Broil 4 to 5 inches from the heat for 5 minutes; turn and brush with remaining oil and fines herbes. Broil for 4 to 6 minutes more or till chicken is tender and no longer pink.

Meanwhile, place French bread halves cut side up. Spread cut sides of bread with margarine or butter; line bottom half of bread with lettuce leaves. Lay bacon slices, overlapping if necessary, over lettuce. Top with hot broiled chicken pieces. Layer cheese slices over chicken; top with a layer of tomato slices. Drizzle salad dressing over tomato layer; add bread top. Cut sandwich crosswise into 4 sections; serve immediately. Makes 4 servings.

Per serving: 589 calories, 40 g protein, 32 g carbohydrate, 32 g total fat (9 g saturated), 96 mg cholesterol, 786 mg sodium, 392 mg potassium

broiled chicken with garlic sauce

4 skinless, boneless chicken breast halves
    (about 1 pound total)
2 tablespoons olive oil or cooking oil
½ cup mayonnaise or salad dressing
2 tablespoons milk
1 tablespoon snipped fresh chives or 1 teaspoon
    dried chives
1½ teaspoon bottled minced garlic
1 teaspoon lemon juice
¼ teaspoon pepper
¼ teaspoon dry mustard

Preheat broiler. Rinse chicken; pat dry. Place chicken pieces on the unheated rack of a broiler pan. Brush with *1 tablespoon* of the olive oil. Broil 4 to 5 inches from the heat for 5 minutes.

Meanwhile, stir together mayonnaise or salad dressing, milk, chives, garlic, lemon juice, pepper, and mustard.

Turn chicken; brush with remaining oil. Broil 4 to 6 minutes more or till chicken is tender and no longer pink. Transfer chicken to heated platter. Spoon some of the garlic sauce over chicken; serve immediately. Pass remaining sauce. Garnish with lemon wedges and fresh chives, if desired. Makes 4 servings.

Be sure to wash your hands before and after handling raw poultry. Also, wash all surfaces, knives, and any utensils used with hot soapy water after they have been used with raw poultry.

Per serving: 387 calories, 22 g protein, 2 g carbohydrate, 32 g total fat (5 g saturated), 76 mg cholesterol, 215 mg sodium, 209 mg potassium

chicken pasta carbonara

8 ounces linguine, spaghettini, or fettuccine

12 ounces skinless, boneless chicken breast halves

1 cup half-and-half or light cream

2 beaten eggs

¼ cup grated Parmesan or Romano cheese

½ teaspoon seasoned salt

¼ teaspoon pepper

1 teaspoon bottled minced garlic

3 tablespoons margarine or butter

2 cups sliced fresh mushrooms

¼ cup cooked bacon pieces

2 tablespoons snipped fresh parsley

In a Dutch oven cook pasta in boiling salted water according to package directions.

Meanwhile, rinse chicken; pat dry. Cut chicken crosswise into ¼-inch strips. In a small bowl stir together cream, eggs, cheese, seasoned salt, and pepper; set aside.

In a large skillet heat *2 tablespoons* of the margarine over medium-high heat. Cook chicken and garlic for 2 to 3 minutes or till chicken is tender and no longer pink. Remove with slotted spoon; cover and keep warm. Cook mushrooms in same skillet 3 minutes.

Meanwhile, drain pasta; return to pan. Toss with remaining 1 tablespoon margarine. Add egg mixture. Cook and stir over medium heat 3 minutes. Add chicken and mushrooms. Transfer to serving platter. Sprinkle with bacon pieces and parsley. Makes 4 servings.

Per serving: 578 calories, 34 g protein, 51 g carbohydrate, 26 g total fat (10 g saturated), 182 mg cholesterol, 551 mg sodium, 472 mg potassium

cajun-style chicken with rice

1 cup quick-cooking white or brown rice

4 skinless, boneless chicken breast halves
   (about 1 pound total)

1 teaspoon Cajun seasoning

1 teaspoon dried thyme, crushed

2 tablespoons cooking oil

1 small red or green sweet pepper, cut into thin strips

1 cup frozen cut okra

⅓ cup dry white wine

⅓ cup chicken broth

Cook rice according to package directions.

Meanwhile, rinse chicken; pat dry. In a small bowl stir together Cajun seasoning and thyme. Rub chicken breasts with seasoning mixture.

In a large skillet cook chicken in hot oil over medium-high heat about 6 minutes or till chicken is tender and no longer pink, turning once. Remove from pan to a serving platter; cover and keep warm. Add red or green pepper and okra to skillet; cook and stir 2 to 3 minutes or till vegetables are crisp-tender. Remove from pan. Add wine and broth to skillet, scraping up any crusty bits in pan. Bring mixture to boiling; boil gently about 3 minutes or until sauce is reduced by half. Return vegetables to skillet; heat through. Serve immediately over chicken with hot cooked rice. Makes 4 servings.

Per serving: 299 calories, 25 g protein, 22 g carbohydrate, 10 g total fat (2 g saturated), 60 mg cholesterol, 170 mg sodium, 379 mg potassium

chicken and artichoke sauté

4 skinless, boneless chicken breast halves
   (about 1 pound total)
¼ cup all-purpose flour
¼ teaspoon salt
¼ teaspoon ground sage
⅛ teaspoon pepper
2 tablespoons cooking oil
½ cup dry white wine
1 14-ounce can artichoke hearts, drained and halved
1 4-ounce can sliced mushrooms, drained
2 tablespoons grated Parmesan or Romano cheese
2 tablespoons snipped fresh parsley

Rinse chicken; pat dry. In a shallow bowl stir together flour, salt, sage, and pepper. Reserve *1 tablespoon* of flour mixture. Dip chicken in flour mixture to coat. In a large skillet cook chicken in hot oil over medium-high heat about 6 minutes or till tender and no longer pink, turning once. Remove from skillet; cover and keep warm. Stir together wine and reserved flour mixture. Drain off any excess oil in skillet. Add artichokes, mushrooms, and wine mixture to skillet, scraping up crusty bits from pan. Cook and stir till thickened and bubbly; cook and stir 2 minutes more. Pour sauce over chicken. Sprinkle with cheese and parsley. Serve immediately. Makes 4 servings.

Remember, if juices are clear when chicken is cut, then it's done; if juices are pink, cook a few minutes longer and test again.

Per serving: 274 calories, 26 g protein, 13 g carbohydrate, 11 g total fat (3 g saturated), 62 mg cholesterol, 654 mg sodium, 432 mg potassium

chicken-couscous salad

1 cup chicken broth

1 cup chopped red or green sweet pepper

2 green onions, sliced

1 cup couscous

¾ cup Italian salad dressing

4 skinless, boneless chicken breast halves
   (about 1 pound total)

1 teaspoon bottled minced garlic

1 tablespoon olive oil or cooking oil

4 cups shredded lettuce or Chinese (napa) cabbage

1 small tomato, cut into wedges

1 cup sliced cucumber

In a medium saucepan combine chicken broth, pepper, and green onion. Bring to boiling; stir in couscous. Cover; remove from heat. Let stand 5 minutes. Stir ¼ *cup* of the dressing into couscous. Transfer to a bowl and place in freezer to quick-chill.

Meanwhile, rinse chicken; pat dry. In a large skillet cook chicken and garlic in hot oil over medium-high heat about 6 minutes or till chicken is tender and no longer pink, turning once. Remove from skillet. Cut diagonally into bite-size strips.

Arrange *1 cup* lettuce on each of 4 dinner plates. Arrange chicken, couscous, tomato, and cucumber atop. Drizzle with remaining dressing. Makes 4 servings.

Couscous is a rice-like grain in the shape of tiny beads. It's made from semolina (the same grain used to make pasta), but it's commonly used in North African cooking in place of rice.

Per serving: 564 calories, 30 g protein, 45 g carbohydrate, 29 g total fat (5 g saturated), 60 mg cholesterol, 609 mg sodium, 537 mg potassium

chicken scallops with green beans and tomatoes

4 skinless, boneless chicken breast halves
       (about 1 pound total)
¼ cup all-purpose flour
1 teaspoon seasoned salt
¼ teaspoon pepper
2 tablespoons cooking oil
1 teaspoon bottled minced garlic
1 16-ounce can diced tomatoes
1½ cups loose-pack frozen French-style green beans
½ cup pitted ripe olives
2 tablespoons snipped fresh parsley
1 teaspoon dried basil, crushed
1 teaspoon dried oregano or thyme, crushed
¼ teaspoon pepper

Rinse chicken; pat dry. Slice breast halves in half horizontally to make a total of 8 thin breast halves. In a shallow bowl stir together flour, seasoned salt, and pepper. Dip slices into flour mixture to coat.

In a 12-inch skillet cook chicken in hot oil over medium-high heat for 4 minutes or till tender and no longer pink, turning once. Remove from pan; cover and keep warm. In same pan cook garlic 1 minute; stir in *undrained* tomatoes, green beans, olives, parsley, basil, oregano or thyme, and pepper. Bring mixture to boiling; reduce heat and simmer, uncovered, for 5 minutes. Return chicken pieces to skillet; cook 2 minutes more to heat through. Makes 4 servings.

Per serving: 270 calories, 25 g protein, 15 g carbohydrate, 13 g total fat (2 g saturated), 59 mg cholesterol, 831 mg sodium, 272 mg potassium

Use a plastic cutting board to cut and slice poultry; it's easier to clean and disinfect than a standard wooden cutting board.

chicken with wine and anchovy sauce

4 skinless, boneless chicken breast halves or turkey breast
    tenderloin steaks (about 1 pound total)

½ teaspoon paprika

¼ teaspoon salt

¼ teaspoon pepper

2 tablespoons margarine or butter

1 tablespoon cooking oil

1 green onion, thinly sliced

3 to 4 anchovy fillets, chopped

1 teaspoon bottled minced garlic

½ cup dry white wine

1 2¼-ounce can sliced ripe olives, drained
    Hot cooked pasta (optional)

Rinse chicken or turkey; pat dry. Slice breast halves in half horizontally to make 8 pieces. In a small bowl combine the paprika, salt, and pepper. Sprinkle on both sides of chicken pieces

In a 12-inch skillet cook chicken in hot margarine and oil over medium-high heat for 3 to 4 minutes or till tender and no longer pink, turning once. Remove from pan; cover and keep warm. In drippings cook onion, anchovies, and garlic for 2 minutes. Stir in wine, scraping up crusty bits from pan. Bring to boiling; reduce heat and simmer 2 minutes. Add olives; heat 1 minute more. If desired, serve with hot cooked pasta. Pour sauce over chicken; serve immediately. Makes 4 servings.

Per serving: 259 calories, 23 g protein, 2 g carbohydrate, 16 g total fat (3 g saturated), 62 mg cholesterol, 468 mg sodium, 236 mg potassium

chicken with oranges and grapes

1 pound skinless, boneless chicken breast halves or
   turkey breast tenderloin steaks
2 tablespoons cooking oil
1 small onion, thinly sliced and separated into rings
½ teaspoon bottled minced garlic
½ cup whipping cream
⅓ cup chicken broth
1 teaspoon finely shredded orange or lemon peel
½ teaspoon salt
¼ teaspoon ground nutmeg
1 11-ounce can mandarin orange sections, drained
1 cup seedless red or green grapes, halved
   Hot cooked rice (optional)

Rinse chicken; pat dry. Slice chicken breasts diagonally
to make 8 pieces. In a 12-inch skillet cook chicken in hot
oil over medium-high heat about 4 minutes or till tender
and no longer pink, turning once. Remove from pan;
cover and keep warm. Add onion and garlic to drippings
in skillet; cook 2 minutes. Stir in cream and chicken
broth; cook and stir over medium heat till thickened. Stir
in orange peel, salt, and nutmeg. Return chicken to pan;
add oranges and grapes. Cover and cook 2 minutes more
to heat through. If desired, serve with hot cooked rice.
Makes 4 servings.

If you are calorie-counting, substitute plain nonfat yogurt or lowfat sour cream for the whipping cream, adding it at the end of the recipe just to heat through, but do not boil.

Per serving: 345 calories, 23 g protein, 15 g carbohydrate, 21 g total fat (9 g saturated),
100 mg cholesterol, 398 mg sodium, 390 mg potassium

Curly wide egg noodles, cooked and tossed with parsley, are a nice complement to this Hungarian take-off.

chicken and potatoes in paprika sauce

12 ounces skinless, boneless chicken breast halves or
   turkey breast tenderloin steaks
2 cups sliced fresh mushrooms
¾ cup chopped onion
2 tablespoons margarine or butter
½ cup dairy sour cream
1 tablespoon paprika
2 teaspoons all-purpose flour
1 cup half-and-half or light cream
1 16-ounce can whole white potatoes, drained and
   halved
¼ teaspoon salt
¼ teaspoon pepper

Rinse chicken; pat dry. Cut chicken or turkey into
¼-inch strips; set aside. In a 4-quart Dutch oven cook and
stir mushrooms and onion in hot margarine till vegetables
are almost tender. Add chicken pieces; cook for 2 to 3
minutes or till tender and no longer pink, stirring
occasionally.

Meanwhile, in a small bowl stir together the sour
cream, paprika, and flour. Add sour cream mixture to
cooked chicken. Slowly stir in cream; bring to boiling,
stirring constantly. Add potatoes, salt, and pepper; heat
through. If desired, garnish with parsley sprigs. Makes
3 servings.

Per serving: 485 calories, 29 g protein, 29 g carbohydrate, 29 g total fat
(13 g saturated), 106 mg cholesterol, 672 mg sodium, 885 mg potassium

honey-glazed chicken stir-fry

12 ounces skinless, boneless chicken breast halves or
     skinless, boneless chicken thighs
2   tablespoons honey
2   tablespoons vinegar
2   tablespoons orange juice
1   tablespoon soy sauce
1   teaspoon cornstarch
2   tablespoons cooking oil
2   cups loose-pack frozen mixed vegetables
3   cups hot cooked rice

Rinse chicken; pat dry. Cut into 1-inch pieces. Set
aside. For sauce, in a small bowl stir together honey,
vinegar, orange juice, soy sauce, and cornstarch; set aside.

Pour cooking oil into a wok or large skillet. (Add
more oil as necessary during cooking.) Preheat over
medium-high heat. Add frozen vegetables; stir-fry for
3 minutes or till vegetables are crisp-tender. Remove. Add
the chicken to the hot wok. Stir-fry for 2 to 3 minutes or
till tender and no longer pink. Push chicken from the
center. Stir sauce. Add sauce to the center. Cook and stir
till thickened and bubbly.

Return the cooked vegetables to the wok. Stir all
ingredients together to coat with sauce. Cook and stir
about 1 minute more or till heated through. Serve
immediately over hot cooked rice. Makes 4 servings.

Per serving: 443 calories, 23 g protein, 66 g carbohydrate, 10 g total fat (2 g saturated),
45 mg cholesterol, 333 mg sodium, 380 mg potassium

cheese-sauced chicken with spaetzle

1 10½-ounce package spaetzle or 8 ounces dried pasta
   such as corkscrew macaroni or bow-ties
12 ounces skinless, boneless chicken breast halves or
   skinless, boneless chicken thighs
2 tablespoons cooking oil
1 cup loose-pack frozen peas and carrots
½ cup chicken broth or water
1 teaspoon dried basil, crushed
½ teaspoon seasoned salt
¼ teaspoon dried dillweed
½ cup whipping cream
½ cup grated Parmesan or Romano cheese

In a large saucepan cook spaetzle according to package directions.

Meanwhile, rinse chicken; pat dry. Cut into thin bite-size strips. In a large skillet cook and stir chicken in hot oil over medium-high heat for 3 minutes or till tender and no longer pink. Remove from pan; cover and keep warm. Add peas and carrots to skillet; stir in broth or water, basil, salt, and dill. Bring to boiling; reduce heat and simmer for 5 minutes or till vegetables are tender. Remove peas and carrots with slotted spoon; keep warm. Simmer liquid in skillet till reduced by half; slowly stir in cream. Heat and stir till thickened, about 2 to 3 minutes. Drain spaetzle; turn into a large serving bowl. Add cooked chicken, peas and carrots, cream sauce, and grated cheese; toss well to coat. Serve immediately. Serves 4.

Per serving: 591 calories, 33 g protein, 53 g carbohydrate, 27 g total fat
(12 g saturated), 160 mg cholesterol, 575 mg sodium, 306 mg potassium

glazed chicken with apples and onions

4 skinless, boneless chicken breast halves
    (about 1 pound total)
2 tablespoons cooking oil
1 cup coarsely chopped red onion
1 medium apple, sliced
¼ cup light or dark raisins
2 tablespoons apple jelly
2 tablespoons vinegar
¼ teaspoon salt
⅛ teaspoon pepper

Rinse chicken; pat dry. In a large skillet cook chicken in hot oil over medium-high heat about 6 minutes or till tender and no longer pink, turning once. Remove from pan; cover and keep warm. In pan drippings cook onion, apples slices, and raisins for 3 minutes or till apples are nearly tender. Stir in apple jelly, vinegar, salt, and pepper. Cook and stir 2 minutes more or till sauce thickens slightly. Add chicken to skillet; spoon sauce over. Cook 1 minute more; serve immediately. If desired, garnish with a fresh herb sprig. Makes 4 servings.

If you'd prefer not to use oil in this dish, start with a nonstick skillet. Spray it generously with non-stick spray coating before heating the pan, and sauté chicken as directed.

Per serving: 270 calories, 22 g protein, 23 g carbohydrate, 10 g total fat (2 g saturated), 59 mg cholesterol, 191 mg sodium, 358 mg potassium

orange and olive chicken salad

4 skinless, boneless chicken breast halves
     (about 1 pound total)
2 tablespoons frozen orange juice concentrate
5 cups shredded romaine or red-tipped leaf lettuce
3 large seedless oranges, peeled, thinly sliced, and halved
12 large black Greek olives or ½ cup pitted ripe olives
1 cup thinly sliced red onion
⅓ cup olive oil or salad oil
⅓ cup orange juice
1 tablespoon lemon juice
1 clove garlic, minced
¼ teaspoon salt
¼ teaspoon pepper

Preheat broiler. Rinse chicken; pat dry. Slice chicken breast halves in half horizontally to make 8 thin slices. Place on a lightly greased, unheated rack of a broiler pan. Brush with orange juice concentrate. Broil 4 to 5 inches from the heat for 7 to 9 minutes or till chicken is tender and no longer pink, turning once. Remove from pan; cool slightly.

Meanwhile, on 4 dinner plates arrange a bed of shredded lettuce. Arrange orange slices on half of the lettuce. Cut chicken into slices and arrange next to orange slices. Sprinkle olives and sliced onion over salad.

For dressing, in a screw-top jar combine oil, orange juice, lemon juice, garlic, salt, and pepper. Cover and shake till well blended; drizzle a few tablespoons of dressing mixture over salad. Pass remaining dressing with salad. Makes 4 servings.

Per serving: 363 calories, 24 g protein, 16 g carbohydrate, 23 g total fat (4 g saturated), 59 mg cholesterol, 252 mg sodium, 616 mg potassium

chicken with orzo, eggplant, and tomatoes

4 skinless, boneless chicken breast halves or turkey breast
   tenderloin steaks (about 1 pound total)

1 14½-ounce can vegetable broth or chicken broth

¾ pound Japanese eggplant or 1 small eggplant,
   unpeeled and cut into 1-inch cubes

⅔ cup orzo (rosamarina)

¼ teaspoon salt

¼ teaspoon pepper

1 14½-ounce can pasta-style chunky tomatoes

1 tablespoon cooking oil

½ cup shredded mozzarella cheese (2 ounces)

Rinse chicken; pat dry. Set aside.

In a large saucepan stir together vegetable or chicken broth, eggplant, orzo, salt, and pepper. Bring mixture to boiling; reduce heat. Simmer, covered, for 10 to 12 minutes or till orzo is tender. Stir in tomatoes. Cook 5 minutes more.

Meanwhile, in a large skillet cook chicken in hot oil over medium-high heat about 6 minutes or till tender and no longer pink, turning once. Cover and keep warm.

To serve, place chicken atop orzo mixture on 4 dinner plates. Sprinkle with cheese. Makes 4 servings.

For a bit of extra herb flavor, substitute a can of Italian-seasoned diced tomatoes, undrained, for the stewed tomatoes.

Per serving: 376 calories, 31 g protein, 39 g carbohydrate, 10 g total fat (3 g saturated), 68 mg cholesterol, 858 mg sodium, 707 mg potassium

chicken and sausage with cabbage

8 ounces skinless, boneless chicken breast halves

8 ounces fully-cooked smoked sausage links, bias-sliced ½-inch thick

6 cups packaged pre-shredded coleslaw mix

½ cup chopped onion

¾ cup chicken broth

2 tablespoons red or white wine vinegar

2 teaspoons stone-ground mustard

1 teaspoon sugar

½ teaspoon caraway seed or fennel seed

¼ teaspoon pepper

2 teaspoons cornstarch

1 tablespoon cold water

Rinse chicken; pat dry. Cut into bite-size pieces and set aside. In a large skillet brown sausage pieces on both sides over medium heat about 3 minutes. Remove sausage pieces. Add chicken to skillet drippings and cook for 4 to 5 minutes or till tender and no longer pink. Remove chicken and drain off excess fat. Add coleslaw mix and onion to skillet. Stir in broth, vinegar, mustard, sugar, caraway seed, and pepper. Bring to boiling; reduce heat. Cover and cook about 5 minutes or till cabbage is crisp-tender. Stir together cornstarch and water. Add to skillet mixture. Cook and stir till thickened and bubbly; cook and stir 2 minutes more. Return meats to skillet and heat through. Makes 4 servings.

Per serving: 312 calories, 22 g protein, 14 g carbohydrate, 20 g total fat (7 g saturated), 68 mg cholesterol, 755 mg sodium, 675 mg potassium

chicken-pepper kabobs with peanut sauce

1 pound skinless, boneless chicken breast halves or turkey breast tenderloins

1 red or yellow sweet pepper, cut into 1-inch squares

1 green pepper, cut into 1-inch squares

2 tablespoons olive oil or cooking oil

½ cup unsweetened coconut milk

¼ cup peanut butter

2 teaspoons brown sugar

2 teaspoons soy sauce

2 teaspoons dry sherry

½ teaspoon chili powder

Hot cooked rice

Preheat broiler. Rinse chicken; pat dry. Cut chicken into 1½-inch pieces. Thread onto 8 short or 4 long skewers alternately with red or yellow and green pepper squares. Place kabobs on unheated rack of a broiler pan. Brush with oil. Broil 4 to 5 inches from the heat for 5 minutes. Turn and broil for 4 to 6 minutes more or till chicken is tender and no longer pink.

Meanwhile, in a small saucepan stir together coconut milk, peanut butter, brown sugar, soy sauce, sherry, and chili powder till combined. Cook and stir over medium heat for 4 minutes or till sauce is smooth and heated through. Brush sauce over broiled kabobs; pass remaining sauce with kabobs. Serve with hot cooked rice. Makes 4 servings.

Per serving: 367 calories, 27 g protein, 9 g carbohydrate, 25 g total fat (9 g saturated), 50 mg cholesterol, 302 mg sodium, 526 mg potassium

If you don't have metal skewers, use bamboo skewers. Soak them in water for 30 minutes before using so they won't burn.

chicken and zucchini in blue cheese sauce

12 ounces skinless, boneless chicken breast halves

⅓ cup whipping cream

⅓ cup chicken broth

¼ cup crumbled blue cheese

2 tablespoons cooking oil

2½ cups sliced zucchini or yellow summer squash
   (3 small squash)

1 cup chopped onion

8 ounce package dried tomato-flavored pasta or regular
   pasta, cooked

¼ cup chopped toasted walnuts

Rinse chicken; pat dry. Cut chicken into ¼-inch strips; set aside.

In a small bowl combine whipping cream, broth, and blue cheese. Set aside.

In a large skillet cook and stir chicken in hot oil over medium-high heat for 2 to 3 minutes or till tender and no longer pink. Remove from pan. Add zucchini and onion; cook and stir 3 to 4 minutes more or till vegetables are crisp-tender. Pour cheese mixture over vegetables. Cook and stir over medium-low heat about 2 minutes or till mixture is heated through and thickened slightly (do not boil). Return chicken to pan; cook 2 minutes more. Toss with cooked pasta. Sprinkle with toasted nuts. Makes 4 servings.

Per serving: 552 calories, 28 g protein, 54 g carbohydrate, 25 g total fat (8 g saturated), 78 mg cholesterol, 236 mg sodium, 507 mg potassium

poached chicken with tomatoes and basil mayonnaise

1 14½-ounce can chicken broth

¼ cup dry white wine

2 bay leaves

¼ teaspoon whole black pepper

4 skinless, boneless chicken breast halves
    (about 1 pound total)

⅔ cup mayonnaise or salad dressing

¼ cup milk

1 tablespoon snipped fresh basil or ½ teaspoon dried
    basil, crushed

1 green onion, chopped

¼ teaspoon dry mustard

¼ teaspoon cracked black pepper
    Lettuce leaves

2 tomatoes, cut up

In a large skillet combine chicken broth, wine, bay leaves, and whole pepper; bring to boiling. Meanwhile, rinse chicken; pat dry. Add chicken to skillet; bring to boiling. Reduce heat; simmer, covered, for 10 to 12 minutes or till chicken is tender and no longer pink.

Meanwhile, in a small bowl stir together mayonnaise or salad dressing, milk, basil, green onion, dry mustard, and cracked black pepper. Arrange lettuce leaves on 4 dinner plates. Remove chicken from cooking liquid; discard liquid. Cut chicken into slices and arrange on lettuce along with tomatoes. Spoon some of the basil mayonnaise over; pass remaining mayonnaise. Serves 4.

Per serving: 433 calories, 25 g protein, 5 g carbohydrate, 34 g total fat (6 g saturated), 82 mg cholesterol, 604 mg sodium, 455 mg potassium

Keep mayonnaise or nonfat mayonnaise dressing on hand for spur-of-the-moment meals. It's a versatile sauce or topping ingredient.

poached chicken with cherry sauce

4 skinless, boneless chicken breast halves
    (about 1 pound total)
1 cup port or burgundy wine
1 cup chicken broth
1 orange slice, halved
1 clove garlic, quartered
¼ teaspoon pepper
1 bay leaf
2 teaspoons cooking oil
⅓ cup sliced green onion
1 tablespoon cornstarch
1 16-ounce can pitted dark sweet cherries
1 tablespoon snipped fresh parsley
    Hot cooked rice

Rinse chicken; pat dry. In a large skillet place chicken breasts; cover with wine and broth. Add orange slice, garlic, pepper, and bay leaf. Bring mixture to boiling; reduce heat. Simmer, covered, for 10 to 12 minutes or till chicken is tender and no longer pink.

Drain chicken; reserve ½ *cup* of the poaching liquid. Keep chicken warm. In the same pan heat oil; cook and stir green onion over medium-high heat for 1 minute. Stir cornstarch into the *undrained* cherries till combined; add to skillet along with reserved poaching liquid. Cook and stir till thickened and bubbly. Cook and stir 2 minutes more. Stir in parsley. Spoon sauce over chicken and serve over rice. Makes 4 servings.

Per serving: 505 calories, 27 g protein, 71 g carbohydrate, 6 g total fat (1 g saturated), 60 mg cholesterol, 242 mg sodium, 510 mg potassium

texas-style pita-wiches

1 pound skinless, boneless chicken thighs or skinless, boneless chicken breast halves

¼ cup bottled hickory smoke-flavored barbecue sauce

1 Granny Smith or other tart apple, chopped

½ cup chopped celery

1 green onion, chopped

2 tablespoons mayonnaise or salad dressing

2 tablespoons bottled hickory smoke-flavored barbecue sauce

4 6-inch pita bread rounds, halved and split

Lettuce leaves

Preheat broiler. Rinse chicken; pat dry. Place chicken pieces on unheated rack of a broiler pan; brush with some of the ¼ cup barbecue sauce. Broil 4 to 5 inches from the heat for 5 minutes. Turn and brush liberally with barbecue sauce. Broil for 4 to 6 minutes more or till chicken is tender and no longer pink, brushing frequently with sauce.

Meanwhile, in a medium bowl combine apple, celery, and green onion. Chop broiled chicken; add to apple mixture with mayonnaise and remaining 2 tablespoons barbecue sauce.

Line pita halves with lettuce leaves; divide chicken mixture equally among pita halves. Serve immediately. Makes 4 servings.

This easy sandwich filling is also great made with leftover barbecued chicken. Cook up some extra at your next barbecue!

Per serving: 327 calories, 21 g protein, 34 g carbohydrate, 12 g total fat (2 g saturated), 58 mg cholesterol, 617 mg sodium, 316 mg potassium

stir-fried chicken with tofu

2 tablespoons water

2 tablespoons soy sauce

1 tablespoon hoisin sauce

1 tablespoon dry sherry

2 teaspoons cornstarch

8 ounces skinless, boneless chicken thighs or skinless, boneless chicken breast halves

2 to 3 tablespoons peanut oil or cooking oil

1½ cups bias-sliced carrots

2 teaspoons chopped, drained pickled ginger

1 teaspoon bottled minced garlic

5 cups shredded Chinese (napa) cabbage

8 ounces tofu (fresh bean curd), cut into ½-inch cubes

In a small bowl stir together water, soy sauce, hoisin sauce, sherry, and cornstarch till combined; set aside. Rinse chicken; pat dry. Cut into 1-inch pieces; set aside.

Pour 1 tablespoon cooking oil into wok or 12-inch skillet. (Add more oil as necessary during cooking.) Preheat over medium-high heat. Stir-fry carrots with ginger and garlic about 3 minutes or till crisp-tender. Add shredded cabbage; stir-fry for 1½ minutes. Remove. Add the chicken to the hot wok. Stir-fry for 2 to 3 minutes or till no longer pink. Push chicken from center of wok. Stir sauce. Add sauce to center of wok. Cook and stir till thickened and bubbly. Cook and stir 1 minute more.

Add tofu and vegetable mixture to the wok. Stir all ingredients together to coat with sauce. Cook and stir about 1 minute more or till heated through. Serves 4.

Per serving: 216 calories, 15 g protein, 13 g carbohydrate, 11 g total fat (2 g saturated), 27 mg cholesterol, 878 mg sodium, 526 mg potassium

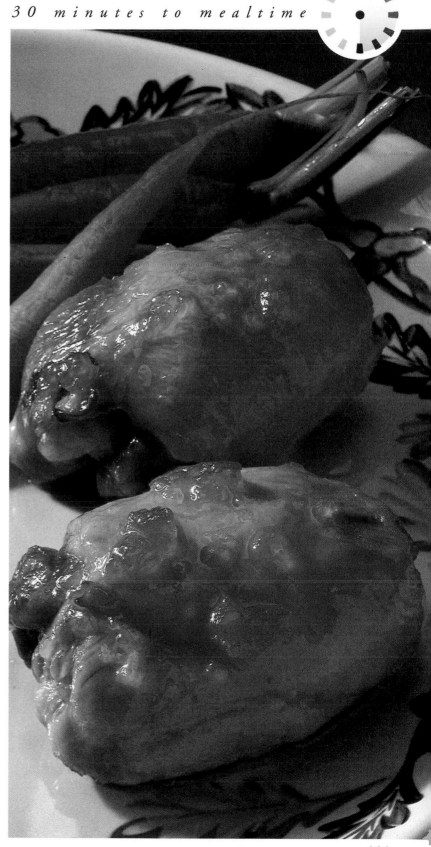

broiled chicken thighs with honey-apricot glaze

1 pound skinless, boneless chicken breast halves

1 tablespoon olive oil or cooking oil

¼ teaspoon garlic salt

⅛ teaspoon pepper

¼ cup apricot preserves

1 tablespoon honey

2 tablespoons vinegar

Preheat broiler. Rinse chicken; pat dry. Place chicken pieces on unheated rack of a broiler pan. Brush with oil and sprinkle with garlic salt and pepper. Broil 4 to 5 inches from the heat for 5 minutes.

Meanwhile, in a small saucepan stir apricot preserves and honey over medium heat till mixture is melted. Remove from heat; stir in vinegar. Brush mixture over chicken pieces; turn and brush with remaining apricot mixture. Broil for 4 to 6 minutes more or till chicken is tender and no longer pink. Serve immediately. If desired, serve with cooked carrots. Makes 4 servings.

To vary the flavor of the sweet-sour glaze, substitute other preserves for the apricot, such as plum or raspberry, or try orange marmalade.

Per serving: 221 calories, 16 g protein, 19 g carbohydrate, 9 g total fat (2 g saturated), 54 mg cholesterol, 185 mg sodium, 169 mg potassium

quick chicken fajitas

8 6- or 7-inch flour tortillas
12 ounces skinless, boneless chicken thighs, or skinless, boneless chicken breast halves
2 tablespoons cooking oil
1 medium red or green sweet pepper, cut into thin strips
1 medium onion, thinly sliced
1 12-ounce jar chunky salsa
½ cup dairy sour cream
1½ cups shredded cheddar cheese

Wrap tortillas in foil; heat in a 350° oven for 5 minutes.

Meanwhile, with a sharp knife, cut chicken into ¼-inch strips. In a large skillet heat *1 tablespoon* of the oil over medium-high heat. Add pepper strips and onion slices; stir-fry 3 minutes or till crisp-tender. Remove from pan.

Add remaining oil to pan; add chicken and stir-fry 2 to 3 minutes or till tender and no longer pink. Add *⅓ cup* of the salsa and the pepper-onion mixture. Cook 1 to 2 minutes or till heated through.

For each serving, arrange 2 warm tortillas on *each* of 4 dinner plates. Fill *each* with some of the chicken mixture. Top with remaining salsa, sour cream, and cheese. Fold tortilla over filling. Makes 4 servings.

If you have extra time, marinate the chicken strips in ½ cup of salsa for 30 minutes. Drain chicken and be sure to discard the marinade.

Per serving: 639 calories, 31 g protein, 50 g carbohydrate, 39 g total fat (16 g saturated), 99 mg cholesterol, 1,136 mg sodium, 772 mg potassium

stir-fried chicken with peanuts

1 pound skinless, boneless chicken thighs

3 tablespoons teriyaki sauce or soy sauce

1 teaspoon cornstarch

⅛ teaspoon ground red pepper

1 tablespoon peanut oil or cooking oil

1 tablespoon grated fresh gingerroot

1½ teaspoons bottled minced garlic

1 green pepper, cut into 1-inch squares

1 red or yellow sweet pepper, cut into 1-inch squares

1 3-ounce can rice noodles or 1½ cups chow mein noodles

¼ cup peanuts

Rinse chicken; pat dry. Cut into 1-inch pieces. Stir together teriyaki sauce, cornstarch, red pepper, and 3 tablespoons *water*; set aside. Pour oil into a wok or large skillet. (Add more oil as necessary during cooking.) Preheat over medium-high heat. Stir-fry gingerroot and garlic in hot oil 15 seconds. Add peppers. Stir fry about 2 minutes or till crisp-tender. Remove. Add *half* of the chicken. Stir-fry for 2 to 3 minutes or till no longer pink. Remove. Repeat with remaining chicken. Return all chicken to wok. Push chicken from the center. Stir sauce. Add sauce to the center. Cook and stir till bubbly. Return vegetable mixture to wok. Stir all ingredients together. Cook and stir about 1 minute more or till hot. Serve over noodles. Sprinkle with peanuts. Makes 4 servings.

Per serving: 274 calories, 21 g protein, 15 g carbohydrate, 15 g total fat (3 g saturated), 54 mg cholesterol, 665 mg sodium, 362 mg potassium

chicken with mushrooms and peppers

1 pound skinless, boneless chicken breast halves

½ cup fine dry seasoned bread crumbs

2 tablespoons grated Parmesan or Romano cheese

1 beaten egg

1 tablespoon water

3 tablespoons cooking oil

2 cups sliced fresh mushrooms

1 cup red or green sweet pepper cut into bite-size strips

1 teaspoon dried basil, crushed

½ teaspoon dried chervil, crushed

½ teaspoon salt

¼ teaspoon pepper

Rinse chicken; pat dry. Halve each chicken piece lengthwise. Place between sheets of plastic wrap. Pound lightly to ¼-inch thickness. In a shallow bowl combine crumbs and cheese. In a second shallow bowl beat egg and water. Dip chicken in egg, then in crumb mixture. In a 12-inch skillet cook chicken in hot oil over medium-high heat about 3 minutes or till tender and no longer pink, turning once. Remove from pan; cover and keep warm. (If necessary, cook half at a time.) In pan drippings cook mushrooms and pepper strips with basil, chervil, salt, and pepper. Cook and stir for 3 minutes, or till peppers are nearly tender. Spoon vegetable mixture over chicken; serve immediately. Makes 4 servings.

Per serving: 308 calories, 22 g protein, 13 g carbohydrate, 19 g total fat (4 g saturated), 110 mg cholesterol, 489 mg sodium, 356 mg potassium

hawaiian stir-fry spinach salad

12 ounces skinless, boneless chicken thighs or skinless, boneless chicken breast halves

1 8-ounce can pineapple chunks (juice pack)

2 tablespoons soy sauce

1 teaspoon cornstarch

½ teaspoon ground ginger

2 tablespoons peanut oil or cooking oil

3 green onions, cut into 1-inch pieces

1 teaspoon bottled minced garlic

1 8-ounce can sliced water chestnuts, drained

10 cups torn spinach

¼ cup chopped peanuts

Rinse chicken; pat dry. Cut chicken crosswise into ¼-inch strips. Drain pineapple, reserving ⅓ cup juice. In a bowl combine reserved pineapple juice, soy sauce, cornstarch, and ginger. Set aside.

Pour *1 tablespoon* oil into a wok or large skillet. (Add more oil as necessary during cooking.) Preheat over medium-high heat. Stir-fry green onions and garlic for 1 minute; remove from wok.

Add chicken to the hot wok. Stir-fry for 2 to 3 minutes or till tender and no longer pink. Push chicken from the center. Stir pineapple juice mixture. Add to the center. Cook and stir till thickened and bubbly. Return onion mixture, pineapple, and water chestnuts to the wok. Stir all ingredients together. Cook 1 minute to heat through. Spoon over spinach in a large salad bowl; toss well. Sprinkle with peanuts. Serve immediately. Makes 4 servings.

Per serving: 286 calories, 22 g protein, 21 g carbohydrate, 14 g total fat (2 g saturated), 45 mg cholesterol, 611 mg sodium, 681 mg potassium

broiled chili-glazed chicken and peppers

4 skinless, boneless chicken breast halves
   (about 1 pound total)
2 medium red, yellow, or green sweet peppers
¼ cup chili sauce
2 tablespoons bottled barbecue sauce
1 tablespoon snipped fresh cilantro or parsley

Preheat broiler. Rinse chicken; pat dry. Place chicken pieces on the unheated rack of a broiler pan. Halve peppers from stem to tip; remove center core. Cut each half into 4 wedges. Place peppers, cut side down, on broiler pan. In a small bowl stir together chili sauce, barbecue sauce, and cilantro or parsley.

Brush chicken and pepper pieces lightly with chili sauce mixture. Broil 4 to 5 inches from the heat for 5 minutes; turn and brush generously with sauce mixture. Broil for 4 to 6 minutes more or till chicken is tender and no longer pink, brushing once or twice more with sauce during cooking. Serve each piece of chicken with 4 pepper wedges. If desired, garnish with sprigs of cilantro or parsley. Makes 4 servings.

Practice boning and skinning bone-in chicken breasts instead of purchasing already-boned and skinned breasts; you'll notice a significant savings per pound.

Per serving: 153 calories, 23 g protein, 7 g carbohydrate, 3 g total fat (1 g saturated), 59 mg cholesterol, 319 mg sodium, 323 mg potassium

chicken, tomato, and corn frittata

4 ounces sliced fully cooked chicken or turkey breast

6 eggs

2 teaspoons snipped fresh basil or ½ teaspoon dried basil, crushed

2 teaspoons snipped fresh thyme or ½ teaspoon dried thyme, crushed

　Few dashes bottled hot pepper sauce

½ cup loose-pack frozen whole kernel corn

1 green onion, sliced

1 tablespoon cooking oil

1 tomato, chopped

½ cup shredded mozzarella, Swiss, or Monterey Jack cheese with jalapeño peppers (2 ounces)

Stack chicken slices; dice. Set aside. In a medium bowl beat together eggs, basil, thyme, and hot pepper sauce.

Preheat broiler. In a large broiler-proof skillet cook corn and onion in hot oil for 3 minutes. Stir in tomato and chicken. Stir egg mixture; pour into skillet over vegetables and meat. Cook over medium heat. As mixture sets, run a spatula around edge of skillet, lifting egg mixture to allow uncooked portions to flow underneath. Continue cooking and lifting edges till egg mixture is almost set (surface will be moist).

Sprinkle cheese over. Place broiler-proof skillet under the broiler 4 to 5 inches from the heat. Broil for 1 to 2 minutes or till top is just set. (Or, if using a regular skillet, remove skillet from the heat; cover and let stand 3 to 4 minutes or till cheese is melted.) Cut into wedges. If desired, garnish with a sprig of fresh herb. Serves 4.

Per serving: 251 calories, 22 g protein, 7 g carbohydrate, 15 g total fat (5 g saturated), 351 mg cholesterol, 186 mg sodium, 289 mg potassium

berried treasure chicken salad

6 cups purchased torn mixed greens for salads

8 ounces sliced fully cooked chicken breast

2 cups mixed fresh berries (sliced strawberries, blueberries, raspberries, or blackberries)

2 oranges, peeled, sliced, and cut into quarters

1 8-ounce container mixed berry or strawberry yogurt

½ cup mayonnaise or salad dressing

Dash ground cinnamon

Orange juice (optional)

½ cup broken walnuts or pecans (optional)

Place lettuce in a large bowl. Stack chicken slices; halve the stack lengthwise. Cut crosswise into ¼-inch strips; add chicken strips to lettuce in bowl. Add fresh berries and orange pieces.

For dressing, in a small bowl stir together yogurt, mayonnaise, and cinnamon. If necessary, add orange juice, *1 teaspoon* at a time, to make of drizzling consistency. Spoon salad onto 4 dinner plates; drizzle with dressing. If desired, sprinkle with walnuts or pecans. Makes 4 servings.

If you're flush with fresh berries, you can puree ½ cup of additional berries to mix with the mayonnaise for the salad dressing instead of using flavored yogurt.

Per serving: 408 calories, 21 g protein, 27 g carbohydrate, 25 g total fat 4 g saturated), 62 mg cholesterol, 237 mg sodium, 532 mg potassium

chicken-broccoli soup with dumplings

1 cup cubed cooked chicken

2 10¾-ounce cans condensed cream of chicken soup

2 cups milk

1½ cups loose-pack frozen cut broccoli

½ cup finely shredded carrot

1 teaspoon Dijon-style mustard

½ teaspoon dried basil, crushed
   Dumplings

½ cup shredded cheddar cheese

In a large saucepan stir together chicken, soup, milk, broccoli, carrot, mustard, and basil. Bring mixture to boiling; reduce heat. Meanwhile, prepare Dumplings. Spoon batter in 4 or 5 mounds atop bubbling soup. Reduce heat. Cover; simmer 10 to 12 minutes or till a toothpick inserted into a dumpling comes out clean. Sprinkle dumplings with cheese. Makes 4 or 5 servings.

Dumplings: In a small mixing bowl combine ⅔ cup *all-purpose flour* and 1 teaspoon *baking powder*. Add ¼ cup *milk* and 2 tablespoons *cooking oil*. Stir just till moistened.

Who says chicken soup has to take hours? For the cooked chicken, use canned chunk-style chicken, drained; purchased deli-cooked chicken, boned and skinned; or your own cut-up leftover chicken.

Per serving: 493 calories, 27 g protein, 38 g carbohydrate, 26 g total fat (9 g saturated), 71 mg cholesterol, 1,445 mg sodium, 578 mg potassium

chicken and couscous on romaine leaves

1½   cups couscous

8   ounces boneless fully cooked smoked or regular
     chicken or turkey breast

1   cup fresh pea pods, halved, or sliced celery

½   cup currants or raisins

4   green onions, sliced

1   2-ounce jar diced pimiento, drained

¼   cup olive oil or cooking oil

3   tablespoons lime or lemon juice

2   tablespoons snipped fresh mint or ¾ teaspoon dried
     mint, crushed

½   teaspoon salt

⅛   teaspoon ground red pepper

8   to 12 large romaine or leaf lettuce leaves

Prepare couscous according to package directions.
Meanwhile, cut chicken into bite-size strips. Transfer to a
large bowl; add pea pods or celery, currants or raisins,
green onion, and diced pimiento. Drain couscous; add to
chicken mixture.

For dressing, in a screw-top jar combine oil, lime or
lemon juice, mint, salt, and ground red pepper. Cover jar
and shake dressing till combined; pour over salad. Toss
well to coat with dressing.

Trim thick center ribs from romaine leaves, if desired.
For each serving, place 2 or 3 romaine leaves on a dinner
plate. Spoon couscous mixture onto romaine. Serves 4.

Per serving: 583 calories, 22 g protein, 75 g carbohydrate, 22 g total fat (4 g saturated),
41 mg cholesterol, 649 mg sodium, 676 mg potassium

chicken-spinach pita pizzas

4 large pita bread rounds
1 8-ounce can pizza sauce
8 ounces sliced fully cooked chicken breast
5 cups torn fresh spinach
1 cup ricotta cheese
2 to 3 tablespoons Italian salad dressing
2 tablespoons grated Parmesan or Romano cheese
1½ cups shredded mozzarella or Monterey Jack cheese
     (6 ounces)

Preheat oven to 425°. Arrange pita bread rounds on a large baking sheet. Spread each with pizza sauce to within ½ inch of edges. Dice chicken breast; set aside.

Chop the spinach. In a medium bowl combine spinach with ricotta cheese and Italian dressing till moistened. Spoon mixture on top of pizza sauce. Sprinkle with chicken and Parmesan cheese. Sprinkle cheese over all. Bake for 8 to 10 minutes or till heated through and cheese is melted. Serve immediately. Makes 4 servings.

For a quick double-crust pizza or a mock calzone, you can add a second pita round to cover the top of each pizza and bake. Or, use two 8-inch pre-baked Italian bread shells, and sandwich them together.

Per serving: 542 calories, 45 g protein, 44 g carbohydrate, 21 g total fat (9 g saturated), 93 mg cholesterol, 1,141 mg sodium, 934 mg potassium

santa barbara chicken pilaf

1 6¼- or 6¾-ounce package quick-cooking long grain
   and wild rice mix
2 cups loose-pack frozen broccoli, corn, and peppers or
   cauliflower, broccoli, and carrots
1½ cups chopped cooked chicken
3 tablespoons Italian salad dressing
   Finely shredded Parmesan cheese (optional)

Prepare rice mix according to package directions. Meanwhile, in a colander run cold water over frozen vegetables till thawed. Stir vegetables, chicken, and salad dressing into cooked rice; cover and cook for 4 minutes more or till vegetables are crisp-tender. Garnish with finely shredded Parmesan cheese, if desired. Serves 4.

To give this recipe lots of different twists, look for interesting rice and seasoning mixes such as curry, saffron, or herb-flavored mixes; Spanish or Oriental-style mixes; or chicken-flavored rice with vermicelli.

Per serving: 339 calories, 22 g protein, 41 g carbohydrate, 10 g total fat (2 g saturated), 51 mg cholesterol, 893 mg sodium, 254 mg potassium

jicama-chicken salad with strawberry vinaigrette

3   cups shredded romaine or leaf lettuce

10 ounces boneless fully cooked smoked chicken or
       turkey

1½ cups jicama, cut into bite-size strips

1½ cups cucumber, cut into half-slices

2   cups strawberries, sliced

2   tablespoons red or white wine vinegar

½   teaspoon sugar
     Dash pepper
     Romaine or leaf lettuce leaves (optional)

Place romaine lettuce in a large bowl. Cube chicken.
Add chicken to romaine along with jicama, cucumber,
and *half* of the sliced berries.

For dressing, in a blender container or food processor
bowl place remaining strawberries, vinegar, sugar, and
pepper. Cover and blend or process till pureed. Pour
dressing over salad; toss to coat well. If desired, serve on
4 dinner plates lined with romaine or lettuce. Serves 4.

Jicama (pronounced HE-kuh-muh), is a root vegetable with thin, pale brown skin and pale white
meat. It's crisp, juicy, and delicious. Use it raw, cut
into sticks, shredded, or lightly cooked in a stir-fry.
And, ½ cup of jicama is just 25 calories!

Per serving: 142 calories, 16 g protein, 15 g carbohydrate, 3 g total fat (1 g saturated),
37 mg cholesterol, 722 mg sodium, 511 mg potassium

pizza new mexico-style

1 16-ounce Italian bread shell (Boboli brand) or one
    10-ounce package refrigerated pizza dough
1 3⅛-ounce can bean dip
4 ounces sliced fully cooked chicken breast or turkey
    breast
½ cup medium salsa
1 cup shredded cheddar, Monterey Jack, mozzarella, or
    Monterey Jack cheese with jalapeño peppers
2 tablespoons snipped fresh cilantro or parsley

Preheat oven to 425°. Place bread shell on a baking sheet or pizza pan. Spread crust with bean dip to within 1 inch of edges. Finely chop chicken; sprinkle over crust. Spoon salsa evenly over chicken; sprinkle with cheese and cilantro. Or, unroll refrigerated dough and press out with hands, starting at center, in a greased 13-inch pizza pan. Bake crust for 8 to 10 minutes or until crust is lightly browned. Then top with beans and other ingredients as for bread shell.

Bake for 8 to 10 minutes or till cheese is bubbly and filling is hot. Makes 4 servings.

If you have more time for the crust, try using 1 loaf of frozen whole wheat bread dough, thawed, or prepare dough from a hot roll mix. Roll the dough to fit pizza pan, top with ingredients, and bake for 25 to 30 minutes.

Per serving: 496 calories, 30 g protein, 54 g carbohydrate, 19 g total fat (6 g saturated), 60 mg cholesterol, 1,054 mg sodium, 250 mg potassium

chicken soup with artichokes and leeks

8 ounces boneless fully cooked smoked chicken or
  turkey breast
½ cup chopped carrots
½ cup sliced leeks or green onions
2 tablespoons cooking oil
¼ cup all-purpose flour
2 cups milk
1 14½-ounce can chicken broth
1 teaspoon dried basil, crushed
½ teaspoon salt
⅛ teaspoon white pepper
1 10-ounce package frozen artichoke hearts
½ cup dry white wine

Cube chicken; set aside. In a large saucepan cook carrots and leeks in hot oil over medium heat for 3 minutes. Sprinkle flour over mixture; slowly stir in milk, chicken broth, basil, salt, and pepper. Add artichoke hearts; bring mixture to boiling, stirring occasionally. Reduce heat; cook 2 minutes longer or till artichokes are tender.

Stir in chicken and wine; cook 2 minutes more or till heated through. Makes 4 servings.

When using leeks, be sure to separate the leaves and thoroughly wash out all of the sand and grit. Slice the white portion only.

Per serving: 363 calories, 20 g protein, 28 g carbohydrate, 18 g total fat (5 g saturated), 51 mg cholesterol, 1,113 mg sodium, 777 mg potassium

avocado, chicken, and pepper salad

  6 cups shredded lettuce
 12 ounces sliced fully cooked chicken breast
  1 red or green sweet pepper, coarsely chopped
  1 yellow summer squash or zucchini, halved lengthwise
    and thinly sliced
  1 medium avocado, halved, seeded, peeled, and sliced
 ⅓ cup lemon juice
  2 tablespoons salad oil
  2 tablespoons water
  1 tablespoon snipped fresh thyme or sage or 1 teaspoon
    dried thyme or sage, crushed
 ¼ teaspoon Worcestershire sauce
  3 dashes bottled hot pepper sauce

Line 4 dinner plates with shredded lettuce. Roll up slices of chicken breast. Arrange chicken breast rolls, red or green sweet pepper, summer squash or zucchini, and avocado slices atop the lettuce. For dressing, in a screw-top jar combine lemon juice, oil, water, thyme or sage, Worcestershire sauce, and hot pepper sauce. Cover and shake well. Spoon dressing over each salad; serve immediately. Makes 4 servings.

Shred lettuce quickly by stacking the washed leaves, rolling them up the long way, and slicing the roll thinly crosswise.

Per serving: 305 calories, 29 g protein, 6 g carbohydrate, 19 g total fat (2 g saturated), 72 mg cholesterol, 83 mg sodium, 830 mg potassium

quick chicken calzone

2 10-ounce packages refrigerated pizza dough

1½ cups chopped cooked chicken

1 cup shredded mozzarella or Monterey Jack cheese (4 ounces)

½ cup pizza sauce or spaghetti sauce

1 2¼-ounce can sliced pitted ripe olives, drained

1 tablespoon olive oil or cooking oil

½ teaspoon dried oregano, crushed

Preheat oven to 425°. On a lightly floured surface unroll pizza dough. Cut each rectangle of dough in half diagonally to make two triangles.

In a medium bowl combine chicken, cheese, pizza sauce, and olives. Place *one-fourth* of the mixture on *half* of each dough triangle, spreading to within ½ inch of edges. Fold dough over filling, making a triangle; pinch edges of dough to seal. With a metal spatula, transfer triangles to a large baking sheet.

Brush dough with olive oil; sprinkle with oregano. Bake for 15 to 18 minutes or till golden brown. Serve hot. If desired, garnish plate with sprigs of parsley. Serves 4.

Classic Italian calzone is like a stuffed pizza— filled with all of your favorite pizza ingredients and with twice the crust! You can reheat any left- over calzone in the oven or microwave the next day for a quick lunch.

Per serving: 546 calories, 32 g protein, 56 g carbohydrate, 22 g total fat (6 g saturated), 67 mg cholesterol, 901 mg sodium, 388 mg potassium

chicken-vegetable ratatouille

8   ounces dried penne, bow tie, or fusilli pasta
1   cup frozen chopped onion
1   teaspoon bottled minced garlic
1   tablespoon olive oil or cooking oil
1   medium eggplant, cut into 1-inch chunks
2   cups loose-pack frozen zucchini, carrots, cauliflower,
      lima beans, and Italian beans
1   14½-ounce can diced tomatoes
1   teaspoon dried Italian seasoning, crushed
¾   teaspoon seasoned salt
¼   teaspoon pepper
1½ cups chopped cooked chicken

In a large saucepan cook pasta according to package directions; drain.

Meanwhile, in a large saucepan cook onion and garlic in hot oil for 2 minutes. Stir in eggplant, frozen vegetables, *undrained* tomatoes, Italian seasoning, seasoned salt, and pepper. Bring mixture to boiling; reduce heat. Simmer, covered, for 12 to 15 minutes or till eggplant is tender.

Add chicken to vegetable mixture; cook 1 minute more to heat through. Serve ratatouille over pasta in shallow bowls. Makes 4 or 5 servings.

Per serving: 438 calories, 28 g protein, 66 g carbohydrate, 7 g total fat (1 g saturated), 44 mg cholesterol, 651 mg sodium, 564 mg potassium

california-style chicken and fruit salad

½ medium pineapple or one 20-ounce can pineapple
   tidbits, drained

1 whole purchased roasted chicken or 3 cups chopped
   cooked chicken

½ cup seedless red or green grapes, halved

½ cup chopped celery

¼ cup piña colada or pineapple yogurt

2 tablespoons mayonnaise or salad dressing
   Lettuce leaves

¼ cup sliced almonds

To prepare the fresh pineapple, remove the crown
from pineapple. Cut off the peel. Remove the eyes from
the fruit by cutting diagonal wedge-shaped grooves in the
pineapple. Cut into quarters; remove the hard center core.
Chop fruit into ½-inch pieces. Measure *2 cups* fruit;
reserve remaining fruit for another use. Remove meat
from whole chicken; cut into ½-inch cubes. In a large
bowl combine the pineapple, chicken, grapes, and celery.
In a small bowl combine the yogurt and mayonnaise or
salad dressing. Pour over the salad mixture and toss to
coat. Spoon salad onto lettuce leaves on 4 dinner plates
and sprinkle with almonds. Serve immediately. Makes
4 servings.

If you like, quarter the pineapple and leave the fronds attached. Hollow out fruit with a paring knife and use the shells as serving containers.

Per serving: 367 calories, 36 g protein, 17 g carbohydrate, 18 g total fat (3 g saturated),
106 mg cholesterol, 163 mg sodium, 553 mg potassium

italian-style enchiladas

1 15-ounce container tomato-basil or marinara
    pasta sauce
2 purchased broiled or roasted chicken breast halves
    (about 8 ounces cooked meat)
3 oil-packed dried tomato halves, drained
1 cup shredded mozzarella or Monterey Jack cheese
    (4 ounces)
1 green onion, sliced
    Nonstick spray coating
6 6-inch flour tortillas
    Sliced green onion (optional)

Preheat oven to 450°. In a small saucepan heat sauce until heated through. Meanwhile, remove bones from chicken; cut meat into bite-size strips. Finely chop dried tomatoes. Toss together the chicken, tomatoes, *½ cup* of the cheese, and onion. To assemble enchiladas, spray a 2-quart rectangular baking dish with nonstick spray coating. Spread *2 tablespoons* of the pasta sauce over bottom of dish. Spoon about *¼ cup* of the chicken mixture just below center of each tortilla. Roll up. Place seam side down in dish.

Pour remaining pasta sauce over all. Sprinkle with remaining cheese. Bake for 10 to 12 minutes or till heated through and cheese is melted. To serve, transfer 2 enchiladas to each dinner plate. If desired, garnish with sliced green onion. Makes 3 servings.

Per serving: 530 calories, 40 g protein, 51 g carbohydrate, 20 g total fat (7 g saturated), 85 mg cholesterol, 1,353 mg sodium, 903 mg potassium

chicken in spicy pasta

1 9-ounce package refrigerated fresh linguine or
   6 ounces dried linguine

4 purchased grilled or roasted chicken breast halves

½ cup water

2 tablespoons soy sauce

1 tablespoon chili sauce

1 teaspoon cornstarch

1 teaspoon sugar

½ teaspoon crushed red pepper

2 tablespoons peanut butter

1 cup shredded cabbage

2 green onions, sliced

Cook linguine according to package directions. Meanwhile, remove bones from chicken; chop meat.

In a small saucepan stir together water, soy sauce, chili sauce, cornstarch, sugar, and crushed red pepper till combined. Cook and stir till thickened and bubbly; cook and stir for 2 minutes more. Remove from heat; stir in peanut butter till combined. Stir in chicken, cabbage, and green onion; heat through.

Drain pasta; turn into a large bowl. Add chicken mixture. Toss till well-coated with sauce. Serve immediately. If desired, garnish with a hot red pepper. Makes 4 servings.

For this recipe, you can also use Oriental noodles such as fresh Chinese noodles or cellophane noodles, cooked and drained.

Per serving: 385 calories, 35 g protein, 40 g carbohydrate, 9 g total fat (2 g saturated), 72 mg cholesterol, 677 mg sodium, 399 mg potassium

chicken and macadamia fruit salad

Lettuce leaves
4 purchased grilled or roasted chicken breast halves
1 papaya or mango seeded, peeled and thinly sliced
2 kiwi fruit, peeled and sliced
1 banana, peeled and bias-sliced
⅓ cup coarsely chopped macadamia nuts, cashews, or peanuts
1 cup plain yogurt
2 tablespoons chutney

Line 4 dinner plates with lettuce leaves. Remove bones from chicken pieces; slice chicken and arrange on lettuce. Arrange papaya or mango, kiwi fruit, and banana slices on plates. Sprinkle nuts over all. For dressing, stir together yogurt and chutney (chop any large pieces in the chutney); pass with salad. Makes 4 servings.

If you don't have poultry shears or kitchen shears among your utensils, this recipe is a good reason to buy a pair. The shears are great for cutting up cooked chicken because they go through skin and the joints of the bones easily.

Per serving: 418 calories, 30 g protein, 40 g carbohydrate, 16 g total fat (3 g saturated), 77 mg cholesterol, 160 mg sodium, 971 mg potassium

chicken and crab gumbo

1 cup chopped red or green sweet pepper

1 cup chopped onion

1 teaspoon bottled minced garlic

2 tablespoons cooking oil

1 tablespoon all-purpose flour

3 cups chicken broth

1 16-ounce can diced tomatoes

1 10-ounce package frozen cut okra or 1½ cups
   sliced okra

¼ cup quick-cooking rice

1 to 2 teaspoons Cajun seasoning

1 bay leaf

2 5-ounce cans or one 12½-ounce can chunk-style
   chicken, drained

1 6½-ounce can crabmeat, drained and cartilage
   removed

In a large saucepan cook red or green sweet pepper,
onion, and garlic in hot oil till vegetables are tender.
Stir in flour. Stir in chicken broth, *undrained* tomatoes,
okra, rice, Cajun seasoning, and bay leaf. Bring mixture to
boiling; reduce heat. Cover and simmer for 6 to 10
minutes or till okra is tender. Stir in chicken and
crabmeat; heat through. Remove bay leaf. If desired, serve
with crackers. Makes 4 or 5 servings.

Okra is a classic ingredient in Louisiana gumbo;
it lends a mild asparagus flavor and also thickens
the brew. For best results, cook the gumbo just till
the okra is tender.

Per serving: 350 calories, 32 g protein, 22 g carbohydrate, 15 g total fat (3 g saturated),
81 mg cholesterol, 1,519 mg sodium, 740 mg potassium

chicken flautas

12 6- or 7-inch flour tortillas
½ cup chopped onion
2 tablespoons snipped fresh cilantro
1 clove garlic, minced
1 tablespoon cooking oil
1 5-ounce can chunk-style chicken, drained and flaked
1 cup canned black beans, rinsed and drained
½ cup salsa
   Cooking oil for deep-fat frying
   Shredded lettuce
   Salsa
   Dairy sour cream

Wrap tortillas tightly in foil; heat in a 350° oven for 10 minutes or till heated through.

Meanwhile, in a medium skillet cook and stir onion, cilantro, and garlic in hot oil for 3 minutes or till vegetables are tender. Stir in chicken, beans, and the ½ cup salsa; heat through.

Place about *2 tablespoons* of the chicken mixture on *each* tortilla. Roll up very tightly, securing with wooden toothpicks. In a large saucepan heat 1½ to 2 inches of cooking oil to 365°. Fry 2 or 3 tortillas at a time for 1 to 2 minutes or till golden brown. Drain on paper towels. Repeat with remaining tortillas while keeping others warm in a 300° oven. Serve hot with shredded lettuce, additional salsa, and sour cream. Makes 4 to 6 servings.

If desired, heat the tortillas in a microwave oven as directed on the package.

Per serving: 541 calories, 20 g protein, 55 g carbohydrate, 29 g total fat (6 g saturated), 28 mg cholesterol, 1,038 mg sodium, 510 mg potassium

spanish-style chicken and rice soup

1 6.8-ounce package Spanish-style rice mix with vermicelli

1 16-ounce can diced tomatoes

3 to 3½ cups chicken broth

2 5-ounce cans or one 12½-ounce can chunk-style chicken, flaked

1 cup loose-pack frozen cut green beans

½ cup loose-pack frozen whole kernel corn

½ cup shredded Monterey Jack cheese or Monterey Jack cheese with jalapeño peppers (2-ounces)

Bottled hot pepper sauce (optional)

In a large saucepan prepare rice mix according to package directions using *undrained* tomatoes. When rice is done, stir in chicken broth; bring to boiling. Stir in *undrained* chicken, green beans, and corn. Heat through.

To serve, ladle soup into bowls; top with shredded cheese. If desired, pass hot pepper sauce. Serves 5 or 6.

If you like, substitute leftover cooked, shredded chicken or purchased deli-cooked chicken for the canned chicken. Figure that one 5-ounce can of chunk-style chicken is equivalent to a generous ½ cup of diced, cooked fresh chicken.

Per serving: 338 calories, 25 g protein, 36 g carbohydrate, 10 g total fat (4 g saturated), 43 mg cholesterol, 1,567 mg sodium, 525 mg potassium

chicken thermidore

2 cups baby carrots

2 shallots, peeled and sliced or ¼ cup chopped onion

1 tablespoon margarine or butter

2 tablespoons all-purpose flour

1¾ cups half-and-half, light cream, or milk

2 cups chopped cooked chicken

2 tablespoons dry sherry

1 tablespoon snipped fresh parsley

½ teaspoon dried tarragon, crushed

½ teaspoon dry mustard

¼ teaspoon salt

¼ teaspoon white pepper

4 slices white bread, toasted and quartered

2 tablespoons grated Parmesan or Romano cheese

Cut carrots in half diagonally. Cook in a small amount of boiling water for 8 to 10 minutes, or till tender. Drain.

Meanwhile, in a large skillet cook shallots in margarine or butter till tender but not brown. Stir in flour. Add cream or milk all at once; cook and stir till thickened and bubbly. Stir in chicken, carrots, sherry, parsley, tarragon, mustard, salt, and pepper. Cook over low heat for 5 minutes or till heated through. Arrange 4 toast quarters on each of 4 dinner plates. Divide chicken mixture evenly over toast. Sprinkle Parmesan or Romano cheese over top. Serve immediately. Makes 4 servings.

Per serving: 444 calories, 30 g protein, 28 g carbohydrate, 23 g total fat (10 g saturated), 109 mg cholesterol, 498 mg sodium, 525 mg potassium

chicken-tortellini soup

½ cup frozen chopped onion

1 teaspoon bottled minced garlic

1 tablespoon cooking oil

1 9-ounce package refrigerated fresh cheese tortellini or
   4 ounces dried cheese tortellini

6 cups chicken broth

2 cups desired loose-pack frozen mixed vegetables

2 5-ounce cans or one 12½-ounce can chunk-style
   chicken

1 teaspoon bouquet garni seasoning, or fines herbes

¼ teaspoon pepper

   Grated Parmesan or Romano cheese (optional)

In a Dutch oven cook onion and garlic in hot oil for
2 minutes. Stir in tortellini, chicken broth, vegetables,
undrained chicken, bouquet garni seasoning, and pepper.
Bring mixture to boiling; reduce heat. Simmer for 5 to 10
minutes for fresh tortellini and 15 to 20 minutes for dried
tortellini or till pasta is tender. Serve topped with
Parmesan or Romano cheese, if desired. Makes 5 or 6
servings.

Bouquet garni seasoning is a tied bundle of herbs such as thyme, parsley, and bay leaf wrapped in cheesecloth. You can purchase bouquet garni seasoning pre-wrapped in convenient bundles or make your own.

Per serving: 352 calories, 28 g protein, 29 g carbohydrate, 13 g total fat (3 g saturated),
34 mg cholesterol, 1,585 mg sodium, 448 mg potassium

tortellini with tomato, chicken, and basil sauce

1 9-ounce package refrigerated fresh cheese tortellini or
   4-ounces dried cheese tortellini
1 14½-ounce can pasta-style chunky tomatoes
1 cup cubed cooked chicken
1 tablespoon chopped fresh basil or 1 teaspoon dried
   basil, crushed
¼ teaspoon pepper
   Grated Parmesan or Romano cheese
   Fresh basil leaves (optional)

In a large saucepan cook pasta according to package directions; drain. Turn into serving dish; cover and keep warm. Meanwhile, in another pan heat tomatoes with chicken, basil, and pepper till boiling. Spoon over pasta; sprinkle with Parmesan cheese and garnish with fresh basil leaves, if desired. Makes 3 servings.

Agnolotti, pronounced "ahn-yo-LOT-ee," is a delightful shaped pasta that literally translated means "little fat lambs." Actually, it's very similar to tortellini or ravioli and can be found with a meat, chicken, or cheese filling.

Per serving: 408 calories, 30 g protein, 47 g carbohydrate, 11 g total fat (2 g saturated), 91 mg cholesterol, 826 mg sodium, 532 mg potassium

chicken minestrone

1 cup frozen chopped onion

½ teaspoon bottled minced garlic

1 tablespoon cooking oil

2 cups chicken broth

1 15-ounce can tomato puree

½ of a 15-ounce can garbanzo beans, drained

½ cup dried corkscrew macaroni, small shells, or
      elbow macaroni

1 teaspoon dried Italian seasoning, crushed

¼ teaspoon salt

2 5-ounce cans or one 12½-ounce can chunk-style
      chicken

1 small zucchini or yellow summer squash, halved
      lengthwise and sliced

   Grated Parmesan or Romano cheese

In a large saucepan cook onion and garlic in hot oil
for 2 minutes. Add broth, tomato puree, garbanzo beans,
pasta, Italian seasoning, and salt. Bring to boiling. Reduce
heat. Cover and simmer for 10 minutes. Stir in *undrained*
chicken and squash. Cover and simmer 5 minutes more
or till pasta is tender and zucchini is crisp-tender. Serve
with Parmesan cheese. If desired, garnish with a sprig of
basil. Makes 5 servings.

For a low-salt version of this dish, use sodium-
reduced chicken broth and tomato puree canned
without salt. Also, rinse the garbanzo beans before
using and use salt substitute for the salt.

Per serving: 266 calories, 20 g protein, 25 g carbohydrate, 10 g total fat (2 g saturated),
34 mg cholesterol, 1,259 mg sodium, 731 mg potassium

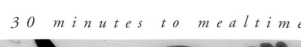

pecan-coated turkey tenderloins

4 turkey breast tenderloin steaks (about 1 pound total)
4 teaspoons Dijon-style mustard
½ cup chopped pecans
3 tablespoons fine dry seasoned bread crumbs
2 tablespoons grated Parmesan cheese
2 tablespoons margarine or butter, melted

Preheat oven to 425°. Rinse turkey; pat dry. Place turkey steaks in a shallow baking pan. Brush *each* tenderloin steak with *1 teaspoon* of the mustard; set aside. In a small bowl combine chopped pecans, bread crumbs, Parmesan cheese, and margarine. Sprinkle evenly over turkey. Bake for 18 to 20 minutes or till turkey is tender and no longer pink. If desired, serve with green beans. Makes 4 servings.

When roasting a turkey breast or breast portions, you can check for doneness by cutting into the turkey (juices should run clear and meat should no longer be pink), or you can use a meat thermometer and roast the breast to 170°.

Per serving: 293 calories, 25 g protein, 7 g carbohydrate, 19 g total fat (3 g saturated), 52 mg cholesterol, 436 mg sodium, 292 mg potassium

salsa-broiled turkey with avocado dressing

1 small ripe avocado, halved, seeded, and peeled
⅔ cup chunky salsa
2 tablespoons snipped fresh cilantro
1 teaspoon lemon juice
4 turkey breast tenderloin steaks (about 1 pound total)
6 cups purchased torn mixed greens for salads
2 green onions, chopped

Preheat broiler. In a small bowl mash avocado; stir in *2 tablespoons* of the salsa, the cilantro, and lemon juice. Set aside.

Rinse turkey; pat dry. Place turkey pieces on unheated rack of a broiler pan. Brush with salsa. Broil 4 to 5 inches from the heat for 5 minutes; turn and brush with remaining salsa. Broil for 4 to 6 minutes more or till turkey is tender and no longer pink. Slice diagonally into 1-inch slices. Place salad greens on 4 dinner plates; arrange turkey atop. Sprinkle with green onions. Serve with avocado mixture. Makes 4 servings.

For a soft turkey taco, heat tortillas wrapped in foil at 350° for 5 minutes. Broil turkey as directed and cut into thin strips. Fill tortillas with turkey, shredded cheese, shredded lettuce, and onion slices. Top with salsa and avocado.

Per serving: 209 calories, 24 g protein, 5 g carbohydrate, 11 g total fat (1 g saturated), 50 mg cholesterol, 205 mg sodium, 858 mg potassium

tortellini with turkey and spinach pesto

1 9-ounce package refrigerated fresh cheese tortellini
1 cup torn spinach
⅓ cup grated Parmesan or Romano cheese
2 tablespoons pine nuts, chopped walnuts, or almonds
1 teaspoon dried basil, crushed
1 teaspoon bottled minced garlic
4 tablespoons olive oil or cooking oil
8 ounces turkey breast tenderloins
1 red and/or yellow sweet pepper, cut into
    thin, bite-size strips
    Grated Parmesan or Romano cheese

In a large saucepan cook tortellini according to package directions. Meanwhile, for pesto, in a blender container or food processor bowl combine spinach, the ⅓ cup cheese, nuts, basil, garlic, and ¼ teaspoon *salt*. Cover and blend or process with several on-off turns till a paste forms, stopping the machine several times and scraping the sides. With the machine running slowly, gradually add *3 tablespoons* of the oil; blend or process to the consistency of soft butter. Set aside.

Rinse turkey; pat dry. Cut into ½-inch pieces. In a skillet cook and stir pepper over medium-high heat in remaining oil for 1 to 2 minutes or till crisp-tender. Remove from skillet. Add turkey. Cook and stir 3 minutes or till turkey is no longer pink. Drain pasta; add pepper, turkey, and pesto; toss well. Serve immediately with additional cheese. Makes 4 servings.

Per serving: 438 calories, 26 g protein, 28 g carbohydrate, 25 g total fat (5 g saturated), 34 mg cholesterol, 757 mg sodium, 279 mg potassium

szechuan-fried turkey tenderloins

¼ cup soy sauce

1 teaspoon grated fresh gingerroot

1 teaspoon sugar

½ teaspoon chili oil

4 turkey breast tenderloin steaks (about 1 pound total)

½ cup all-purpose flour

2 tablespoons cooking oil

4 green onions, cut into slivers

3 cups hot cooked rice

Red peppers (optional)

In a shallow dish stir together soy sauce, gingerroot, sugar, and chili oil; set aside. Rinse turkey; pat dry. Place turkey between pieces of plastic wrap; pound with meat mallet to ¼-inch thickness.

Dip turkey into soy sauce mixture, then in flour to coat thoroughly on both sides. Heat oil in a large skillet over medium-high heat; fry *half* of the turkey pieces at a time for 2 to 3 minutes per side or till no longer pink. Drain well on paper towels; cover and keep warm while cooking remaining turkey. Garnish turkey with onions and serve with hot cooked rice. If desired, garnish with red peppers. Makes 4 servings.

Sometimes called the "filet mignon" of turkey, turkey breast tenderloins are skinless, boneless cuts of turkey from the eye of the breast. The steaks are the same cut, split lengthwise.

Per serving: 442 calories, 28 g protein, 57 g carbohydrate, 10 g total fat (2 g saturated), 50 mg cholesterol, 1,077 mg sodium, 340 mg potassium

sesame turkey

2 tablespoons sesame seed paste (tahini)

1 tablespoon lemon juice

1 tablespoon soy sauce

⅛ teaspoon ground red pepper

1 green onion, sliced

4 turkey breast tenderloin steaks (about 1 pound total)

1 tablespoon grated fresh gingerroot

1 teaspoon bottled minced garlic

2 tablespoons cooking oil

1 teaspoon sesame seed

For sauce, in a small bowl stir together sesame paste, lemon juice, and soy sauce. Stir in red pepper and green onion till combined. Set aside.

Rinse turkey; pat dry. In a 12-inch skillet cook turkey steaks with ginger and garlic in hot oil over medium-high heat about 6 minutes or till turkey is tender and no longer pink, turning once. Transfer to serving plates; spoon sauce over. Sprinkle with sesame seed. Makes 4 servings.

Tahini, available in larger supermarkets and in Middle-Eastern markets, is a smooth paste made from sesame seeds. It's a distinctive ingredient used in Middle-Eastern cuisine and adds a toasted nut flavor to sauces and dressings.

Per serving: 195 calories, 23 g protein, 3 g carbohydrate, 10 g total fat (2 g saturated), 50 mg cholesterol, 278 mg sodium, 282 mg potassium

turkey piccata with fettuccine

4 ounces fettuccine or linguine

¼ cup all-purpose flour

½ teaspoon lemon-pepper seasoning or pepper

4 turkey breast tenderloin steaks (about 1 pound total)

2 tablespoons olive oil or cooking oil

⅓ cup dry white wine

2 tablespoons lemon juice

2 tablespoons water

½ teaspoon instant chicken bouillon granules

1 tablespoon capers, rinsed and drained (optional)

2 tablespoons snipped fresh parsley

1 lemon, thinly sliced

In a large saucepan cook pasta according to package directions. Meanwhile, in a shallow bowl stir together flour and lemon-pepper seasoning or pepper.

Rinse turkey; pat dry. Place between sheets of plastic wrap; pound to ⅛-inch thickness. Dip turkey slices in flour mixture to coat. In a 12-inch skillet cook turkey steaks in hot oil over medium-high heat about 2 minutes per side, or till light golden brown and no longer pink. Remove from pan; cover and keep warm. Add wine, lemon juice, water, and bouillon granules to skillet, scraping up crusty bits from bottom of pan. Stir in capers, if desired; bring mixture to boiling. Simmer 2 minutes. Remove from heat. Add parsley.

To serve, drain pasta; divide pasta among 4 dinner plates. Arrange turkey over pasta; spoon sauce over. Garnish with lemon; serve immediately. Makes 4 servings.

Per serving: 331 calories, 26 g protein, 31 g carbohydrate, 10 g total fat (2 g saturated), 50 mg cholesterol, 292 mg sodium, 308 mg potassium

turkey tenderloins with almond butter sauce

4 turkey breast tenderloin steaks (about 1 pound total)
1 clove garlic, halved
2 tablespoons margarine or butter
3 tablespoons slivered almonds
½ teaspoon finely shredded lemon peel
3 cups hot cooked couscous or rice
1 green onion, sliced

Preheat broiler. Rinse turkey; pat dry. Rub cut garlic clove over turkey pieces. Mince garlic and set aside. Place turkey on unheated rack of a broiler pan. Broil 4 to 5 inches from the heat for 5 minutes; turn. Broil 4 to 6 minutes more or till turkey is tender and no longer pink.

Meanwhile, in a small skillet melt margarine. Cook almonds and garlic in margarine for 2 minutes or till almonds are golden brown. Stir in lemon peel. Remove from heat; cover and keep warm.

Spoon couscous onto 4 dinner plates; place a turkey steak over each serving. Spoon almond sauce over turkey and sprinkle with green onion. Makes 4 servings.

Complement this dish with a mixed green salad tossed with a creamy dressing and hot steamed asparagus or baby carrots. Serve with chenin blanc or a white bordeaux wine.

Per serving: 343 calories, 28 g protein, 33 g carbohydrate, 11 g total fat (2 g saturated), 50 mg cholesterol, 119 mg sodium, 343 mg potassium

turkey with pea pods

⅓ cup chicken broth or water

2 tablespoons soy sauce

2 tablespoons dry sherry

2 teaspoons cornstarch

12 ounces turkey breast tenderloins

6 ounces fresh pea pods or 6-ounce package frozen pea pods, thawed and well drained

2 tablespoons peanut oil or cooking oil

1 8-ounce can sliced water chestnuts, drained

1 8-ounce can sliced straw mushrooms or one 6-ounce can sliced mushrooms, drained

2¼ cups hot cooked rice

For sauce, in a small bowl stir together chicken broth or water, soy sauce, sherry, and cornstarch. Set aside.

Rinse turkey; pat dry. Cut into thin bite-size strips. Set aside. Remove strings from fresh pea pods; cut pea pods diagonally in half. Set aside.

Pour cooking oil into a wok or large skillet. (Add more oil as necessary during cooking.) Preheat over medium-high heat. Add fresh pea pods, if using; stir-fry 1 minute. Remove. Add turkey. Stir-fry turkey for 2 to 3 minutes or till no longer pink. Push turkey from the center. Stir sauce. Add sauce to the center of the wok. Cook and stir till thickened and bubbly. Add water chestnuts, mushrooms, and pea pods. Cover and cook 2 minutes or till heated through. Serve immediately over hot cooked rice. Makes 3 or 4 servings.

If you have leftover stir-fry and rice, toss it with shredded Chinese cabbage and a few drops of vinegar for a salad the next day.

Per serving: 470 calories, 26 g protein, 59 g carbohydrate, 13 g total fat (2 g saturated), 49 mg cholesterol, 1,025 mg sodium, 487 mg potassium

turkey breakfast hash

¼ cup cooking oil

1 pound ground turkey sausage

1 cup chopped onion

1 24-ounce package loose-pack frozen hash brown
  potatoes with onion and peppers

¼ cup chili sauce or catsup

Apple wedges (optional)

In a 12-inch skillet heat *2 tablespoons* of the oil. Cook
sausage and onion till browned; remove from pan,
reserving drippings.

Add remaining oil to skillet. Cook potatoes, covered,
over medium heat for 5 minutes. Uncover; cook and stir
5 to 8 minutes more or till tender.

Return turkey mixture to skillet along with chili sauce
or catsup; cook and stir 2 minutes more or till heated
through. If desired, serve with apple wedges. Serves 4.

*You'll find that turkey sausage is a great breakfast
add-on. If you have leftover cooked potatoes and
fresh sweet peppers, chop them and substitute them
for the frozen hashbrowns used in this recipe.*

Per serving: 631 calories, 28 g protein, 40 g carbohydrate, 41 g total fat
(13 g saturated), 43 mg cholesterol, 1,112 mg sodium, 960 mg potassium

spaghetti squash with turkey marinara

1 3- to 4-pound spaghetti squash, quartered
1 pound ground raw turkey or chicken
1 teaspoon bottled minced garlic
¼ teaspoon seasoned salt
¼ teaspoon pepper
1 15-ounce can meatless spaghetti sauce (2 cups)
   Grated Parmesan or Romano cheese

Place squash pieces in a 4½-quart Dutch oven; add water to a depth of 2 inches. Bring to boiling; reduce heat and simmer, partially covered, for 20 minutes or till squash strands separate from rind.

Meanwhile, in a 10-inch skillet cook ground turkey and garlic for 3 minutes or till turkey is no longer pink. Stir in seasoned salt, pepper, and spaghetti sauce; cook 2 minutes more or till heated through.

With tongs, remove squash from pan; drain. Using two forks, remove strands of squash from rind; pile on a serving platter. Spoon turkey and sauce mixture over squash; sprinkle with grated cheese. Serve immediately. Makes 4 servings.

Spaghetti squash, a hard-shelled bright yellow squash filled with mildly sweet spaghetti-strands of pulp, is a superb low-cal substitute for pasta. A fork will separate the strands from the shell.

Per serving: 322 calories, 21 g protein, 30 g carbohydrate, 13 g total fat (4 g saturated), 47 mg cholesterol, 709 mg sodium, 463 mg potassium

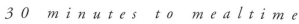

turkey and zucchini sloppy joes

12 ounces ground raw turkey or chicken

1 teaspoon bottled minced garlic

1 tablespoon cooking oil

½ cup chopped red or green sweet pepper

1 16-ounce can zucchini with tomato sauce

1 2¼-ounce can sliced pitted ripe olives, drained

½ teaspoon dried Italian seasoning, crushed

4 onion rolls or hamburger buns, split

½ cup shredded cheddar, American, or mozzarella cheese (optional)

In a large skillet cook ground turkey and garlic in hot oil till turkey is browned. Add pepper; cook 2 minutes more. Stir in zucchini with sauce, olives, and Italian seasoning. Cook 2 minutes more or till heated through.

Toast rolls or buns, if desired. Spoon turkey mixture into rolls. Sprinkle with cheese, if desired. Serve immediately. Makes 4 servings.

If you want all light or dark meat in your ground turkey, choose breasts for light meat or thighs for the dark. Ask your butcher to grind it with or without the skin, as desired.

Per serving: 312 calories, 16 g protein, 30 g carbohydrate, 15 g total fat (3 g saturated), 32 mg cholesterol, 871 mg sodium, 677 mg potassium

new mexico turkey and rice salad

¾ cup quick-cooking brown rice or quick-cooking rice
1 pound ground raw turkey or chicken
4 green onions, sliced
2 teaspoons cooking oil
1½ cups salsa
3 cups shredded lettuce
Avocado slices
Shredded cheddar cheese
Green onion, sliced

Cook rice according to package directions. Meanwhile, in a large skillet cook turkey and the 4 green onions in hot oil till browned. Drain off excess fat. Stir in salsa.

Place lettuce on 4 dinner plates; spoon turkey mixture over lettuce. Spoon rice in center of turkey mixture. Garnish each plate with avocado slices, shredded cheese, and additional sliced green onion. Makes 4 servings.

The amount of fat in purchased ground turkey will vary considerably from brand to brand. Some types contain more or less white meat and may also contain the skin. Check with your butcher on the content.

Per serving: 335 calories, 22 g protein, 17 g carbohydrate, 22 g total fat (6 g saturated), 57 mg cholesterol, 479 mg sodium, 688 mg potassium

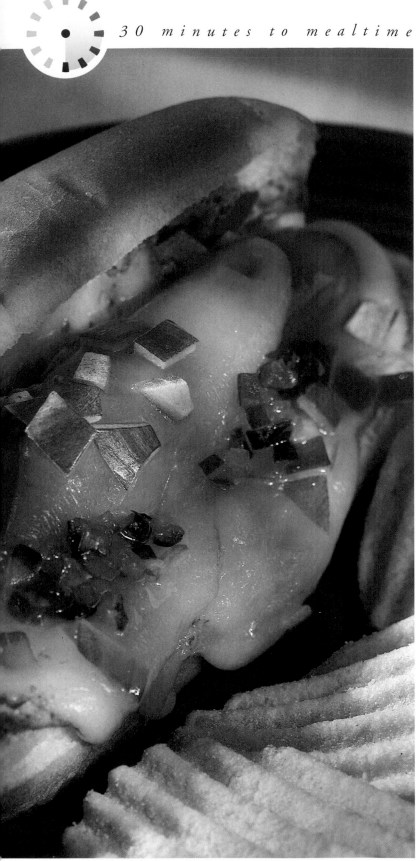

muenster-baked turkey franks

4 frankfurter buns, split
1 tablespoon brown or Dijon-style mustard
4 slices muenster cheese (4 ounces)
4 fully cooked turkey franks
½ cup chopped red onion

Preheat oven to 375°. Tear off four 10-inch pieces of foil; place a split bun on each foil piece. Spread buns with mustard. Cut each cheese slice into 3 pieces. Arrange 2 pieces on each bun. Top each with a frankfurter and another piece of cheese. Sprinkle onion over franks.

Wrap each frank in foil; place packets on a baking sheet. Bake 12 to 15 minutes or till heated through. Serve with pickle relish and potato chips, if desired. Makes 4 servings.

Turkey franks boast the all-American flavor of conventional hot dogs without the calories and high fat content. Of course, recipes vary by brand, but most cooked turkey franks are made by blending lean turkey with seasonings and then smoking the meat.

Per serving: 331 calories, 17 g protein, 23 g carbohydrate, 19 g total fat (9 g saturated), 75 mg cholesterol, 1,111 mg sodium, 191 mg potassium

newfangled turkey salad

Romaine or spinach leaves

1 16-ounce can peach slices

10 ounces fully cooked smoked turkey, cut into thin strips

2 kiwi fruit, peeled and sliced

1 cup halved seedless red or green grapes

½ cup vanilla yogurt

¼ teaspoon ground nutmeg

¼ cup sliced toasted almonds

Line 4 dinner plates with romaine leaves. Drain peaches, reserving *1 tablespoon* syrup. On each plate arrange turkey strips, peach slices, kiwi fruit, and grapes. For dressing, stir together yogurt, nutmeg, and reserved peach syrup. Spoon over salad; sprinkle with almonds. Makes 4 servings.

To make this salad ahead, arrange all salad ingredients except kiwi fruit on a serving platter; prepare dressing and store in a separate container. Add kiwi fruit slices just before serving the salad.

Per serving: 297 calories, 19 g protein, 44 g carbohydrate, 7 g total fat (2 g saturated), 39 mg cholesterol, 748 mg sodium, 779 mg potassium

turkey and cheddar sandwich loaf

1 18-inch long unsliced loaf Italian, French, or
     sourdough bread
8 ounces thinly sliced fully cooked smoked turkey or
     chicken breast
1 6-ounce package sliced cheddar, mozzarella, or Swiss
     cheese
⅓ cup pimiento-stuffed olives, chopped
2 tablespoons olive oil or cooking oil
1 teaspoon dried oregano or rosemary, crushed

Preheat oven to 400°. Cut a piece of foil about 24 inches long. Cut bread crosswise into ¾-inch-thick slices, cutting to, but not through, bottom crust. Place bread in center of foil. Stack sliced turkey; cut meat slices into thirds. Repeat with cheese slices. Fill every other cut made in bread with meat and cheese slices; spoon olives between bread and filling. Brush loaf with olive oil; sprinkle with crushed oregano. Wrap loaf loosely in foil using more foil as needed; place on baking sheet. Bake about 12 to 15 minutes, or till cheese melts and bread is heated through. To serve, cut through unfilled cuts to form sandwiches. Serve immediately. Makes 8 to 10 servings.

Per serving: 304 calories, 16 g protein, 29 g carbohydrate, 14 g total fat (6 g saturated), 35 mg cholesterol, 894 mg sodium, 171 mg potassium

turkey and winter fruit salad

Lettuce leaves

8 ounces sliced fully cooked turkey or chicken breast

1 apple, sliced

1 ripe medium pear, sliced

1 orange, peeled, halved, and thinly sliced

1 cup seedless red or green grapes, halved

1 8-ounce carton lemon or vanilla yogurt

3 tablespoons milk

¼ teaspoon five-spice powder or ground cinnamon

Line 4 dinner plates with lettuce leaves. Roll up each turkey slice; place on plates. Arrange apple, pear, and orange slices decoratively on plates. Sprinkle grapes over all. For dressing, in a small bowl stir together yogurt, milk, and five-spice powder to make of drizzling consistency. Drizzle mixture over salad. Serve at once. Makes 4 servings.

No matter what the season, you can prepare this colorful salad using the fruits that are at their ripe and ready peak. If it's appropriate, substitute a fruit-flavored yogurt that complements the fruit you've chosen.

Per serving: 230 calories, 20 g protein, 30 g carbohydrate, 4 g total fat (2 g saturated), 43 mg cholesterol, 77 mg sodium, 498 mg potassium

turkey, bacon, tomato, and avocado sandwiches

8   slices bacon

8   slices sourdough, whole wheat, or rye bread, toasted
    Lettuce leaves

8   ounces sliced fully cooked smoked turkey or chicken
    breast

¼   cup thousand island, mayonnaise, or creamy ranch
    salad dressing

4   tomato slices

1   avocado, halved, seeded, peeled, and sliced

In skillet cook bacon till crisp; drain. Arrange bread slices on a flat surface. Arrange lettuce leaves on *half* of the bread slices. Top with sliced turkey. Spread *1 tablespoon* salad dressing on each sandwich. Top each sandwich with *one* tomato slice, *two* bacon strips, and *one-fourth* of the avocado slices. Add second slice of bread. Cut sandwiches into quarters if desired; secure with toothpicks if necessary. Makes 4 servings.

Use these same ingredients to create a classic California Cobb salad. Add crumbled blue cheese, hard-cooked egg wedges, and a blue cheese salad dressing.

Per serving: 376 calories, 21 g protein, 28 g carbohydrate, 20 g total fat (3 g saturated), 39 mg cholesterol, 1,119 mg sodium, 630 mg potassium

sesame turkey-noodle salad

⅓ cup peanut oil or cooking oil

⅓ cup rice vinegar or cider vinegar

3 tablespoons sugar

½ teaspoon salt

½ teaspoon pepper

8 ounces sliced fully cooked turkey or chicken breast

2 cups shredded Chinese (napa) cabbage or lettuce

2 cups shredded red cabbage

1 3-ounce package ramen noodles

½ cup slivered almonds

2 green onions, sliced

2 tablespoons sesame seeds

1 tablespoon peanut oil or cooking oil

For dressing, in a screw-top jar combine ⅓ cup oil, the vinegar, sugar, salt, and pepper. Cover and shake well; set aside.

Dice cooked chicken; place in a large salad bowl with Chinese and red cabbage. Remove seasoning packet from noodles; reserve for another use. Crumble ramen noodles into cabbage mixture.

In a small skillet cook almonds, green onions, and sesame seeds in the 1 tablespoon hot oil over medium-high heat for 2 to 3 minutes or till nuts and seeds are golden brown. Spoon over salad. Shake dressing well; pour over salad. Toss well to coat. Serve immediately. Makes 4 servings.

Per serving: 539 calories, 24 g protein, 30 g carbohydrate, 38 g total fat (5 g saturated), 39 mg cholesterol, 691 mg sodium, 478 mg potassium

turkey-asparagus puffed omelet

4 egg whites
4 beaten egg yolks
1 tablespoon margarine or butter
8 ounces sliced fully cooked smoked turkey breast
1 10-ounce package frozen cut asparagus or green beans
½ of a red or green sweet pepper, cut into thin strips
2 tablespoons olive oil or cooking oil
½ teaspoon dried fines herbes or dried basil, crushed
   Sauce

Preheat oven to 325°. Beat egg whites and 2 table-spoons water on high speed of electric mixer for 1 to 1½ minutes or till stiff peaks form (tips stand straight). Fold in beaten egg yolks. In a large ovenproof skillet heat margarine till a drop of water sizzles. Pour in egg mixture, mounding it slightly higher at the sides. Cook over low heat for 8 to 10 minutes, or till puffed, set, and golden brown on the bottom. Bake for 8 to 10 minutes or till a knife inserted off center comes out clean.

For filling, cut turkey into thin strips. In a large skillet cook and stir asparagus and pepper in hot oil for 4 to 5 minutes. Stir in turkey and herb; heat through.

Loosen sides of omelet. Make a shallow cut slightly off center across omelet. Spoon filling onto larger side of omelet. Spoon Sauce over filling. Fold omelet over filling. Turn out onto plattter. Cut into 4 pieces. Makes 4 servings.

Sauce: Combine ½ cup *dairy sour cream,* 1 teaspoon *Worcestershire sauce,* and 1 teaspoon *prepared mustard.*

Per serving: 304 calories, 21 g protein, 7 g carbohydrate, 22 g total fat (7 g saturated), 250 mg cholesterol, 713 mg sodium, 455 mg potassium

turkey and spinach sunshine salad

1 10-ounce package fresh spinach, torn

8 ounces sliced fully cooked turkey breast or chicken breast

2 grapefruit, peeled and sectioned

2 oranges, peeled and sectioned

⅓ cup orange juice

¼ cup olive oil or cooking oil

1 teaspoon honey

½ teaspoon poppy seed

¼ teaspoon salt

¼ teaspoon paprika

¼ teaspoon dry mustard

Place spinach in a large bowl. Stack turkey slices; roll up the long way. Cut roll crosswise into ¼-inch strips; add to spinach with grapefruit and orange sections.

For dressing, in screw-top jar combine orange juice, oil, honey, poppy seeds, salt, paprika, and dry mustard. Cover and shake well. Pour the dressing over salad and toss. Makes 4 servings.

If you're using fresh spinach that's not already washed, rinse it thoroughly in water before using because it tends to be very sandy. Change the water and rinse the leaves several times.

Per serving: 309 calories, 21 g protein, 23 g carbohydrate, 16 g total fat (3 g saturated), 39 mg cholesterol, 226 mg sodium, 890 mg potassium

turkey and spinach muffins with hollandaise

1 10-ounce package frozen chopped spinach
1 1-ounce package hollandaise sauce mix
4 English muffins, split
   Margarine or butter (optional)
8 ounces sliced fully cooked smoked turkey or chicken
   breast
1 tablespoon cooking oil
   Paprika

In saucepan cook spinach according to package directions; drain well. Prepare hollandaise sauce mix according to package directions; cover and keep warm.

Toast muffins; spread with margarine, if desired. Place 2 muffin halves on each of 4 dinner plates. In a skillet cook turkey slices in hot oil over medium heat for 1 minute or till heated through.

Spoon spinach over muffins; top with hot turkey slices. Spoon hollandaise sauce over; sprinkle with paprika. Serve immediately. If desired, garnish with fresh strawberries. Makes 4 servings.

In place of the English muffins, try using split toasted bagels or split warmed croissants. Substitute sautéed potato slices, steamed asparagus spears, drained pineapple rings, or a fresh tomato slice for the spinach leaves.

Per serving: 444 calories, 20g protein, 39 g carbohydrate, 24 g total fat (12 g saturated), 77 mg cholesterol, 1,332 mg sodium, 814 mg potassium

turkey tostadas with avocado dressing

4 8-inch flour tortillas

4 ounces sliced fully cooked turkey or chicken breast

3 cups shredded lettuce

½ of a 15-ounce can garbanzo or pinto beans, drained

2 tomatoes, cut into wedges

1 2¼-ounce can sliced pitted ripe olives, drained

1 cup shredded cheddar or Monterey Jack cheese
    (4 ounces)

1 ripe avocado, halved, seeded, peeled, and diced

⅓ cup dairy sour cream

1 tablespoon lemon or lime juice

¼ teaspoon bottled hot pepper sauce

Preheat oven to 350°. Place tortillas on a baking sheet. Bake 10 minutes or till crisp.

Stack the turkey slices; dice. Place *one* crisp tortilla on each of 4 dinner plates. Place *one-fourth* of the shredded lettuce on each tortilla. Top each with *one-fourth* of the turkey, beans, tomato wedges, olives, and shredded cheese.

For dressing, in a blender container or food processor bowl place avocado, dairy sour cream, lemon or lime juice, and hot pepper sauce. Cover and blend or process until pureed. Dollop avocado mixture on top of each tostada. Makes 4 servings.

Per serving: 453 calories, 21 g protein, 34 g carbohydrate, 28 g total fat (8 g saturated), 56 mg cholesterol, 881 mg sodium, 815 mg potassium

pasta with chicken, sausages and peppers

1 pound skinless, boneless chicken thighs

8 ounces fresh hot or mild Italian sausage links, sliced

2 red, yellow, or green sweet peppers, cut into thin strips

1 medium onion, cut into wedges

1 16-ounce can diced tomatoes

½ cup dry red or white wine

1 teaspoon dried Italian seasoning, crushed

½ teaspoon salt

¼ teaspoon pepper

1 tablespoon cornstarch

¼ cup tomato juice or water

3 cups hot cooked pasta

Rinse chicken; pat dry. Cut into thin bite-size strips; set aside. In a 12-inch skillet cook sausage for 5 minutes stirring to brown on all sides. Remove from skillet, reserving 2 tablespoons drippings. In same skillet cook chicken for 2 to 3 minutes or till browned; remove from skillet. Cook peppers and onion in remaining drippings for 3 minutes. Return sausage and chicken to skillet; add *undrained* tomatoes, wine, Italian seasoning, salt, and pepper. Bring to boiling; reduce heat. Simmer, covered, for 10 minutes.

Stir cornstarch into tomato juice or water; stir into skillet. Cook and stir till mixture thickens and bubbles; cook and stir 2 minutes more. Serve sauce over pasta. Makes 4 servings.

Per serving: 470 calories, 33 g protein, 40 g carbohydrate, 17 g total fat (5 g saturated), 87 mg cholesterol, 960 mg sodium, 722 mg potassium

Tip: If turkey breast tenderloin steaks are not available, slice whole turkey tenderloins in half horizontally. Steaks should be ½- to ¾-inch thick.

chicken with grilled vegetables

2 medium carrots, cut into 1-inch slices

2 medium zucchini or yellow summer squash, cut into 1-inch chunks

1 medium red onion, cut into thick wedges

¼ cup frozen orange juice concentrate, thawed

2 tablespoons olive oil or cooking oil

2 cloves garlic, minced

1 teaspoon dried rosemary, crushed

1 teaspoon dried basil, crushed

½ teaspoon salt

⅛ teaspoon pepper

4 skinless, boneless chicken breast halves or turkey breast tenderloin steaks (about 1 pound total)

Start grill. Meanwhile, cook carrots in boiling water, covered, for 5 minutes. Add zucchini and onion wedges and cook 2 to 3 minutes more till vegetables are crisp-tender; drain. Thread vegetables alternately on 4 skewers; place on a baking sheet. In a small bowl whisk together orange juice concentrate, oil, garlic, rosemary, basil, salt, and pepper until combined.

Rinse chicken; pat dry. Brush with orange juice mixture. Place on a grill rack of an uncovered grill directly over *medium* coals. Grill for 6 minutes, brushing frequently with orange juice mixture. Turn chicken; place vegetable skewers on grill. Brush chicken and vegetables with orange juice mixture. Grill chicken and vegetables for 6 to 9 minutes more or till chicken is tender and no longer pink; turn vegetables frequently. Makes 4 servings.

Per serving: 245 calories, 23 g protein, 15 g carbohydrate, 10 g total fat (2 g saturated), 59 mg cholesterol, 346 mg sodium, 548 mg potassium

almond chicken

⅓ cup slivered almonds

1 pound skinless, boneless chicken breast halves

2 tablespoons cooking oil

1½ cups julienne carrots

½ cup chopped onion

1 clove garlic, minced

1 cup chicken broth

2 tablespoons dry sherry

½ teaspoon seasoned salt

　Dash pepper

1 8-ounce carton dairy sour cream

2 tablespoons all-purpose flour

2 to 3 cups hot cooked rice

Preheat oven to 350°. Spread almonds on a baking sheet. Toast in the oven for 5 to 10 minutes, stirring once or twice, till golden brown. Set aside.

Rinse chicken; pat dry. Cut chicken breast halves into quarters; set aside. Pour *1 tablespoon* of the oil into a large skillet. Heat over medium-high heat. Add carrots, onion, and garlic; cook about 5 minutes, stirring occasionally. Remove vegetables. Add remaining oil and chicken to the hot skillet. Cook about 3 minutes, turning until browned on all sides. Add vegetables, chicken broth, sherry, seasoned salt, and pepper. Bring to boiling; reduce heat and simmer 10 minutes or till chicken is tender and no longer pink. Combine sour cream and flour. Stir into chicken mixture. Cook and stir till thickened and bubbly; cook and stir 1 minute more. Serve over hot cooked rice. Sprinkle with almonds. Makes 4 to 6 servings.

Per serving: 557 calories, 31 g protein, 44 g carbohydrate, 28 g total fat (10 g saturated), 85 mg cholesterol, 475 mg sodium, 581 mg potassium

pesto chicken

4 skinless, boneless chicken breast halves
   (about 1 pound total)
   Pesto
½ cup shredded Monterey Jack or Swiss cheese
¼ cup all-purpose flour
1 slightly beaten egg
½ cup fine dry seasoned bread crumbs
2 tablespoons olive oil or cooking oil
⅔ cup chicken broth

Rinse chicken; pat dry. Place chicken between sheets of plastic wrap; pound to form ⅛-inch-thick rectangles. Spread *one-fourth* of the Pesto over each to within ¼ inch of edges. Sprinkle *2 tablespoons* cheese over *half* of the pesto on each. Fold breast over cheese half; secure with wooden toothpicks, if necessary.

Coat chicken with flour; dip in a mixture of beaten egg and 2 teaspoons *water*. Coat with seasoned crumbs. Heat oil in a large skillet; brown chicken on all sides over medium heat about 5 minutes. Carefully add broth; bring to boiling. Reduce heat; cover and simmer about 15 minutes or till chicken is tender and no longer pink. Makes 4 servings.

Pesto: In blender container place ½ cup *each* loosely packed fresh *parsley sprigs* and fresh *basil leaves;* ¼ cup grated *Parmesan or Romano cheese;* 2 tablespoons *pinenuts, walnuts,* or *almonds;* 2 cloves *garlic,* quartered; and 3 tablespoons *olive oil* or *cooking oil*. Cover; blend with on-off turns to form a paste, stopping and scraping sides frequently. Blend on low speed till nearly smooth.

Per serving: 488 calories, 34 g protein, 18 g carbohydrate, 31 g total fat (8 g saturated), 130 mg cholesterol, 766 mg sodium, 372 mg potassium

chicken pitas indienne

½ of a small cucumber, chopped (½ cup)

1 medium tomato, chopped (⅔ cup)

½ teaspoon dried dillweed

12 ounces skinless, boneless chicken breast halves or skinless, boneless chicken thighs

2 tablespoons olive oil or cooking oil

½ teaspoon salt

½ teaspoon ground turmeric

¼ teaspoon ground cumin

¼ teaspoon pepper

1 small onion, sliced

4 6- or 8-inch pita bread rounds, or flour tortillas

½ cup plain yogurt

In colander combine cucumber and tomato; sprinkle with dill. Drain while preparing sandwiches.

Rinse chicken; pat dry. Cut into bite-size strips. Place in bowl. Sprinkle oil, salt, turmeric, cumin, and pepper over chicken; toss to coat. Let stand 15 minutes.

In a large skillet cook and stir chicken over medium-high heat 2 to 3 minutes or till tender and no longer pink. Remove from skillet. In drippings cook and stir onion till tender but not brown; drain. Add chicken and toss with onion to heat through. To assemble sandwiches, top each pita round or tortilla with *one-fourth* of the chicken mixture and *one-fourth* of the cucumber mixture. Top each sandwich with yogurt. Fold pita or tortilla in half to serve. Makes 4 servings.

Per serving: 297 calories, 22 g protein, 27 g carbohydrate, 11 g total fat (2 g saturated), 48 mg cholesterol, 546 mg sodium, 416 mg potassium

plum-sauced chicken kabobs

1 8-ounce can pineapple chunks (juice pack)

⅓ cup bottled plum sauce

2 tablespoons vinegar

2 small zucchini and/or yellow summer squash, cut into
   ½-inch slices

1 pound skinless, boneless chicken breast halves or
   turkey breast tenderloins

4 ounces fresh mushrooms, trimmed

8 cherry tomatoes
   Hot cooked rice (optional)

Drain pineapple, reserving *2 tablespoons* juice. Mix plum sauce, vinegar, and reserved pineapple juice; set aside. Cook zucchini in boiling water 1 minute. Drain.

Preheat broiler. Rinse chicken; pat dry. Cut chicken into 1½-inch pieces. On 8 skewers alternately thread chicken, mushrooms, pineapple chunks, and zucchini slices. Place skewers on the unheated rack of a broiler pan. Brush lightly with plum sauce mixture.

Broil 4 to 5 inches from the heat for 5 minutes; turn and brush liberally with sauce mixture. Broil 4 to 6 minutes more or till chicken is tender and no longer pink, adding cherry tomatoes to end of each skewer the last minute of broiling. Serve immediately with rice, if desired. Makes 4 servings.

Remember, if you are starting with frozen chicken, thaw it in the refrigerator—never at room temperature, where bacteria can form.

Per serving: 204 calories, 23 g protein, 21 g carbohydrate, 3 g total fat (1 g saturated), 59 mg cholesterol, 65 mg sodium, 531 mg potassium

bacon-wrapped chicken breasts

4 slices thick-sliced bacon

4 skinless, boneless, chicken breast halves
   (about 1 pound total)

4 1-ounce slices provolone cheese

½ cup chicken broth

2 tablespoons dry red wine

1 10½-ounce can tomato puree

1 teaspoon dried thyme, crushed

½ teaspoon sugar

¼ teaspoon dried basil, crushed

¼ teaspoon dried oregano, crushed
   Hot cooked mafalda or fusilli pasta

In a large skillet cook bacon over medium heat till cooked but not crisp. Drain, reserving *1 tablespoon* drippings in pan. Set aside. Rinse chicken; pat dry. Place chicken between sheets of plastic wrap; pound to form ⅛-inch-thick rectangles. Sprinkle with ¼ teaspoon *salt* and dash *pepper*. Place *1 slice* of cheese atop each chicken breast near one edge. Fold in long sides of chicken and roll up jelly roll-style, starting from edge with cheese. Wrap a bacon slice around each chicken roll, securing with wooden toothpicks.

Brown chicken on all sides in bacon drippings over medium heat. Add broth, wine, tomato puree, thyme, sugar, basil, and oregano. Bring to boiling; reduce heat. Simmer, covered, for 15 minutes; uncover and simmer 5 to 10 minutes more or until tender and no longer pink. Serve with sauce over pasta. Makes 4 servings.

Per serving: 456 calories, 38 g protein, 41 g carbohydrate, 15 g total fat (7 g saturated), 85 mg cholesterol, 936 mg sodium, 680 mg potassium

When the seasons change, vary the vegetables in this rich soup. Try tiny new potatoes, asparagus, corn, or green beans.

herbed cream of chicken soup

12 ounces skinless, boneless chicken breast halves or
    skinless, boneless chicken thighs
5 cups chicken broth
1 bay leaf
¼ teaspoon whole black peppers
1½ cups julienne-sliced carrots
¾ cup chopped onion
¾ cup sliced celery
1 teaspoon dried basil, crushed
1 teaspoon dried thyme, crushed
½ cup long grain rice
1 cup half-and-half or light cream
1 tablespoon all-purpose flour
1 egg yolk

Rinse chicken; pat dry. In a Dutch oven place chicken. Add broth, bay leaf, and peppers; bring mixture to boiling. Reduce heat and simmer for 10 to 15 minutes or till chicken is tender and no longer pink. Remove chicken and cool. Strain broth through a double thickness of 100% cotton cheesecloth and discard bay leaf and peppers. Return broth to pan. Skim fat from broth. Add carrots, onion, celery, basil, thyme, and ¼ teaspoon *salt.* Bring to boiling; stir in uncooked rice. Reduce heat and simmer, covered, for 20 minutes or till rice is tender.

Meanwhile, cut cooked chicken into thin strips. In a small bowl whisk together cream, flour, and egg yolk. Add cream mixture to soup. Stir in the chicken strips. Cook and stir till mixture thickens slightly and comes to a boil. Makes 4 to 6 servings.

Per serving: 468 calories, 28 g protein, 34 g carbohydrate, 24 g total fat
(13 g saturated), 165 mg cholesterol, 1,237 mg sodium, 782 mg potassium

chicken and zucchini parmagiana

12 ounces skinless, boneless chicken breast halves

2 tablespoons cooking oil

⅓ cup chopped onion

2 cloves garlic, minced

1 15-ounce can tomato puree

⅓ cup tomato paste

2 teaspoon dried Italian seasoning, crushed

3 cups zucchini slices cut ¼-inch-thick

1½ cups shredded mozzarella cheese (6 ounces)

½ cup grated Parmesan or Romano cheese

Rinse chicken; pat dry. Cut chicken into bite-size strips. In a large skillet stir-fry chicken in *1 tablespoon* of the oil until no longer pink. Drain and set aside.

In same skillet heat remaining oil; cook onion and garlic for 2 minutes. Stir in cooked chicken, tomato puree, tomato paste, and Italian seasoning; simmer, covered, 5 minutes.

Preheat oven to 425°. Steam zucchini over simmering water for 5 minutes; drain well. In a lightly greased 2-quart rectangular baking dish arrange *half* of the zucchini slices; spoon *half* of the chicken-tomato sauce mixture over. Sprinkle *half* of the cheeses over top. Repeat layers, ending with cheeses. Cover and bake for 10 to 12 minutes or till heated through. Makes 6 servings.

Per serving: 266 calories, 23 g protein, 14 g carbohydrate, 13 g total fat (6 g saturated), 52 mg cholesterol, 608 mg sodium, 694 mg potassium

coachella chicken salad

1 pound skinless, boneless chicken breast halves or
    skinless, boneless chicken thighs

1 14½-ounce can chicken broth

2 sprigs fresh parsley

1 apple, cored and chopped

½ cup chopped dates or raisins

½ cup chopped walnuts or pecans

½ cup chopped celery

½ cup mayonnaise or salad dressing

2 tablespoons frozen orange juice concentrate, thawed

⅛ teaspoon ground nutmeg

    Lettuce leaves

Rinse chicken; pat dry. In a large skillet combine chicken with broth and parsley. Bring mixture to boiling; reduce heat and simmer 15 to 18 minutes or till chicken is tender and no longer pink. Drain; cool 10 minutes.

Meanwhile, in a medium bowl toss together apple, dates, walnuts, and celery. For dressing, in a small bowl stir together mayonnaise, orange juice concentrate, and nutmeg till combined. Chop chicken; add to date mixture. Spoon dressing over salad; toss well to coat. Cover and quick-chill in the freezer for 10 minutes. Serve on lettuce-lined plates. Makes 4 servings.

The name "Coachella" is taken from the California desert valley where the dates are grown.

Per serving: 512 calories, 25 g protein, 30 g carbohydrate, 33 g total fat (5 g saturated), 76 mg cholesterol, 280 mg sodium, 542 mg potassium

chicken stroganoff

12 ounces skinless, boneless chicken breast halves

 2 tablespoons margarine or butter

1½ cups quartered mushrooms

 ⅓ cup sliced green onion

 2 tablespoons all-purpose flour

 1 cup chicken broth

 ¼ cup dry white wine or vermouth

 1 4-ounce jar diced pimiento, drained

 1 teaspoon fines herbes or dried basil, crushed

 ⅓ cup dairy sour cream

    Croustades

Prepare Croustades. Rinse chicken; pat dry. Cut chicken into bite-size pieces. In a large skillet heat margarine. Add chicken; cook and stir 4 to 5 minutes or till tender and no longer pink. Remove with slotted spoon. Add mushrooms and onion to skillet; cook and stir for 2 to 3 minutes.

Sprinkle flour over mixture. Add broth and wine. Cook and stir till thickened and bubbly; cook and stir 1 minute more. Stir in pimiento and fines herbes; gradually add sour cream. Stir in chicken; heat through but *do not boil.* Serve mixture in Croustades. Serves 4.

Croustades: Preheat oven to 375°. Using 1 loaf unsliced *white or wheat bread*, cut 4 slices 1½ inches thick; reserve remaining bread for another use. Trim crusts. With tip of a knife, hollow out centers from slices leaving a ¼- to ½-inch-thick shell on bottom and sides. (Use trimmings to make bread crumbs.) Brush with 1 tablespoon melted *margarine* and place on baking sheet. Bake for 10 to 12 minutes or till golden.

Per serving: 458 calories, 26 g protein, 45 g carbohydrate, 18 g total fat (6 g saturated), 53 mg cholesterol, 760 mg sodium, 510 mg potassium

pesto-stuffed chicken breasts

4 medium chicken breast halves (about 1½ pounds total)
¼ cup purchased pesto
1 teaspoon cooking oil
⅛ teaspoon salt
　Dash pepper
2 tablespoons margarine or butter (optional)
⅓ cup sliced almonds or pinenuts (optional)
1 tablespoon snipped fresh parsley (optional)

　Preheat oven to 425°. Rinse chicken; pat dry. With fingers, gently separate skin from meat along rib edge, leaving skin attached at breast bone. Spread *1 tablespoon* of the pesto between skin and meat of each breast. Place chicken, skin side up, in a lightly greased roasting pan. Brush chicken skin with oil; sprinkle with salt and pepper. Bake for 35 to 40 minutes or till chicken is tender and no longer pink.

　If desired, in a small skillet melt margarine or butter; add almonds or pinenuts and stir over medium heat until golden brown. Stir in parsley. Spoon almond mixture over baked chicken to serve. If desired, serve with carrots and garnish with fresh basil. Makes 4 servings.

Variation: You can also use this mixture to stuff a whole turkey breast. Gently separate the skin from the meat with your fingers, leaving the skin attached, then spread the mixture in between.

Per serving: 312 calories, 31 g protein, 3 g carbohydrate, 19 g total fat (2 g saturated), 85 mg cholesterol, 252 mg sodium, 240 mg potassium

chicken and artichoke bake

1½ cups sliced fresh mushrooms

⅓ cup chopped shallots or sliced green onions

2 tablespoons cooking oil

1 10-ounce package frozen artichoke hearts

8 ounces thinly sliced Canadian-style bacon or fully cooked ham

8 ounces sliced fully cooked chicken or turkey breast

2 tablespoons margarine or butter

2 tablespoons all-purpose flour

1 cup milk

½ cup shredded Gruyère or Swiss cheese (2 ounces)

¼ teaspoon salt

¼ teaspoon white pepper

¾ cup soft bread crumbs (1 slice)

1 tablespoon margarine or butter, melted

Preheat oven to 425°. In a large skillet cook and stir mushrooms and shallots in hot oil for 2 minutes. Add artichokes; cook 4 minutes more, stirring frequently to separate artichoke hearts. Spoon mixture into a 2-quart rectangular baking dish. Layer Canadian-style bacon and chicken or turkey slices over vegetables.

For sauce, in a small saucepan melt 2 tablespoons margarine; stir in flour. Add milk all at once; cook and stir until thickened and bubbly. Stir in cheese, salt, and pepper till cheese melts. Pour sauce over chicken. Toss crumbs with 1 tablespoon margarine. Sprinkle atop casserole. Bake, uncovered, for 15 minutes or till heated through. Serve with a slotted spoon. If desired, serve with fresh fruit. Makes 6 servings.

Per serving: 351 calories, 27 g protein, 15 g carbohydrate, 21 g total fat (6 g saturated), 69 mg cholesterol, 900 mg sodium, 583 mg potassium

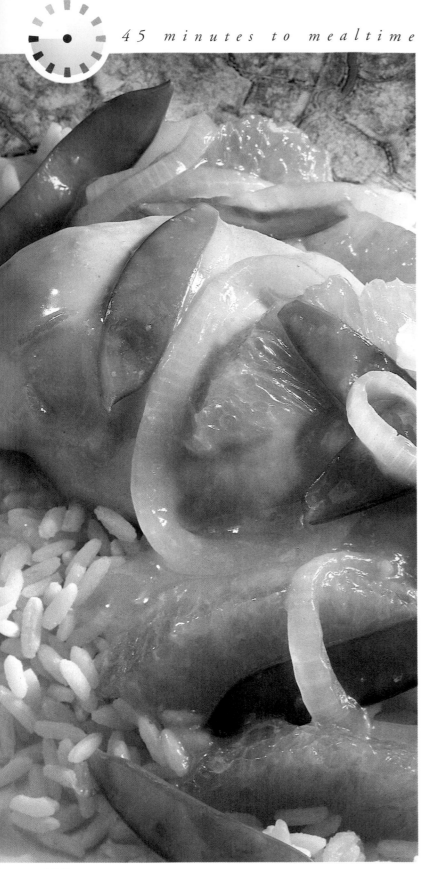

orange chicken with snow peas

4 skinless, boneless chicken breast halves
   (about 1 pound total)

4 oranges

1 cup sliced onion

¼ cup water

1 clove garlic, minced

2 tablespoons cornstarch

½ cup chicken broth

½ teaspoon dried basil, crushed (optional)

¼ teaspoon salt
   Dash pepper

1 6-ounce package frozen pea pods or 1½ cups fresh pea
   pods with strings removed

2 cups hot cooked rice

Rinse chicken; pat dry. Finely shred peel of *one* of the oranges. Squeeze juice from *two* of the oranges; measure *¾ cup*. Peel and section the 2 remaining oranges. In a large skillet combine ¾ cup orange juice, *half* of the shredded peel, onion, water, and garlic. Bring to boiling; add chicken and reduce heat. Simmer, covered, 15 to 18 minutes or till chicken is tender and no longer pink.

Remove chicken to serving platter; cover and keep warm. Reserve liquid in skillet with the onion. Stir cornstarch into chicken broth; add to poaching liquid in skillet with basil (if used), remaining peel, salt, and pepper. Cook and stir till mixture is thickened and bubbly. Stir in pea pods; cook and stir 2 minutes more. Add orange sections; heat through. Spoon sauce over chicken and hot cooked rice. Makes 4 servings.

Per serving: 346 calories, 28 g protein, 48 g carbohydrate, 4 g total fat (1 g saturated), 60 mg cholesterol, 290 mg sodium, 523 mg potassium

spicy chicken nuggets

1 pound skinless, boneless chicken breast halves or
    skinless, boneless chicken thighs
¼ cup margarine or butter, melted
¼ cup fine dry bread crumbs
2 tablespoons snipped fresh cilantro
1 to 2 tablespoons Cajun seasoning
3 cloves garlic, minced
1 cup peach or apricot preserves
2 tablespoons prepared mustard
2 tablespoons vinegar
1 teaspoon prepared horseradish

Tip: Make a double batch of the spice-coated nuggets and freeze half. They'll be ready to roll in butter and bake. Just add 5 to 10 minutes to the baking time.

Preheat oven to 375°. Rinse chicken; pat dry. Cut chicken into 1½-inch pieces. Place melted margarine in a shallow bowl. In a plastic bag combine bread crumbs, cilantro, Cajun seasoning, and garlic.

Roll chicken pieces in margarine; then shake several pieces at a time in crumb mixture to coat. Place pieces, not touching, in a lightly greased shallow baking pan. Bake for 30 minutes or till chicken is tender and no longer pink.

Meanwhile, for dipping sauce, in a small saucepan combine preserves, mustard, vinegar, and horseradish. Heat through. If desired, arrange chicken nuggets on a plate lined with salad greens. Serve chicken with sauce. Makes 4 to 5 servings.

Per serving: 481 calories, 23 g protein, 63 g carbohydrate, 15 g total fat (3 g saturated), 59 mg cholesterol, 1,307 mg sodium, 310 mg potassium

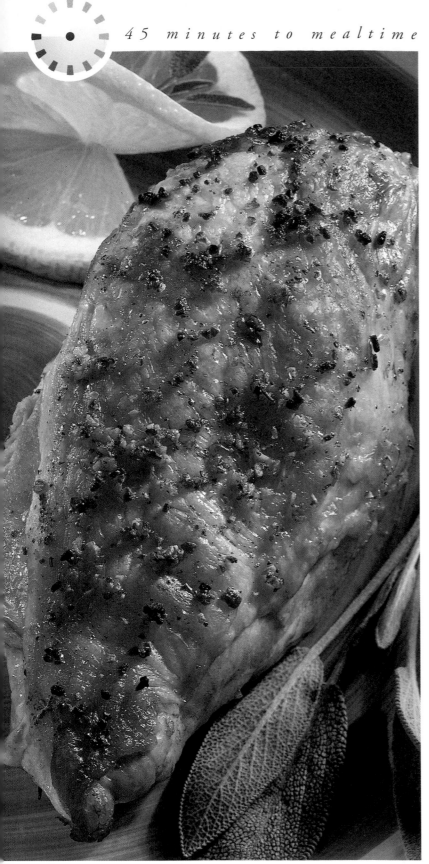

garlic-roasted chicken

4 large chicken breast halves (about 2 pounds total)
1 tablespoon lemon juice
1 teaspoon olive oil or cooking oil
4 cloves garlic, minced
½ teaspoon seasoned salt
½ teaspoon ground sage

Preheat oven to 425°. Rinse chicken; pat dry. Place chicken, skin side up, in a lightly greased roasting pan. In a small bowl combine lemon juice, olive oil, garlic, seasoned salt, and ground sage. Brush mixture on the chicken breast halves.

Bake for about 35 minutes or till chicken is tender and no longer pink. Garnish with lemon slices and sage leaves, if desired. Makes 4 servings.

If you are on a low-salt diet, garlic, lemon, and sage are just a few of the seaonings you will want to try to enhance the taste of chicken and other meats. Use a seasoned salt substitute instead of the salt in this recipe, if you prefer.

Per serving: 137 calories, 22 g protein, 1 g carbohydrate, 4 g total fat (1 g saturated), 59 mg cholesterol, 213 mg sodium, 192 mg potassium

chicken rolls

4 skinless, boneless chicken breast halves
   (about 1 pound total)
¾ cup herb-seasoned stuffing mix
1 2½-ounce jar mushroom stems and pieces, drained
1 tablespoon snipped fresh parsley
2 to 3 tablespoons chicken broth
1 tablespoon margarine or butter, melted
2 tablespoons cooking oil
¾ cup chicken broth
½ teaspoon ground sage
¾ cup half-and-half or light cream
4 teaspoons all-purpose flour
2 tablespoons snipped fresh chives
2 cups corkscrew macaroni, cooked and drained

Rinse chicken; pat dry. Place chicken between sheets of plastic wrap; pound to form ⅛-inch-thick rectangles.

Toss together stuffing mix, mushrooms, parsley, and dash pepper. Toss with 2 to 3 tablespoons broth and margarine. Spoon *one-fourth* of mixture onto small end of each chicken breast. Fold in long sides of chicken and roll up jelly roll-style, starting from the short edge. Secure with wooden toothpicks.

In a medium skillet brown chicken on all sides in hot oil. Add ¾ cup broth and sage; bring to boiling. Reduce heat; simmer, covered, about 15 minutes or till no longer pink, turning rolls halfway through cooking. Remove chicken rolls; keep warm. Stir cream into flour; add to drippings. Cook and stir till thickened and bubbly, cook and stir 1 minute more. Stir in chives. Return chicken to pan; heat through. Serve over macaroni. Serves 4.

Per serving: 486 calories, 31 g protein, 45 g carbohydrate, 20 g total fat (6 g saturated), 76 mg cholesterol, 566 mg sodium, 345 mg potassium

skillet chicken with cukes and tomatoes

4 skinless, boneless chicken breast halves
    (about 1 pound total)
½ cup chopped onion
1 clove garlic, minced
1 tablespoon cooking oil
½ cup chicken broth
1 teaspoon dried dillweed
1 teaspoon dried basil, crushed
½ teaspoon dried thyme, crushed
½ teaspoon salt
¼ teaspoon pepper
1 medium cucumber, halved lengthwise and sliced
1½ cups halved cherry tomatoes
½ cup dairy sour cream

Rinse chicken; pat dry. In a large skillet cook chicken with onion and garlic in hot oil till chicken is browned. Stir in broth, dillweed, basil, thyme, salt, and pepper. Cover and simmer for 5 to 6 minutes or till chicken is tender and no longer pink. Stir in cucumbers and tomatoes and cook for 1 minute. With a slotted spoon remove chicken and vegetables to serving platter; cover and keep warm. Bring liquid in skillet to boiling. If necessary, reduce to ⅓ cup. Stir in sour cream; heat through but *do not boil.* Serve sauce over chicken and vegetables. Makes 4 servings.

Per serving: 251 calories, 24 g protein, 9 g carbohydrate, 13 g total fat (5 g saturated), 72 mg cholesterol, 443 mg sodium, 534 mg potassium

chicken with cashew rice

12 ounces skinless, boneless chicken breast halves or
   skinless, boneless chicken thighs

2 tablespoons cooking oil

2 cups broccoli flowerets

2 cloves garlic, minced

1 teaspoon grated fresh gingerroot

2 cups chicken broth

⅔ cup long grain rice

2 tablespoons snipped fresh cilantro or parsley

1 tablespoon soy sauce

¼ teaspoon crushed red pepper

½ cup cashews

Rinse chicken; pat dry. Cut into bite-size strips; set aside. In a large skillet heat *1 tablespoon* of the oil. Add broccoli; stir fry over medium-high heat for 3 to 4 minutes or till crisp-tender. Remove from skillet; set aside. Heat remaining tablespoon of oil in skillet; add chicken, garlic, and gingerroot. Stir-fry 2 minutes. Carefully add broth; bring to boiling. Stir in uncooked rice, cilantro, or parsley, soy sauce, and crushed red pepper. Reduce heat and simmer, covered, 20 minutes. Stir in broccoli and cashews; heat through. Makes 4 servings.

If you like to keep fresh gingerroot around for use in recipes, store a piece in the freezer. When you need some, peel off part of the skin and grate it, then refreeze any remaining gingerroot.

Per serving: 399 calories, 25 g protein, 34 g carbohydrate, 18 g total fat (4 g saturated), 45 mg cholesterol, 810 mg sodium, 530 mg potassium

chicken and asparagus risotto

3½ to 4 cups chicken broth

12 ounces skinless, boneless chicken breast halves

 2 tablespoons margarine or butter

 1 10-ounce package frozen cut asparagus

 1 medium carrot, shredded

 1 cup chopped fresh mushrooms

 1 cup Arborio rice or long grain rice

 1 teaspoon dried basil, crushed

 2 cloves garlic, minced

 ½ teaspoon ground sage

 ¼ cup grated Parmesan or Romano cheese

In a medium saucepan bring chicken broth to boiling. Meanwhile, rinse chicken; pat dry. Cut chicken into bite-size pieces; set aside.

In a large saucepan cook chicken in margarine or butter over medium heat for 3 to 5 minutes or till tender and no longer pink. Add asparagus, carrot, mushrooms, uncooked rice, *1 cup* of the hot broth, basil, garlic, and sage. Cook over medium heat, stirring constantly, till nearly all liquid is absorbed.

Add *1 cup* additional hot broth, cooking and stirring till liquid is nearly absorbed. Repeat, adding broth and cooking it down till rice is tender and nearly all liquid has been absorbed, about 18 to 25 minutes. Remove from heat; stir in cheese. Makes 4 servings.

Per serving: 303 calories, 27 g protein, 22 g carbohydrate, 12 g total fat (3 g saturated), 50 mg cholesterol, 917 mg sodium, 577 mg potassium

tomato-sauced chicken 'n' pasta

1 8-ounce can tomato sauce

⅓ cup oil-packed dried tomatoes, drained
    (reserve 2 tablespoons oil)

½ cup lightly packed fresh basil leaves

1 teaspoon sugar

2 cloves garlic, minced

¼ teaspoon pepper

12 ounces skinless, boneless chicken breast halves

2 tablespoons cooking oil

2 cups chopped fresh vegetables (such as mushrooms,
    summer squash, sweet pepper, or carrots)

½ cup chopped onion

½ cup chicken broth

8 ounces pasta, cooked and drained

1 to 2 tablespoons grated Parmesan or Romano cheese

In a food processor bowl or blender container place tomato sauce, drained tomatoes, reserved tomato oil, basil, sugar, garlic, and pepper. Cover and process or blend till nearly smooth. Set aside.

Rinse chicken; pat dry. Cut into bite-size strips. In a large skillet heat *1 tablespoon* of the oil. Cook chicken for 2 to 3 minutes till tender and no longer pink. Remove from pan; add more oil if necessary. Cook and stir vegetables and onion for 3 to 5 minutes or till crisp-tender. Add chicken, tomato mixture, and broth to vegetables. Bring to boiling; reduce heat. Cover; simmer 10 minutes. Toss sauce with pasta in a large bowl. Sprinkle with Parmesan or Romano cheese. Serves 4.

Per serving: 515 calories, 28 g protein, 58 g carbohydrate, 19 g total fat (3 g saturated), 46 mg cholesterol, 538 mg sodium, 806 mg potassium

grilled chicken and mushrooms

1 pound skinless, boneless chicken breast halves

8 fresh medium mushrooms (3 cups)

1 medium red, yellow, or green sweet pepper, cut into 1½-inch pieces

3 green onions, cut into 1-inch pieces

½ cup salsa-style catsup

2 tablespoons jalapeño jelly
    Shredded lettuce (optional)

Start grill. Meanwhile, rinse chicken; pat dry. Cut chicken into strips lengthwise about ½-inch thick. On 4 long or 8 short skewers loosely thread chicken accordion style alternately with mushrooms, peppers, and onions. In a small saucepan heat catsup and jelly. Brush over chicken and vegetables.

Place skewers on the grill rack of an uncovered grill directly over medium coals. Grill for 10 to 12 minutes till chicken is tender and no longer pink, turning once and brushing with sauce. (*Or,* preheat broiler. Place skewers on unheated rack of a broiler pan. Broil 4 to 5 inches from heat for 12 to 14 minutes, turning once and brushing with sauce.) If desired, serve on a bed of shredded lettuce. Makes 4 servings.

Watch for sales on fresh chicken and stock up on the parts you use most often. Freeze recipe-size batches of chicken pieces in freezer bags so you can pull out the right quantity when needed.

Per serving: 190 calories, 23 g protein, 17 g carbohydrate, 4 g total fat (1 g saturated), 59 mg cholesterol, 315 mg sodium, 540 mg potassium

chicken curry with rice

12 ounces skinless, boneless chicken breast halves or skinless, boneless chicken thighs

1 tablespoon all-purpose flour

1 tablespoon curry powder

½ teaspoon dried thyme, crushed

½ teaspoon ground cinnamon

½ teaspoon ground ginger

¼ teaspoon salt

3 tablespoons cooking oil

1½ cups sliced onion

1½ cups chopped red or green sweet pepper

2 cloves garlic, minced

⅔ cup chicken broth

½ cup cashews pieces

½ cup raisins or mixed dried fruit bits

3 cups hot cooked rice

¼ cup dairy sour cream or plain yogurt

Rinse chicken; pat dry. Cut chicken into bite-size strips. In a bowl stir together flour, curry powder, thyme, cinnamon, ginger, and salt. Add chicken pieces; toss to coat with flour mixture. Let stand 15 minutes.

In a large skillet, heat *2 tablespoons* of the oil. Cook chicken, turning frequently to brown. Remove from pan. Add remaining oil to pan drippings; cook and stir onion, pepper, and garlic for 5 minutes. Add chicken and broth. Bring mixture to boiling; reduce heat. Simmer, covered, for 10 minutes. Heat through. Serve over hot cooked rice. Top with sour cream and sprinkle lightly with curry powder, if desired. Makes 4 servings.

Per serving: 573 calories, 25 g protein, 65 g carbohydrate, 25 g total fat (6 g saturated), 51 mg cholesterol, 320 mg sodium, 650 mg potassium

fruit-and-nut stuffed chicken

4 skinless, boneless chicken breast halves
1 8-ounce can crushed pineapple (juice pack)
¼ cup finely chopped macadamia nuts or walnuts
¼ cup coconut (optional)
¼ teaspoon ground cinnamon
⅛ teaspoon salt
⅓ cup fine dry bread crumbs
2 tablespoons cooking oil
   Sauce

Rinse chicken; pat dry. Drain pineapple, reserving
⅓ cup juice. In a small bowl stir together pineapple, nuts,
coconut if desired, cinnamon, salt, and dash *pepper.*

Place chicken between sheets of plastic wrap; pound
with to ⅛-inch thickness. Spoon *one-fourth* of the
pineapple mixture onto each breast half. Fold in long sides
of chicken and roll up jelly roll-style, starting from short
edge. Secure with wooden toothpicks.

Roll chicken in crumbs to coat. In a large skillet heat
oil; brown chicken rolls on all sides over medium heat
about 5 minutes. Carefully add ⅔ cup *water;* bring to
boiling. Reduce heat and simmer, covered, for 20 minutes
or till chicken is tender and no longer pink. Meanwhile,
prepare Sauce; spoon over chicken. Serve with pea pods,
if desired. Makes 4 servings.

Sauce: In small saucepan melt 1 tablespoon *margarine;*
stir in 2 teaspoons *cornstarch.* Add ⅓ cup reserved
pineapple juice, ¼ cup *dry white wine* or *water,* 1 teaspoon
sugar, and ½ teaspoon *instant chicken bouillon granules.*
Cook and stir till bubbly; cook and stir 2 minutes more.

Per serving: 356 calories, 24 g protein, 19 g carbohydrate, 20 g total fat (3 g saturated),
59 mg cholesterol, 325 mg sodium, 304 mg potassium

chicken little rarebit

2 slices bacon

12 ounces skinless, boneless chicken breast halves

1 14½-ounce can chicken broth

1 bay leaf

2 tablespoons margarine or butter

1 tablespoon cooking oil

3 tablespoons all-purpose flour

½ teaspoon seasoned salt

¼ teaspoon dry mustard

2 cups milk

1½ cups shredded sharp cheddar or American cheese

4 slices rye bread, toasted and halved diagonally

1 tomato, cut into wedges

In a large skillet cook bacon slices till crisp. Drain on paper towels. Break in half. Wipe grease from skillet. Rinse chicken; pat dry. Add chicken broth and bay leaf to skillet. Bring to boiling. Add chicken; reduce heat. Simmer, covered, for 10 to 12 minutes or till chicken is tender and no longer pink. Drain; cool 5 minutes. Chop chicken. Discard broth and bay leaf.

In a medium saucepan heat margarine and oil. Stir in flour, seasoned salt, and mustard; add milk all at once. Cook and stir over medium heat till mixture is thickened and bubbly. Cook and stir 1 minute more. Stir in cheese till melted, but do not boil. Stir in chicken; heat through.

For each serving, spoon sauce over 2 toast triangles. Serve with tomato wedges and a bacon piece. If desired, sprinkle with sliced green onion. Makes 4 servings.

Per serving: 516 calories, 35 g protein, 24 g carbohydrate, 31 g total fat (13 g saturated), 101 mg cholesterol, 866 mg sodium, 519 mg potassium

thai chicken-coconut soup

1 pound skinless, boneless chicken breast halves or skinless, boneless chicken thighs

4 cups chicken broth

2 tablespoons fish sauce (optional)

2 tablespoons lemon or lime juice

1 tablespoon grated fresh gingerroot

1 teaspoon ground cumin

1½ cups broccoli flowerets

1 cup julienne-sliced red, yellow, or green sweet pepper

1 jalapeño pepper, seeded and chopped

3 green onions, sliced into ½-inch pieces

2 tablespoons snipped fresh cilantro

1 14-ounce can unsweetened coconut milk

Rinse chicken; pat dry. Cut chicken into bite-size strips. In a Dutch oven stir together chicken broth, chicken, fish sauce (if using), lemon or lime juice, gingerroot, and cumin.

Bring mixture to boiling; reduce heat. Simmer, covered, for 10 minutes. Stir in broccoli, sweet pepper, jalapeño pepper, onions, and cilantro. Simmer, covered, for 10 minutes more or till vegetables are tender. Add coconut milk; heat through, but do not boil. Makes 4 servings.

Fish sauce is a traditional Thai table sauce; you'll find it in Oriental markets.

Per serving: 461 calories, 31 g protein, 9 g carbohydrate, 33 g total fat (22 g saturated), 60 mg cholesterol, 857 mg sodium, 986 mg potassium

grilled chicken burgers with red onions

1 slightly beaten egg

½ cup fine dry seasoned bread crumbs

1 tablespoon coarse-grain brown mustard

1 pound ground raw chicken or turkey

4 ½-inch-thick slices red or yellow onion

1 tablespoon olive oil or cooking oil

½ teaspoon dried basil, crushed

4 Kaiser or onion rolls, split

   Lettuce

8 thin slices tomato

   Coarse-grain brown mustard (optional)

Start grill. In a medium bowl combine egg, crumbs, and 1 tablespoon mustard. Add ground chicken or turkey; mix well. With hands, shape mixture into 4 patties, ¾ inch thick. Set aside.

Thread 2 bamboo or metal skewers horizontally through each onion slice. Combine olive oil and basil. Brush over onions.

Grill chicken patties on the grill rack of an uncovered grill directly over *medium* coals for 7 minutes. Turn patties; add onions on skewers and grill 7 to 11 minutes more or till onions are crisp-tender and juices of patties run clear. Place lettuce and *two* tomato slices on bottom half of each roll; top with chicken burgers. Serve each burger with a grilled onion slice. Pass additional mustard, if desired. Makes 4 servings.

This recipe brings out the succulent flavor of red onions. Grill them till they are slightly charred on both sides.

Per serving: 378 calories, 25 g protein, 40 g carbohydrate, 13 g total fat (3 g saturated), 108 mg cholesterol, 803 mg sodium, 367 mg potassium

feta-stuffed chicken breasts

4 medium chicken breast halves (about 1½ pounds total)

½ cup crumbled feta cheese (2 ounces)

1 2¼-ounce can chopped pitted ripe olives, drained

½ teaspoon dried basil, crushed or 1½ teaspoons snipped fresh basil

¼ teaspoon dried rosemary, crushed or ½ teaspoon snipped fresh rosemary

¼ teaspoon salt

⅛ teaspoon pepper

3 tablespoons margarine or butter, melted

2 tablespoons lemon juice

1 teaspoon sesame seed

Preheat oven to 425°. Rinse chicken; pat dry. With fingers, separate skin from meat, without removing skin. In a small bowl stir together feta cheese, olives, basil, and rosemary till combined. Spread *one-fourth* of the mixture under skin of each breast half. Place chicken, skin side up, in a lightly greased baking dish. Sprinkle with salt and pepper. Bake for 35 to 40 minutes or till chicken is tender and no longer pink.

Meanwhile, combine margarine, lemon juice, and sesame seed. Brush mixture over chicken frequently during the last 20 minutes of baking. Serve with broccoli flowerets, if desired. Makes 4 servings.

If you prefer the dark meat of chicken thighs, purchase boneless ones and stuff them as you would the breasts.

Per serving: 302 calories, 30 g protein, 2 g carbohydrate, 19 g total fat (6 g saturated), 90 mg cholesterol, 457 mg sodium, 259 mg potassium

tequila and lime-grilled chicken

¼ cup tequila

¼ cup lime or lemon juice

3 cloves garlic, minced

¼ teaspoon seasoned salt

¼ teaspoon pepper

4 skinless, boneless chicken breast halves
   (about 1 pound total)
   Warmed flour tortillas

Start grill. In a shallow non-metal dish stir together tequila, lime or lemon juice, garlic, seasoned salt, and pepper. Rinse chicken; pat dry. Place chicken in tequila mixture; turn to coat with marinade. Cover and let stand 20 minutes.

Drain chicken; reserve tequila mixture. Grill on the grill rack of an uncovered grill directly over *medium* coals for 12 to 15 minutes or till chicken is tender and no longer pink, turning once and basting with tequila mixture halfway through grilling time. Serve chicken with warm flour tortillas. Garnish with lime slices and salsa, if desired. Makes 4 servings.

To carry out the South American theme of this entrée, serve the chicken with spicy black beans or corn-on-the-cob brushed with chili-spiked butter.

Per serving: 264 calories, 24 g protein, 20 g carbohydrate, 5 g total fat (1 g saturated), 59 mg cholesterol, 249 mg sodium, 234 mg potassium

chicken ravioli

6 ounces ground raw chicken or turkey

1 8-ounce container soft-style cream cheese with chives and onion

¼ cup shredded carrot

24 3½-inch wonton wrappers

⅓ cup chopped onion

1 clove garlic, minced

1 tablespoon margarine or butter

1 14½-ounce can whole Italian-style tomatoes, cut up

2 tablespoons tomato paste

½ teaspoon dried Italian seasoning, crushed

¼ teaspoon sugar

1 tablespoon cooking oil

For filling, in a medium bowl stir together chicken or turkey, cream cheese, and carrot. To shape ravioli, place about *1 tablespoon* filling in center of each wonton wrapper. Brush edges with water. Fold 1 corner over to the opposite corner, forming a triangle. Set aside.

In a medium saucepan cook onion and garlic in hot margarine till tender but not brown. Carefully stir in *undrained* tomatoes, tomato paste, Italian seasoning, sugar, dash salt, and dash pepper. Simmer, uncovered, 5 to 10 minutes to desired consistency, stirring occasionally.

Meanwhile, in a Dutch oven bring a large amount of water and the oil to boiling. Drop ravioli, 4 or 5 at a time, into the boiling water. Reduce heat. Simmer, uncovered, for 3 to 4 minutes or till chicken or turkey is no longer pink. Remove ravioli using a slotted spoon, drain on paper towels. Place ravioli on 4 dinner plates and spoon sauce atop. Makes 4 servings.

Per serving: 456 calories, 16 g protein, 35 g carbohydrate, 28 g total fat (12 g saturated), 110 mg cholesterol, 467 mg sodium, 520 mg potassium

chicken with sweet potatoes

1 pound sweet potatoes, peeled, cut into 1-inch chunks

4 skinless, boneless chicken breast halves
   (about 1 pound total)

1 tablespoon cooking oil

1 medium onion, cut into wedges

1 medium red sweet pepper, cut into thin strips

1 or 2 cloves garlic, minced

1 8-ounce can pineapple chunks (juice pack)

1 8-ounce can stewed tomatoes

½ teaspoon ground cinnamon

½ teaspoon ground cumin

1 tablespoon cornstarch

In a saucepan cook potatoes in boiling water 15 to 20 minutes till just tender; drain. Rinse chicken; pat dry. In a large skillet cook chicken in oil over medium heat for about 5 minutes or till browned; remove from pan.

In pan drippings cook onion, pepper, and garlic for 3 minutes. Add *undrained* pineapple, browned chicken pieces, *undrained* tomatoes, cinnamon, cumin, ½ teaspoon *salt*, and ⅛ teaspoon *pepper*. Bring mixture to boiling; reduce heat. Simmer, covered, for 15 minutes or till chicken is tender and no longer pink.

Stir cornstarch into 1 tablespoon *cold water;* add to skillet. Cook and stir till mixture is thickened and bubbly; cook and stir 2 minutes more. Add potatoes to skillet; heat through. Serve mixture over hot cooked rice, if desired. Makes 4 servings.

Per serving: 319 calories, 24 g protein, 40 g carbohydrate, 7 g total fat (1 g saturated), 59 mg cholesterol, 476 mg sodium, 768 mg potassium

honey-glazed drumsticks

1½ pounds chicken drumsticks or thighs
3 tablespoons honey
2 tablespoons lemon or lime juice
½ teaspoon ground ginger
¼ teaspoon salt
¼ teaspoon garlic powder
  Dash pepper

Preheat oven to 425°. Skin chicken, if desired. Rinse chicken; pat dry. Place drumsticks or thighs in a baking pan. Bake for 20 minutes.

Meanwhile, in a small bowl stir together honey, lemon or lime juice, ginger, salt, garlic powder, and pepper. Brush mixture over drumsticks; bake 15 to 20 minutes more or till tender and no longer pink, brushing several times with honey mixture. If desired, serve with lightly cooked zucchini and red sweet peppers and garnish with parsley. Makes 4 servings.

When you're using a sweetener like honey, brown sugar, or molasses in a brush-on sauce for meats, wait until the last half of the roasting or grilling time to use it. Otherwise, the sugar will blacken and the meat will have a burned flavor.

Per serving: 247 calories, 22 g protein, 14 g carbohydrate, 11 g total fat (3 g saturated),
77 mg cholesterol, 207 mg sodium, 212 mg potassium

chicken thighs with cabbage and apples

8 skinless chicken thighs (2 to 2½ pounds total)

2 tablespoons cooking oil

1 cup chopped red or yellow onion

1 clove garlic, minced

½ cup chicken broth

3 tablespoons red or white wine vinegar

1 tablespoon snipped fresh rosemary or ½ teaspoon dried rosemary, crushed

¼ teaspoon salt

¼ teaspoon pepper

2 apples, thinly sliced

3 cups pre-shredded coleslaw mix

Rinse chicken; pat dry. In a large skillet brown chicken on all sides in hot oil. Remove chicken from skillet. In drippings cook and stir onion and garlic for 2 minutes; return chicken to skillet. Add broth, vinegar, rosemary, salt, and pepper.

Bring mixture to boiling; reduce heat. Cover and simmer 15 minutes. Add apples and coleslaw mix. Cook 10 to 15 minutes more or till chicken is tender and no longer pink. Serve with a slotted spoon. Makes 4 servings.

If you can't find a pre-packaged coleslaw mix, substitute a mixture of 1 cup shredded green cabbage, 1 cup shredded red cabbage, and 1 cup grated carrot.

Per serving: 351 calories, 28 g protein, 20 g carbohydrate, 18 g total fat (4 g saturated), 93 mg cholesterol, 329 mg sodium, 566 mg potassium

baked chicken thighs in spicy sauce

8   chicken thighs (2 to 2½ pounds total)
2   tablespoons cooking oil
⅓   cup bottled barbecue sauce
⅓   cup sweet and sour sauce
1   tablespoon chili powder
    Several dashes bottled hot pepper sauce

Preheat oven to 425°. Skin chicken, if desired. Rinse chicken; pat dry. Arrange chicken thighs, not touching, in a lightly greased shallow baking pan. Brush with oil.

Bake for 35 to 45 minutes or till chicken is tender and no longer pink.

Meanwhile, in a small bowl combine barbecue sauce, sweet and sour sauce, chili powder, and hot pepper sauce. Brush mixture frequently over chicken after the first 15 minutes of baking time. Makes 4 servings.

Use the same sauce mixture to make spicy chicken wings, or "buffalo" wings for your next party. Bake, then sprinkle with sesame seed and sliced green onion.

Per serving: 386 calories, 29 g protein, 22 g carbohydrate, 20 g total fat (5 g saturated), 103 mg cholesterol, 774 mg sodium, 376 mg potassium

athenian chicken

1 pound skinless, boneless chicken thighs

1 tablespoon lemon juice

½ teaspoon salt

Dash pepper

1 tablespoon olive oil or cooking oil

1 cup chopped red onion

1 clove garlic, minced

1 4-ounce can whole or sliced mushrooms, drained

½ cup chicken broth

¼ cup dry white wine

¼ teaspoon ground cinnamon

⅛ teaspoon ground cloves

1 9-ounce package frozen French-style green beans

2 medium tomatoes, cut into wedges

3 cups hot cooked rice

¼ cup crumbled feta cheese (optional)

Rinse chicken; pat dry. Cut thigh pieces into quarters. Toss chicken with lemon juice, salt, and dash pepper. In a large skillet cook chicken in hot oil over medium high heat about 3 minutes, turning to brown on all sides. Add onion and garlic and cook for 3 minutes more or till onion is tender, stirring occasionally. Add mushrooms, broth, wine, cinnamon, and cloves to skillet. Bring to boiling; reduce heat. Simmer, covered, for 15 minutes.

Meanwhile, run cool water over beans to thaw and separate. Add beans to skillet; cook, covered, about 5 minutes more or till chicken is tender and no longer pink. Stir in tomatoes; heat through. If desired, season with salt and pepper. Serve over rice. Sprinkle with feta, if desired. Makes 4 servings.

Per serving: 437 calories, 24 g protein, 56 g carbohydrate, 12 g total fat (3 g saturated), 61 mg cholesterol, 636 mg sodium, 558 mg potassium

calypso pineapple chicken

2½ to 3 pounds meaty chicken pieces (breasts, thighs,
    and drumsticks)

1 tablespoon cooking oil

¼ teaspoon salt

⅛ teaspoon ground red pepper

1 15¼-ounce can pineapple tidbits, drained

½ cup chopped red onion

½ cup chopped red or green sweet pepper

1 jalapeño pepper, seeded and finely chopped

1 tablespoon snipped fresh cilantro

1 tablespoon lemon or lime juice

¼ teaspoon pepper

Preheat oven to 425°. Skin chicken, if desired. Rinse
chicken; pat dry. Arrange chicken pieces in a lightly
greased 13x9x2-inch baking pan; brush with oil. Sprinkle
with salt and ground red pepper. Bake for 25 minutes.

Meanwhile, in a medium bowl stir together pineapple
tidbits, onion, sweet pepper, jalapeño pepper, cilantro,
lemon or lime juice, and pepper. Spoon mixture over
chicken. Bake 10 to 15 minutes more or till chicken is
tender and no longer pink. Makes 4 to 6 servings.

*When using fresh chiles, wear gloves to protect
your hands from the oils. Or, wash hands thoroughly with soapy water after handling.*

Per serving: 430 calories, 43 g protein, 20 g carbohydrate, 19 g total fat (5 g saturated),
130 mg cholesterol, 250 mg sodium, 525 mg potassium

chicken with succotash

2½ to 3 pounds meaty chicken pieces (breasts, thighs,
    and drumsticks)
1 tablespoon cooking oil
½ teaspoon seasoned salt
¼ teaspoon ground sage
4 slices bacon
1 cup chopped onion
1 10-ounce package frozen lima beans,
1 10-ounce package frozen whole kernel corn
1 cup chicken broth
1 tablespoon all-purpose flour
½ teaspoon salt
¼ teaspoon pepper

Preheat oven to 425°. Skin chicken, if desired. Rinse
chicken; pat dry. Arrange chicken pieces in a lightly
greased 3-quart rectangular baking dish; brush with oil.
Sprinkle with seasoned salt and sage. Bake for 35 to 40
minutes or till chicken is tender and no longer pink.

Meanwhile, in a large skillet cook bacon till crisp;
drain, reserving *2 tablespoons* drippings in pan. Crumble
bacon; set aside. Cook onion, lima beans, and corn in
reserved drippings over medium heat for 5 minutes,
stirring occasionally. Combine chicken broth and flour;
stir into skillet. Cook and stir till mixture is thickened and
bubbly. Stir in salt and pepper. Reduce heat. Cover and
simmer for 10 minutes or till vegetables are tender. Stir in
crumbled bacon. Cover and keep warm.

To serve, arrange chicken on a serving platter. Pour
vegetable mixture over chicken. Makes 6 servings.

Per serving: 411 calories, 35 g protein, 23 g carbohydrate, 20 g total fat (6 g saturated),
94 mg cholesterol, 584 mg sodium, 622 mg potassium

normandy apple chicken

2½ to 3 pounds meaty chicken pieces (breasts, thighs,
    and drumsticks)

2 tablespoons cooking oil

½ teaspoon seasoned salt

1 tablespoon margarine or butter

2 medium red apples, cored and thinly sliced

1 medium onion, cut into wedges

½ cup apple juice

1 tablespoon apple brandy, cognac, or brandy

1 tablespoon all-purpose flour

¼ teaspoon salt

¾ cup half-and-half or light cream

2 tablespoons snipped fresh watercress or parsley

Preheat oven to 425°. Skin chicken, if desired. Rinse
chicken; pat dry. Arrange chicken in a lightly greased
3-quart rectangular baking dish. Brush with *1 tablespoon*
of the oil; sprinkle with seasoned salt and dash *pepper.*
Bake for 35 to 40 minutes or till chicken is tender and no
longer pink.

Meanwhile, in a medium skillet heat remaining oil
and margarine or butter. Cook and stir apples and onion
for 5 minutes. With a slotted spoon remove from skillet;
cover and keep warm. Stir in apple juice and apple
brandy. Bring to boiling; reduce heat. Simmer until liquid
is reduced by half. Stir flour, salt, and dash *pepper* into
cream; add to skillet. Cook and stir till thickened and
bubbly; cook and stir 1 minute more. Stir in watercress or
parsley. To serve, spoon apples and onions onto plate.
Drizzle with sauce. Top with chicken. Makes 6 servings.

Per serving: 368 calories, 30 g protein, 13 g carbohydrate, 21 g total fat (6 g saturated),
102 mg cholesterol, 317 mg sodium, 383 mg potassium

chicken with mole sauce

2½ to 3 pounds meaty chicken pieces (breasts, thighs,
   and drumsticks)

2 tablespoons cooking oil

¾ cup slivered almonds

¼ cup chopped onion

1 6-inch flour tortilla, torn or 1 slice dry bread, torn

1 clove garlic, minced

¼ teaspoon ground cinnamon

⅛ teaspoon ground cloves

1 10-ounce can tomatoes with green chili peppers

1 cup chicken broth

1 ounce unsweetened chocolate, cut up

¼ teaspoon salt

Preheat oven to 425°. Rinse chicken; pat dry. Arrange
chicken in a lightly greased shallow baking pan. Brush
with *1 tablespoon* of the oil. Bake for 35 to 40 minutes or
till chicken is tender and no longer pink.

Meanwhile, in a large skillet heat remaining oil. Add
almonds, onion, tortilla or bread, garlic, cinnamon, and
cloves. Cook over medium heat, stirring frequently, about
5 minutes or till nuts are slightly toasted. Cool 5 minutes.
Place almond mixture in a blender container or food
processor bowl. Cover and blend or process till finely
chopped. Add *undrained* tomatoes, broth, chocolate, and
salt. Cover; blend till nearly smooth. Pour mixture into
skillet. Bring to boiling; reduce heat. Simmer, uncovered,
5 minutes or till thickened, stirring frequently. Spoon
some of the mole sauce over chicken; pass remainder.
Serve with warmed flour tortillas, if desired. Serves 6.

Per serving: 364 calories, 33 g protein, 9 g carbohydrate, 22 g total fat (5 g saturated),
87 mg cholesterol, 505 mg sodium, 448 mg potassium

honey-mustard baked chicken

2½ to 3 pounds meaty chicken pieces (breasts, thighs, and drumsticks)
 1 tablespoon cooking oil
 ⅓ cup brown mustard
 1 tablespoon soy sauce
 1 to 2 tablespoons honey

Preheat oven to 425°. Rinse chicken; pat dry. Skin chicken, if desired. Place chicken in a lightly greased shallow baking pan. Bake for 15 minutes.

Meanwhile, in a small bowl stir together mustard, soy sauce, and honey to taste. Brush mixture generously over chicken pieces. Bake 20 to 25 minutes more or till chicken is tender and no longer pink, brushing frequently with mustard mixture. If desired, serve with steamed green beans. Makes 6 servings.

Are "free-range" chickens worth the extra cost? These chickens have been raised without hormones or additives and are processed in small batches. Try one and decide for yourself.

Per serving: 259 calories, 29 g protein, 4 g carbohydrate, 14 g total fat (3 g saturated), 86 mg cholesterol, 426 mg sodium, 232 mg potassium

caribbean-style oven-fried chicken

2½ to 3 pounds meaty chicken pieces (breasts, thighs, and drumsticks)

¼ cup margarine or butter, melted

1 teaspoon lemon juice

3 cloves garlic, minced

¼ teaspoon bottled hot pepper sauce

¾ cup fine dry bread crumbs

1 tablespoon snipped fresh parsley

1½ teaspoons paprika

1½ teaspoons pepper*

½ teaspoon salt

Preheat oven to 425°. Skin chicken, if desired. Rinse chicken; pat dry. In a shallow bowl stir together melted margarine, lemon juice, garlic, and hot pepper sauce. In another shallow bowl stir together bread crumbs, parsley, paprika, pepper, and salt.

Dip chicken first in margarine mixture, then in bread crumb mixture to coat. Place on an unheated rack of a broiler pan or on a rack in a roasting pan. Bake for 35 to 40 minutes or till tender and no longer pink. If desired, serve with fresh fruit. Makes 6 servings.

Yes, the amount of pepper is correct!

Per serving: 336 calories, 30 g protein, 10 g carbohydrate, 19 g total fat (5 g saturated), 86 mg cholesterol, 437 mg sodium, 259 mg potassium

five-spice chicken

2½ to 3 pounds meaty chicken pieces (breasts, thighs, and drumsticks)
2 tablespoons cooking oil
1½ teaspoons purchased five-spice powder*
¼ teaspoon garlic powder

Preheat oven to 425°. Skin chicken, if desired. Rinse chicken; pat dry. Arrange chicken in a 13x9x2-inch baking pan. Brush with oil; sprinkle with five-spice powder and garlic powder. Bake for 35 to 40 minutes or till chicken is tender and no longer pink. If desired, serve with Chinese egg noodles tossed with shredded carrot and sliced green onion. Makes 6 servings.

*If purchased five spice powder is not available, you can easily make your own. In a blender container combine 3 tablespoons ground cinnamon, 2 teaspoons aniseed, 1½ teaspoons fennel seed, 1½ teaspoons whole szechuan or black pepper, and ¾ teaspoon ground cloves. Cover and blend to a fine powder. Or, use a mortar and pestle to crush all of the seeds. Store in a tightly covered container. Makes about ⅓ cup.

Per serving: 257 calories, 28 g protein, 1 g carbohydrate, 15 g total fat (4 g saturated), 86 mg cholesterol, 77 mg sodium, 216 mg potassium

chicken with lemon and caper sauce

2 to 2½ pounds meaty chicken pieces (breasts, thighs, and drumsticks)
1 clove garlic, halved
1 tablespoon cooking oil
1 teaspoon lemon-pepper seasoning
¾ cup water
¼ cup dry white wine
½ teaspoon instant chicken bouillon granules
2 tablespoons all-purpose flour
1 tablespoon lemon juice
1 teaspoon drained capers
Asparagus spears (optional)

Preheat oven to 425°. Skin chicken, if desired. Rinse chicken; pat dry. Arrange chicken pieces in a 3-quart rectangular baking dish. Rub chicken with garlic; discard garlic. Brush chicken with oil; sprinkle lemon-pepper seasoning over chicken. Bake for 35 to 40 minutes or till chicken is tender and no longer pink.

Meanwhile, in a small saucepan stir together water, wine, and chicken bouillon granules. Stir in flour and lemon juice; bring mixture to boiling. Reduce heat; cook and stir till mixture is thickened and bubbly. Stir in capers; cook and stir 1 minute more. Spoon the sauce over chicken to serve. If desired, serve with asparagus spears. Makes 4 servings.

Per serving: 315 calories, 34 g protein, 4 g carbohydrate, 16 g total fat (4 g saturated), 104 mg cholesterol, 486 mg sodium, 277 mg potassium

Lemon-pepper seasoning is mainly salt, with black pepper and lemon peel added. It adds a subtle lemon flavor to foods.

You can reuse frying oil if you strain it through a fine strainer after each use and chill tightly covered in the refrigerator. Use again only for chicken-frying.

cornmeal-fried chicken

2½ to 3 pounds meaty chicken pieces (breasts, thighs, and drumsticks)
2 cups water
1 cup yellow cornmeal
¼ cup all-purpose flour
½ teaspoon salt
½ teaspoon garlic powder
¼ teaspoon ground cumin
¼ teaspoon pepper
2 beaten eggs
¾ cup milk
Cooking oil for frying

Skin chicken, if desired. Rinse chicken. Place chicken in a large skillet; pour water over. Bring to boiling; reduce heat and simmer, covered, for 20 to 25 minutes or till just done and no longer pink.

Meanwhile, in a bowl stir together cornmeal, flour, salt, garlic powder, cumin, and pepper. In another bowl beat together egg and milk till combined. Add liquid to cornmeal mixture, stirring till combined.

Drain chicken; pat dry. In a 12-inch skillet heat about 1 inch of cooking oil to 365°. With tongs, dip chicken in cornmeal mixture to coat all sides. Add chicken to hot oil and cook for 10 minutes or till golden brown, turning once. Drain well on paper towels. Makes 6 servings.

Per serving: 438 calories, 33 g protein, 23 g carbohydrate, 22 g total fat (5 g saturated), 160 mg cholesterol, 291 mg sodium, 323 mg potassium

lime chicken

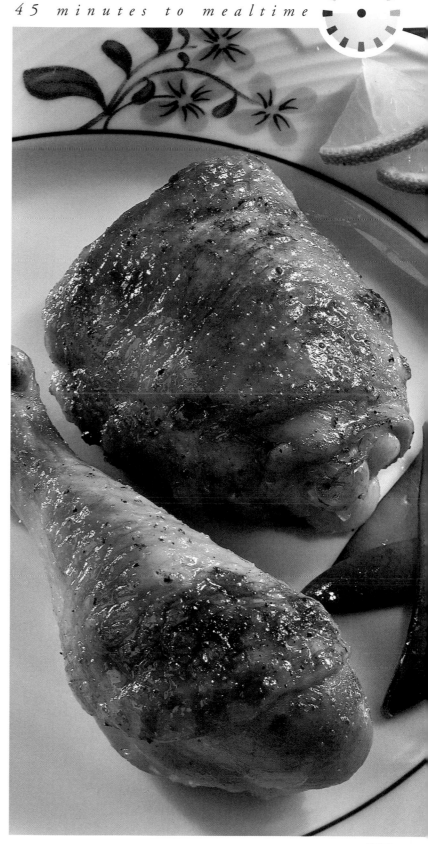

2½ to 3 pounds meaty chicken pieces (breasts, thighs, and drumsticks)
1 tablespoon cooking oil
    Salt
    Pepper
½ cup frozen limeade or lemonade concentrate, thawed
⅛ teaspoon garlic powder
1 lime or lemon, cut into wedges

Preheat oven to 425°. Rinse chicken; pat dry. Place in a lightly greased shallow baking pan. Brush with oil; sprinkle with salt and pepper. Bake for 15 minutes.

Meanwhile, in a small bowl stir together limeade or lemonade concentrate and garlic powder. Brush mixture generously over chicken. Bake 20 to 25 minutes more or till chicken is tender and no longer pink, brushing several times with the limeade mixture. Serve with lime or lemon wedges. Makes 6 servings.

"Key" limes are a well-known variety of the Mexican lime. Highly aromatic, they are usually not available outside of Florida. Persian limes are large, oval, bright green, and tart and are the most widely available limes.

Per serving: 273 calories, 28 g protein, 11 g carbohydrate, 13 g total fat (3 g saturated), 86 mg cholesterol, 165 mg sodium, 230 mg potassium

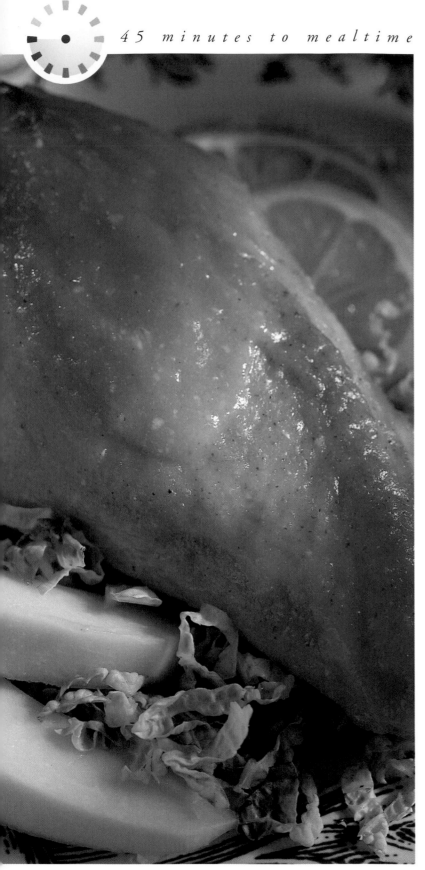

papaya-glazed chicken

2½ to 3 pounds meaty chicken pieces (breasts, thighs, and
    drumsticks)
½ teaspoon seasoned salt
1 cup chopped, peeled papaya
1 tablespoon orange juice
1 tablespoon honey
½ to 1 teaspoon curry powder

Preheat oven to 425°. Skin chicken, if desired. Rinse
chicken; pat dry. Place in a 3-quart rectangular baking
dish. Sprinkle with seasoned salt. Bake for 20 minutes.

Meanwhile, in a blender container or food processor
bowl place papaya chunks, orange juice, honey, and curry
powder. Cover and blend or process till smooth. Remove
chicken from oven; brush papaya mixture liberally over
chicken. Bake 15 to 20 minutes more or till chicken is
tender and no longer pink, brushing several times with
papaya mixture. Makes 6 servings.

Papaya contains an enzyme known as "papain,"
which is an ingredient in commercial meat ten-
derizer. Caribbean cooks have long used chunks of
papaya to tenderize a chicken or meat stew. Select
a papaya that feels somewhat soft.

Per serving: 236 calories, 28 g protein, 6 g carbohydrate, 11 g total fat (3 g saturated),
86 mg cholesterol, 183 mg sodium, 280 mg potassium

chicken and risotto-stuffed peppers

1 6-ounce package risotto mix or saffron-flavored
    rice mix
4 large red, yellow, or green sweet peppers
1½ cups cubed cooked chicken
1 cup cubed Swiss or Monterey Jack cheese (4 ounces)
1 small tomato, peeled, seeded, and chopped
2 tablespoons toasted pinenuts or chopped almonds
2 tablespoons Italian salad dressing
2 tablespoons snipped fresh parsley
½ cup fine dry bread crumbs
2 tablespoons margarine or butter, melted

Prepare risotto or rice mix according to package
directions. Preheat oven to 350°.

Meanwhile, halve peppers lengthwise; remove seeds
and membranes. Cook pepper halves in boiling water for
5 minutes; invert and drain on paper towels. Stir chicken,
cheese, tomato, pinenuts or walnuts, Italian salad dressing,
and parsley into hot cooked rice mixture.

Arrange pepper halves, cut side up, in a 3-quart
rectangular baking dish. Spoon rice mixture into shells.
Combine bread crumbs and melted margarine; sprinkle
atop. Bake, uncovered, for 15 to 20 minutes or till heated
through. For each serving, arrange 2 pepper halves on
each plate. Makes 4 servings.

Per serving: 602 calories, 32 g protein, 52 g carbohydrate, 30 g total fat (8 g saturated),
77 mg cholesterol, 1,164 mg sodium, 422 mg potassium

chicken-stuffed chiles rellenos-style

2 4-ounce cans whole green chili peppers, drained

1 5-ounce can chunk-style chicken, drained and flaked

1 cup shredded Monterey Jack and/or cheddar cheese
  (4 ounces)

4 eggs

⅓ cup all-purpose flour

⅓ cup milk

  Salsa (optional)

Preheat oven to 375°. Slit each chili lengthwise; scrape out seeds and discard. Arrange chili peppers in 4 lightly greased au gratin dishes or a 2-quart square baking dish. Divide chicken evenly among chili peppers; sprinkle cheese over chicken-filled chili peppers.

In a medium bowl beat together eggs, flour, and milk. Pour egg mixture evenly over chili peppers.

Bake individual casseroles for 15 to 20 minutes or the 2-quart baking dish for 25 to 30 minutes or till golden and a knife inserted near center comes out clean. Let stand for 5 minutes before serving. If desired, serve with salsa. Makes 4 servings.

The term "rellenos" (ray-YAY-no) means "stuffing" in Spanish. Mexican chefs make their stuffings with corn, cheese, chiles, shrimp, and vegetables to fill large mild green chiles or bell peppers. This version is baked instead of fried.

Per serving: 290 calories, 23 g protein, 10 g carbohydrate, 17 g total fat (8 g saturated), 259 mg cholesterol, 670 mg sodium, 216 mg potassium

chicken 'n' cheddar puff

1 5-ounce can chunk-style chicken, drained and flaked

1 10-ounce package frozen cut broccoli, cooked and drained

½ cup shredded cheddar or Swiss cheese (2 ounces)

4 eggs

1½ cups milk

2 tablespoons all-purpose flour

½ teaspoon dry mustard

½ teaspoon seasoned salt

⅛ teaspoon pepper

Preheat oven to 375°. Lightly grease 4 individual casserole dishes or 10-ounce custard cups. Divide chicken, cooked broccoli, and cheese evenly among dishes. In a bowl beat together eggs, milk, flour, mustard, seasoned salt, and pepper with a rotary beater or wire whisk till smooth. Pour over chicken mixture in dishes. Bake about 25 minutes or till puffed and set and knife comes out clean. Serve immediately. Makes 4 servings.

Variation: Substitute 1 cup of shredded cooked leftover turkey for the canned chicken. Try frozen asparagus cuts or artichoke hearts, cooked and drained, instead of the broccoli, and use Monterey Jack or muenster cheese.

Per serving: 268 calories, 23 g protein, 11 g carbohydrate, 14 g total fat (6 g saturated), 254 mg cholesterol, 548 mg sodium, 382 mg potassium

chicken and cheddar crustless quiche

Nonstick spray coating

1 tablespoon toasted wheat germ

1 4-ounce can mushroom stems and pieces, drained

1 cup shredded cheddar, Swiss, or Monterey Jack cheese (4 ounces)

1 5-ounce can chunk-style chicken, drained and flaked

4 eggs

½ cup milk

1 teaspoon dried basil, crushed

¼ teaspoon seasoned salt

Preheat oven to 350°. Spray a 9-inch pie plate or 8-inch quiche dish with nonstick coating. Sprinkle the wheat germ into the pie plate or dish. Spread drained mushrooms, cheese, and chicken evenly in bottom of pie plate. In a small bowl beat together eggs, milk, basil, and seasoned salt with a wire whisk until combined. Pour mixture over chicken in pan.

Bake for 25 to 30 minutes or till a knife inserted halfway between center and edge comes out clean. Let stand 5 minutes; cut into wedges. Makes 4 servings.

Per serving: 277 calories, 23 g protein, 5 g carbohydrate, 18 g total fat (9 g saturated), 265 mg cholesterol, 632 mg sodium, 244 mg potassium

chicken-stuffed baked tomatoes

4 large tomatoes

1½ cups finely chopped zucchini

¼ cup sliced green onion

1 tablespoon cooking oil

2 5-ounce cans or one 12-ounce can chunk-style
   chicken, drained and flaked

¼ cup ranch-style or thousand island salad dressing

1 cup cubed cheddar, Monterey Jack, or Swiss cheese
   (4 ounces)

Preheat oven to 400°. Cut tomatoes in half. With a
grapefruit knife or a paring knife hollow out the
tomatoes, leaving a ¼-inch-thick shell. Invert tomato shells
on paper towels to drain.

Meanwhile, in a medium skillet cook zucchini and
onion in hot oil for 3 minutes, stirring occasionally; stir
in chicken and heat through. Remove from heat; stir in salad
dressing and cheese.

Place tomatoes, cut side up, in a lightly greased baking
dish. Spoon chicken mixture into tomatoes. Cover and
bake for 12 to 15 minutes or till heated through. Place
2 tomato halves on each plate. Makes 4 servings.

Next time, use the chicken mixture to stuff par-
tially-cooked sweet pepper, zucchini, or yellow
squash shells.

Per serving: 347 calories, 24 g protein, 8 g carbohydrate, 25 g total fat (9 g saturated),
73 mg cholesterol, 642 mg sodium, 494 mg potassium

mediterranean-
style cornish hens

2 1¼- to 1½-pound Cornish game hens, split
1 tablespoon olive oil or cooking oil
4 cloves garlic, minced
¼ teaspoon seasoned salt
1 14½-ounce can chicken broth
1 tablespoon margarine or butter
1 cup finely chopped carrot
½ cup chopped green sweet pepper
½ teaspoon dried thyme, crushed
¼ teaspoon salt
¼ teaspoon pepper
¾ cup couscous
⅓ cup sliced green onion

Preheat broiler. Rinse hens; pat dry. Place hens, skin side down, on the unheated rack of a lightly greased broiler pan. Combine oil and garlic. Brush hens with *half* of the oil mixture. Sprinkle with seasoned salt. Broil hens, bone side up, 5 to 6 inches from the heat for 20 minutes. Turn hens, skin side up, and broil 5 minutes more. Brush with remaining oil mixture and broil 5 to 10 minutes more or till hens are tender and no longer pink.

Meanwhile, in a medium saucepan bring chicken broth and margarine to boiling. Add carrot, green pepper, thyme, salt, and pepper. Return to boiling; reduce heat. Simmer, covered, for 7 to 8 minutes or till carrot is tender. Add couscous and green onion. Cover. Remove from heat and let stand 5 minutes. Fluff couscous lightly with fork before serving with hens. Makes 4 servings.

Per serving: 576 calories, 44 g protein, 34 g carbohydrate, 30 g total fat (6 g saturated), 120 mg cholesterol, 703 mg sodium, 304 mg potassium

apricot and mint-broiled cornish hens

2 1¼- to 1½-pound Cornish game hens, split
   Cooking oil
¼ teaspoon salt
   Dash pepper
⅓ cup apricot or peach preserves
1 teaspoon lemon juice
1½ teaspoons snipped fresh mint or ½ teaspoon dried
    mint, crushed
   Hot cooked orzo or rice (optional)

Preheat broiler. Rinse hens; pat dry. Place hens, skin side down, on the unheated rack of a lightly greased broiler pan. Brush hens lightly with oil; sprinkle with salt and pepper. Broil hens, bone side up, 5 to 6 inches from the heat for 20 minutes.

Meanwhile, in a small saucepan melt preserves; stir in lemon juice and mint. Turn hens skin side up. Broil 15 minutes longer till hens are tender and no longer pink. Brush with apricot mixture and broil 2 minutes longer. If desired, serve with pasta or rice. Makes 4 servings.

This easy broiling method for Cornish hens is a great way to slash the cooking time. You can use the same method on the grill, too.

Per serving: 380 calories, 30 g protein, 19 g carbohydrate, 21 g total fat (5 g saturated), 100 mg cholesterol, 211 mg sodium, 26 mg potassium

broiled turkey with vegetables

4 turkey breast tenderloin steaks (about 1 pound total)

2 tablespoons cooking oil

½ teaspoon seasoned salt

1½ cups sliced parsnips

1 cup sliced carrots

1 cup brussels sprouts, halved

½ cup sliced celery

½ cup sliced onion

¼ cup mayonnaise or salad dressing

½ teaspoon dried basil, crushed

½ teaspoon dried dillweed

½ teaspoon dried thyme, crushed

¼ teaspoon salt

¼ teaspoon pepper

Preheat broiler. Rinse turkey; pat dry. Place turkey on the unheated rack of a broiler pan; brush both sides with *1 tablespoon* of the oil. Sprinkle with seasoned salt. Broil 4 to 5 inches from the heat for 8 to 10 minutes or till tender and no longer pink, turning once. Remove to a serving platter; keep warm.

Meanwhile, in a steamer basket over simmering *water*, steam next 4 vegetables for 8 to 10 minutes or till tender. Remove vegetables from steamer; keep warm. Reserve *¼ cup* steaming liquid; discard remaining liquid. In same pan heat remaining 1 tablespoon oil; cook and stir onion for 3 minutes. Stir together reserved liquid, mayonnaise, herbs, salt, and pepper. Add to onion mixture in pan. Return vegetables to pan; stir to coat with sauce. Spoon vegetables over broiled turkey. Makes 4 servings.

Per serving: 359 calories, 24 g protein, 21 g carbohydrate, 21 g total fat (3 g saturated), 58 mg cholesterol, 469 mg sodium, 709 mg potassium

grilled turkey tenderloins with onion-cilantro relish

½ cup chopped onion

¼ cup cilantro sprigs

⅛ teaspoon salt

⅛ teaspoon pepper

4 turkey breast tenderloin steaks (about 1 pound total)

3 tablespoons lime or lemon juice

Lime or lemon wedges (optional)

Start grill. In a blender container or food processor bowl blend or process onions with cilantro, salt, and pepper till mixture is very finely chopped.

Rinse turkey; pat dry. Dip turkey in lime or lemon juice. Place turkey on grill rack of an uncovered grill directly over medium coals. Grill for 7 minutes. Turn; brush with lime juice. Spread the onion mixture over turkey. Grill 8 to 11 minutes more or till turkey is tender and no longer pink.

Serve tenderloins with lime or lemon wedges and garnish with cilantro, if desired. Makes 4 servings.

Per serving: 124 calories, 22 g protein, 3 g carbohydrate, 2 g total fat (1 g saturated), 50 mg cholesterol, 113 mg sodium, 267 mg potassium

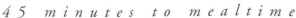

turkey soup with barley

1 pound turkey breast tenderloins or skinless, boneless
    chicken breast halves or thighs

2 tablespoons cooking oil

1 cup chopped onion

1 cup chopped red or green sweet pepper

1 clove garlic, minced

4 cups chicken broth

1 10-ounce package frozen cut green beans

1 cup loose-pack frozen, whole kernel corn or
    one 8-ounce can whole kernel corn, drained

⅔ cup quick-cooking barley

1 teaspoon sugar

1 teaspoon dried thyme, crushed

1 teaspoon dried basil, crushed

½ teaspoon salt

¼ teaspoon pepper

1 bay leaf

    Rinse turkey; pat dry. Cut turkey into bite-size strips. In a Dutch oven cook and stir turkey in hot oil for 5 minutes. With a slotted spoon remove from pan. In pan drippings cook onion, sweet pepper, and garlic for 3 minutes, stirring occasionally. Drain off excess fat.

    Return turkey to pan with chicken broth, beans, corn, barley, sugar, thyme, basil, salt, pepper, and bay leaf. Bring to boiling; reduce heat. Simmer, covered, for 15 to 20 minutes or till barley is cooked. Discard bay leaf. Makes 4 or 5 servings.

Per serving: 411 calories, 33 g protein, 45 g carbohydrate, 12 g total fat (2 g saturated), 51 mg cholesterol, 1,108 mg sodium, 780 mg potassium

turkey milano with pistachio sauce

4 turkey breast tenderloin steaks or skinless, boneless
   chicken breast halves (about 1 pound total)
¼ cup olive oil
¼ cup white wine vinegar
2 cloves garlic, minced
1 tablespoon snipped fresh chives
¼ teaspoon salt
   Dash pepper
⅓ cup margarine or butter
1 cup chopped onion
1 medium red sweet pepper, cut into strips
⅓ cup pistachio nuts or slivered almonds
¼ cup dry white wine
   Hot cooked fettuccine or linguine

Rinse turkey; pat dry. Place turkey in a shallow non-metal dish. In a small bowl stir together oil, vinegar, garlic, chives, salt, and pepper; pour over turkey. Let stand 20 minutes. Meanwhile, preheat broiler. Drain turkey, reserving marinade. Place on the unheated rack of a broiler pan. Broil 4 to 5 inches from the heat for 5 minutes. Turn and brush with marinade. Broil 4 to 6 minutes more or till tender and no longer pink.

Meanwhile, in a small skillet melt margarine or butter. Cook onion, sweet pepper, and pistachios for 3 minutes, stirring frequently. Stir in wine; simmer 2 minutes more. Season to taste with *salt* and *pepper*. Spoon sauce over turkey and pasta. Makes 4 servings.

Per serving: 576 calories, 28 g protein, 33 g carbohydrate, 37 g total fat (6 g saturated), 50 mg cholesterol, 493 mg sodium, 534 mg potassium

spicy grilled turkey tenderloins

4 turkey breast tenderloin steaks (about 1 pound total)
1 teaspoon finely shredded orange peel
¼ cup orange juice
2 tablespoons olive oil or cooking oil
1 teaspoon ground cumin
1 teaspoon dried thyme, crushed
½ teaspoon salt
¼ teaspoon pepper
¼ teaspoon crushed red pepper
   Hot cooked rice (optional)

Start grill. Rinse turkey; pat dry. Place turkey in a shallow non-metal dish. In a measuring cup stir together orange peel, orange juice, oil, cumin, thyme, salt, pepper, and crushed pepper. Pour mixture over turkey; let stand 20 minutes.

Drain turkey, reserving marinade. Place turkey on grill rack of an uncovered grill directly over *medium* coals. Grill for 12 to 15 minutes or till turkey is tender and no longer pink, turning once and basting with reserved marinade halfway through grilling time. If desired, serve with rice. Makes 4 servings.

Delicious and versatile, turkey easily adapts to a variety of seasonings. Next time, in place of the cumin, thyme, and red pepper, try ginger, allspice, and nutmeg or combine thyme, garlic, and fennel.

Per serving: 182 calories, 22 g protein, 2 g carbohydrate, 9 g total fat (2 g saturated), 50 mg cholesterol, 315 mg sodium, 260 mg potassium

turkey-black bean chili

- 1 pound turkey breast tenderloins or skinless, boneless chicken breast halves or thighs
- 2 tablespoons cooking oil
- 1 cup chopped green sweet pepper
- 1 cup chopped onion
- 2 cloves garlic, minced
- 2 28-ounce cans tomatoes, cut up
- 2 15-ounce cans black beans or great northern beans, drained
- 1 12-ounce can beer
- 2 tablespoons red wine vinegar
- 1 tablespoon chili powder
- 1 teaspoon dried oregano, crushed
- 1 teaspoon ground cumin
- ¼ teaspoon bottled hot pepper sauce
- 1 bay leaf
- 1 cup shredded Monterey Jack or cheddar cheese

Rinse turkey; pat dry. Cut into bite-size strips. In a Dutch oven cook turkey or chicken in hot oil over medium heat till no longer pink; remove from pan. In pan drippings cook green pepper, onion, and garlic for 3 minutes, stirring occasionally; drain off excess fat.

Return turkey to pan. Add *undrained* tomatoes, drained beans, beer, vinegar, chili powder, oregano, cumin, hot pepper sauce, bay leaf, 1 teaspoon *salt*, and ¼ teaspoon *pepper*. Bring to boiling; reduce heat. Simmer, covered, for 20 minutes or till turkey is tender, stirring occasionally. Discard bay leaf. Sprinkle cheese over each serving. Makes 6 servings.

Per serving: 377 calories, 31 g protein, 38 g carbohydrate, 13 g total fat (5 g saturated), 50 mg cholesterol, 1,286 mg sodium, 1,167 mg potassium

Dijon mustard has a distinctive clean, sharp flavor that comes from a blend of brown or black mustard seeds, white wine, and spices.

turkey with mustard sauce

4 turkey breast tenderloin steaks or skinless, boneless
   chicken breasts halves (about 1 pound total)
2 tablespoons olive oil or cooking oil
4 shallots, sliced, or ½ cup chopped green onion
½ cup dry white wine
½ cup chicken broth
1 teaspoon dried basil, crushed
1 teaspoon dried tarragon, crushed
   Dash pepper
1 10-ounce package frozen asparagus spears or tiny
   whole carrots
2 tablespoons Dijon-style mustard
¼ cup dairy sour cream

Rinse turkey; pat dry. In a large skillet cook turkey and shallots in hot oil over medium heat about 5 minutes or until turkey is browned, turning once. Stir in wine, broth, basil, tarragon, and pepper. Bring to boiling; reduce heat. Simmer, covered, for about 5 minutes or till turkey is tender and no longer pink. Meanwhile, cook asparagus or carrots till crisp-tender; drain.

Transfer turkey to a serving platter; cover and keep warm. Bring liquid in skillet to boiling. Continue boiling about 5 minutes or till mixture is reduced to ½ cup. Stir mustard and sour cream into pan juices; heat through but do not boil. Arrange cooked asparagus or carrots alongside turkey; spoon sauce over turkey. Makes 4 servings.

Per serving: 271 calories, 25 g protein, 8 g carbohydrate, 13 g total fat (4 g saturated), 57 mg cholesterol, 386 mg sodium, 491 mg potassium

poached turkey with cranberry-orange sauce

4 turkey breast tenderloin steaks (1 pound total)

½ small onion, sliced

2 teaspoons instant chicken bouillon granules

½ cup frozen cranberry-orange relish, thawed

1 tablespoon lemon juice

1 tablespoon honey

1 teaspoon cornstarch

¼ teaspoon salt

Hot cooked long grain and wild rice (optional)

Rinse turkey; pat dry. Place turkey pieces in a large skillet. Add enough *water* to cover turkey. Add sliced onion and bouillon granules. Bring mixture to boiling; reduce heat. Simmer, covered, for 12 to 15 minutes or till turkey is tender and no longer pink.

Remove turkey; cover and keep warm. Reserve the poaching liquid. Strain liquid and reserve *½ cup;* discard remaining liquid. Return reserved liquid to skillet. Add cranberry-orange relish, lemon juice, honey, cornstarch, and salt. Cook and stir till mixture is thickened and bubbly. Cook and stir 2 minutes more. Arrange tenderloins on a serving platter; spoon sauce over. If desired, serve with hot cooked long grain and wild rice. Makes 4 servings.

Per serving: 167 calories, 22 g protein, 13 g carbohydrate, 2 g total fat (1 g saturated), 50 mg cholesterol, 615 mg sodium, 269 mg potassium

creamed turkey and mushrooms

4 frozen patty shells or 4 slices white bread, halved
    diagonally and toasted

1 pound turkey breast tenderloins or skinless, boneless
    chicken breast halves or thighs

2 tablespoons olive oil or cooking oil

2 tablespoons margarine or butter

8 ounces fresh mushrooms, sliced (3 cups)

1 cup chopped onion

3 tablespoons all-purpose flour

½ teaspoon salt

½ teaspoon paprika

¼ teaspoon pepper

1 cup chicken broth

½ cup half-and-half, light cream, or milk

¼ cup grated Parmesan or Romano cheese

2 tablespoons snipped fresh parsley
    Cooked carrots (optional)

If using frozen patty shells, prepare according to
package directions. Rinse turkey; pat dry. Cut turkey into
bite-size strips. In a 12-inch skillet, cook turkey in hot oil
about 5 minutes or till tender and no longer pink, turning
frequently. Remove from pan.

To pan drippings, add margarine; cook mushrooms
and onions for 5 minutes, stirring frequently. Stir in flour,
salt, paprika, and pepper. Add broth and cream all at
once; cook and stir till mixture is thickened and bubbly.
Cook and stir 1 minute more. Stir in turkey, cheese, and
parsley. Cook 2 minutes more. Serve in patty shells or
over toast. If desired, serve with carrots. Makes 4 servings.

Per serving: 562 calories, 31 g protein, 29 g carbohydrate, 36 g total fat (8 g saturated),
64 mg cholesterol, 806 mg sodium, 462 mg potassium

poached turkey with watercress sauce

4 turkey breast tenderloin steaks (about 1 pound total)

1 cup dry white wine

1 carrot, quartered

¼ teaspoon whole black peppercorns

1 bay leaf

2 tablespoons margarine or butter

4 shallots, chopped, or ⅓ cup chopped onion

1 teaspoon dried basil, crushed

1 cup watercress sprigs, chopped, or 1 cup chopped spinach

1 tablespoon all-purpose flour

½ cup half-and-half, light cream, or milk

   Hot cooked pasta (optional)

Rinse turkey; place in a large skillet. Add wine and enough *water* to cover turkey. Add carrot, peppercorns, and bay leaf. Bring to boiling; reduce heat. Simmer, covered, 12 to 15 minutes or till turkey is no longer pink.

Remove turkey; cover, and keep warm. Reserve the poaching liquid. Strain liquid and reserve *½ cup;* discard remaining liquid. In same pan melt margarine; cook shallots, basil, ¼ teaspoon *salt,* and ⅛ teaspoon *white pepper* for 3 minutes. Add watercress; cook 2 minutes more. Sprinkle flour over mixture; stir till dissolved. Add the ½ cup reserved poaching liquid and cream all at once; cook and stir till thickened and bubbly; cook and stir 1 minute more. Spoon sauce over chicken. If desired, serve with pasta. Makes 4 servings.

Per serving: 228 calories, 23 g protein, 6 g carbohydrate, 11 g total fat (4 g saturated), 59 mg cholesterol, 267 mg sodium, 361 mg potassium

chicken burgers with pineapple salsa

1 8¼-ounce can crushed pineapple, drained

½ cup chopped red or green sweet pepper

½ cup sliced green onion

2 tablespoons snipped fresh cilantro or parsley

2 cloves garlic, minced

1 jalapeño or serrano pepper, seeded and finely chopped

1 egg

¼ cup fine dry bread crumbs

1 teaspoon dried basil, crushed

½ teaspoon ground sage

½ teaspoon seasoned salt

⅛ teaspoon pepper

1 pound ground raw chicken or turkey

Start grill. For salsa, in a medium bowl combine crushed pineapple, sweet pepper, *half* of the green onion, the cilantro, garlic, and jalapeño. Cover; chill till serving time.

In another medium bowl combine the egg, bread crumbs, remaining onion, basil, sage, seasoned salt, and pepper. Add ground chicken; mix well. Shape into four ¾-inch-thick patties. Grill patties on the grill rack of an uncovered grill directly over *medium* coals for 14 to 18 minutes or till juices run clear and burgers are no longer pink, turning halfway through grilling. *(Or,* preheat broiler. Broil 4 to 5 inches from heat on an unheated rack of broiler pan for 10 to 12 minutes.) Serve burgers with salsa. Makes 4 servings.

Per serving: 228 calories, 18 g protein, 16 g carbohydrate, 10 g total fat (3 g saturated), 95 mg cholesterol, 273 mg sodium, 336 mg potassium

turkey meatball soup

1   slightly beaten egg

⅓ cup fine dry seasoned bread crumbs

1   pound ground raw turkey or chicken

2   tablespoons cooking oil

4   cups chicken broth

1   10-ounce package frozen peas and carrots

2   cups diced peeled potatoes

2   cups shredded fresh kale or spinach

2   teaspoons dried basil, crushed

½ teaspoon ground sage

¼ teaspoon pepper

In a medium bowl combine egg and bread crumbs. Add turkey and mix well. With hands, shape mixture into twenty-four 1-inch meatballs.

In a Dutch oven heat oil; brown meatballs on all sides. Drain off excess fat. Add broth, peas and carrots, potatoes, kale, basil, sage, and pepper. Bring to boiling; reduce heat. Simmer, covered, for 15 to 20 minutes or till vegetables are tender and meatballs are no longer pink. Serves 6.

Here are three meatball-shaping methods you can try: 1) Use a small ice cream scoop. 2) Shape the meat mixture into two 1-inch-diameter logs; cut off slices from the log and roll them into balls. 3) Pat the meat mixture into a 1-inch-thick square on waxed paper. Cut into 1-inch cubes and shape each cube into a ball.

Per serving: 249 calories, 18 g protein, 21 g carbohydrate, 10 g total fat (2 g saturated), 64 mg cholesterol, 763 mg sodium, 587 mg potassium

maple-glazed chicken and vegetables

2½ to 3 pounds meaty chicken pieces (breasts, thighs, and
     drumsticks)
1 tablespoon cooking oil
3 cups sliced or cut vegetables (such as carrots, potatoes,
     sweet potatoes, rutabaga, turnips, or parsnips),
     cut ½-inch thick
1 large onion, cut into wedges
½ teaspoon salt
¼ teaspoon pepper
½ cup chicken broth
1 tablespoons margarine or butter
⅓ cup maple or maple-flavored syrup

Preheat oven to 425°. Skin chicken. Rinse chicken; pat
dry. Place in a lightly greased shallow baking pan; brush
chicken with oil. Sprinkle sliced vegetables and onion
around chicken. Sprinkle with salt and pepper. Pour broth
over vegetables. Bake for 20 minutes.

Meanwhile, in a small saucepan melt margarine; stir in
syrup and heat through. Brush mixture over chicken and
vegetables; bake 15 to 20 minutes more or till chicken is
tender and no longer pink, brushing frequently with
maple syrup mixture.

Transfer chicken and vegetables to serving platter;
keep warm. Skim fat from pan drippings; pass pan
drippings with chicken. Makes 6 servings.

Per serving: 352 calories, 30 g protein, 24 g carbohydrate, 15 g total fat (4 g saturated),
86 mg cholesterol, 364 mg sodium, 891 mg potassium

phyllo-crusted chicken pot pie

1½ cups coarsely chopped potatoes

2½ cups loose-pack frozen mixed vegetables

12 ounces skinless, boneless chicken breast halves

½ cup chopped onion

2 cloves garlic, minced

1 tablespoon olive oil or cooking oil

1 12-ounce jar chicken gravy

1 teaspoon dried basil, crushed

4 sheets frozen phyllo dough, thawed

2 tablespoons margarine or butter, melted

In medium saucepan cook potatoes in boiling water to cover for 10 minutes. Add frozen vegetables; cook 5 minutes more. Drain vegetables. Preheat oven to 400°.

Meanwhile, rinse chicken; pat dry. Chop the chicken. In a large skillet cook chicken, onion, and garlic in hot oil about 5 minutes or till chicken is no longer pink. Drain off excess fat. Stir in gravy and basil; heat till bubbly. Stir in cooked vegetables. Turn mixture into a lightly greased 2-quart square baking dish.

Brush each sheet of phyllo dough with the margarine or butter and layer on top of each other. Lay the stack of phyllo sheets over the filling. With kitchen shears, trim phyllo dough edges as necessary to overlap 1 inch around edge of dish. Fold under to fit edge of dish.

Bake for 20 to 25 minutes or until crust is golden brown and filling is heated through. Cut into squares and spoon onto serving plates. Makes 4 servings.

Per serving: 399 calories, 23 g protein, 38 g carbohydrate, 18 g total fat (4 g saturated), 46 mg cholesterol, 720 mg sodium, 593 mg potassium

chicken enchiladas

1 pound skinless, boneless chicken breast halves or
   skinless, boneless chicken thighs

1 tablespoon cooking oil

½ teaspoon seasoned salt

3 cups shredded cheddar or Monterey Jack cheese
   (12 ounces)

1 cup sliced pitted ripe olives

1 cup sliced green onions

1 14-ounce can enchilada sauce

8 8-inch flour tortillas

Be sure to assemble this dish just before baking, since the tortillas tend to become soggy if they're not baked soon after they've been dipped in the sauce.

Preheat oven to 375°. Rinse chicken; pat dry. Cut into bite-size strips. In a large skillet cook chicken in hot oil until browned and no longer pink. Remove from heat; drain off excess fat. Toss chicken with salt.

Reserve *1½ cups* cheese, *⅓ cup* olives, and *1 tablespoon* onion for topping. To assemble enchiladas, spoon *½ cup* of the enchilada sauce in the bottom of a lightly greased 3-quart rectangular baking dish.

Lay each tortilla on a flat surface; fill with some of the cooked chicken, remaining cheese, onions, and olives, dividing ingredients evenly among tortillas. Fold tortillas over filling; place seam side down in sauce. Pour the remaining enchilada sauce over filled tortillas; sprinkle reserved cheese, olives, and green onions over top.

Bake, covered, for 15 minutes. Uncover, bake 10 to 15 minutes more or till heated through. Makes 8 servings.

Per serving: 375 calories, 25 g protein, 22 g carbohydrate, 22 g total fat
(10 g saturated), 75 mg cholesterol, 778 mg sodium, 174 mg potassium

oriental sesame-baked chicken

6 medium chicken breast halves (about 2½ pounds total)
3 tablespoons teriyaki sauce
2 teaspoons grated fresh gingerroot
¼ cup fine dry bread crumbs
3 tablespoons sesame seed
⅛ teaspoon pepper
   Hot cooked rice (optional)

Preheat oven to 425°. Skin chicken, if desired. Rinse chicken; pat dry. In a shallow bowl combine teriyaki sauce and gingerroot; set aside.

In another shallow bowl stir together bread crumbs, sesame seed, and pepper. Roll chicken in teriyaki mixture then roll in bread crumb mixture to coat on all sides. In a 13x9x2-inch baking pan, arrange chicken pieces, meaty side up, so pieces don't touch.

Bake for 35 to 40 minutes, or till chicken is tender and no longer pink. Do not turn. If desired, serve with hot cooked rice. Makes 6 servings.

This method of "oven-frying" coated chicken in a hot oven simulates fried chicken without the added fat of deep-frying. For this method to result in crispy chicken, allow space between the pieces or they will steam instead of baking up crisp.

Per serving: 234 calories, 32 g protein, 5 g carbohydrate, 9 g total fat (2 g saturated), 87 mg cholesterol, 448 mg sodium, 286 mg potassium

jamaican jerk chicken

4 skinless, boneless chicken breast halves

½ cup chopped onion

2 tablespoons lime juice

1 teaspoon salt

1 teaspoon crushed red pepper

½ teaspoon ground allspice

¼ teaspoon curry powder

⅛ teaspoon dried thyme, crushed

⅛ teaspoon ground red pepper

⅛ teaspoon ground ginger

2 cloves garlic, quartered

1 medium red, yellow, or green sweet pepper, cut into
      1½-inch pieces

1 small zucchini, sliced ½ inch thick

1 tablespoon cooking oil

You can use 1 tablespoon purchased Jamaican Jerk seasoning in place of the crushed red pepper, allspice, curry powder, ground red pepper, ginger, thyme, and black pepper.

Start grill. Rinse chicken; pat dry. In a blender container combine onion, lime juice, salt, crushed red pepper, allspice, curry, thyme, red pepper, ginger, garlic, and ¼ teaspoon *black pepper*. Cover and process till pureed. Place chicken in non-metal shallow dish. Add puree; turn to coat both sides. Cover; chill 30 minutes.

Meanwhile, thread sweet pepper and zucchini pieces on four 8- to 10-inch skewers. Brush with oil and sprinkle with ¼ teaspoon *coarsely ground pepper*. Remove chicken from puree. Grill on the rack of an uncovered grill directly over *medium* coals for 12 to 15 minutes or till tender and no longer pink, turning and brushing once with puree. Add vegetables to grill the last 10 minutes of cooking; turn frequently. Makes 4 servings.

Per serving: 173 calories, 22 g protein, 5 g carbohydrate, 7 g total fat (1 g saturated), 59 mg cholesterol, 596 mg sodium, 309 mg potassium

oriental foil-wrapped chicken with vegetables

1 10-ounce package frozen tiny whole carrots
4 skinless, boneless chicken breast halves
     (about 1 pound total)
1 4-ounce can whole mushrooms, drained
1 small red sweet pepper, cut into bite-size strips
3 tablespoons hoisin sauce
2 cloves garlic, minced
1 teaspoon grated gingerroot
   Dash ground red pepper
¼ cup sliced green onions
   Hot cooked rice (optional)

Preheat oven to 425°. Run carrots under cold water to
thaw. Drain well. Rinse chicken; pat dry. Place 1 chicken
breast half in the center of an 18x12-inch piece of heavy
foil. Repeat with remaining chicken and 3 additional foil
pieces. Divide carrots, mushrooms, and red pepper evenly
among foil packets. Stir together hoisin sauce, garlic,
ginger, and ground red pepper. Drizzle over chicken and
vegetables. Bring up two opposite sides of foil and seal
with a double fold. Fold remaining ends to completely
enclose the chicken and vegetables, leaving space for
steam to build. Repeat with each foil packet. Place on a
15x10x1-inch baking pan. Bake for 30 minutes or till
chicken is tender and no longer pink.

To serve, carefully open foil packets. Sprinkle with
green onions. If desired, serve over hot cooked rice. Spoon
some of the cooking juices over all. Makes 4 servings.

Per serving: 152 calories, 23 g protein, 8 g carbohydrate, 3 g total fat (1 g saturated),
59 mg cholesterol, 494 mg sodium, 342 mg potassium

easy chicken cassoulet

8 ounces bulk pork sausage

½ cup chopped onion

1 clove garlic, minced

1¾ pounds meaty chicken pieces (breasts, thighs, and drumsticks)

1 15-ounce can tomato puree

1 cup fresh or frozen cut green beans

1 10-ounce package frozen lima beans

1 teaspoon dried thyme, crushed

½ teaspoon seasoned salt

¼ teaspoon dried savory, crushed

¼ teaspoon pepper

1 bay leaf

To vary this dish, experiment with different types of sausages, such as veal, chicken, or turkey in place of the pork.

In a 12-inch skillet break up pork sausage; add onion and garlic. Cook and stir till sausage is brown and onion is tender. Drain, reserving *2 tablespoons* drippings in pan. Set sausage aside. Skin chicken, if desired. Rinse chicken; pat dry. Cook chicken in reserved drippings about 10 minutes or till lightly browned, turning to brown evenly. Drain off excess fat.

Return sausage to skillet. Add tomato puree, green beans, lima beans, thyme, salt, savory, pepper, and bay leaf. Bring mixture to boiling; reduce heat. Simmer, covered, for 35 minutes or till chicken is tender and no longer pink. Discard bay leaf. Makes 6 servings.

Per serving: 341 calories, 34 g protein, 34 g carbohydrate, 8 g total fat (3 g saturated), 68 mg cholesterol, 667 mg sodium, 1,149 mg potassium

chicken mazatlan with roasted green onions

4 chicken breast halves or legs (drumstick-thigh piece) (about 2 pounds total)

1½ cups crushed tortilla chips

2 teaspoons chili powder

¼ teaspoon garlic salt

¼ teaspoon onion salt

1 slightly beaten egg

¼ cup milk

8 green onions

1 teaspoon cooking oil

Dash salt

Preheat oven to 425°. Skin chicken, if desired. Rinse chicken; pat dry. In a shallow dish stir together crushed chips, chili powder, garlic salt, and onion salt. In another shallow dish whisk together egg and milk.

Dip chicken pieces in egg mixture, then roll in chip mixture to coat on all sides. In a 13x9x2-inch baking pan arrange chicken pieces, skin side up, so pieces don't touch. Sprinkle any remaining chips atop.

Bake for 35 to 40 minutes or till chicken is tender and no longer pink. Do not turn.

Meanwhile, trim onions leaving about 2 inches of green. Arrange green onions on a baking sheet. Brush with oil; sprinkle with salt. Place in oven with chicken during the last 10 minutes of roasting time. Serve 2 onions with each serving of chicken. Makes 4 servings.

Per serving: 325 calories, 37 g protein, 16 g carbohydrate, 12 g total fat (3 g saturated), 146 mg cholesterol, 512 mg sodium, 403 mg potassium

chicken-stuffed cabbage rolls

12 green cabbage leaves
 1 pound skinless, boneless chicken breast halves
 ⅓ cup sliced green onion
 1 clove garlic, minced
 1 tablespoon cooking oil
 1 cup cooked white or brown rice
 1 cup chopped tomato
 1 teaspoon dried basil, crushed
 ½ teaspoon dried thyme, crushed
 ½ cup chicken broth

Preheat oven to 400°. In a Dutch oven pour water to a depth of 1½ inches. Bring to boiling; immerse cabbage leaves. Reduce heat; simmer 5 minutes. Drain on paper towels. Meanwhile, rinse chicken; pat dry. Dice chicken. In a large skillet cook chicken, onion, and garlic in hot oil till chicken is no longer pink. Drain off fat. Stir in rice, tomato, basil, thyme, ½ teaspoon *salt,* and ¼ teaspoon *pepper;* heat through. Remove from heat. Spoon *2 rounded tablespoons* of filling onto stem end of each cabbage leaf. Fold sides of leaf over stuffing; roll up jelly roll-style. Place rolls seam side down in a shallow baking pan; pour chicken broth over rolls. Bake, covered, for 20 to 25 minutes or till hot. Spoon Sauce over rolls. Serves 6.

Sauce: In a saucepan melt 1 tablespoon *margarine or butter;* stir in 1 tablespoon *all-purpose flour.* Add ¾ cup *milk* all at once; cook and stir till mixture is thickened and bubbly. Cook and stir 1 minute. Stir in ¼ cup grated *Parmesan cheese* and 1 tablespoon snipped fresh *parsley.* Season to taste with *salt* and *pepper.*

Per serving: 222 calories, 19 g protein, 17 g carbohydrate, 9 g total fat (3 g saturated), 45 mg cholesterol, 375 mg sodium, 387 mg potassium

chicken, ham, and cheese-stuffed shells

16 jumbo pasta shells

8 ounces skinless, boneless chicken breast halves or skinless, boneless chicken thighs

1 tablespoon cooking oil

1 cup finely chopped fully cooked ham

1 beaten egg

2 cups shredded mozzarella cheese (8 ounces)

1 15-ounce container ricotta cheese

1 28-ounce jar zesty tomato or tomato and herb pasta sauce

¼ cup grated Parmesan or Romano cheese

Cook pasta in boiling salted water according to package directions till tender; drain. Invert shells on paper towels; set aside. Preheat oven to 425°.

Meanwhile, rinse chicken; pat dry. Finely chop chicken. In a medium skillet cook chicken in hot oil till no longer pink. Add ham; cook 2 minutes more. Remove from heat. Drain off excess fat.

In a large bowl stir together egg, mozzarella cheese, and ricotta cheese till mixed. Stir in chicken and ham.

Fill shells with cheese mixture; place filled side up in a lightly greased 3-quart rectangular baking dish. Pour pasta sauce over shells. Sprinkle grated Parmesan cheese over sauce. Bake, covered, for 15 minutes. Uncover; bake 10 to 15 minutes more or till bubbly and heated through. If desired, serve with green beans. Makes 8 servings.

Per serving: 401 calories, 28 g protein, 31 g carbohydrate, 19 g total fat (8 g saturated), 82 mg cholesterol, 969 mg sodium, 598 mg potassium

chicken with roasted peppers

3 red, yellow, and/or green sweet peppers

4 skinless, boneless chicken breast halves
   (about 1 pound total)

1 tablespoon cooking oil

1½ cups chopped, seeded tomatoes (2 medium)

1 cup sliced onion

2 cloves garlic, minced

1 teaspoon dried basil, crushed

1 teaspoon dried oregano, crushed

½ teaspoon salt

¼ teaspoon pepper

   Grated Parmesan or Romano cheese (optional)

If you are in a hurry, you can skip the pepper-roasting step; just use a purchased jar of roasted red peppers, drained.

Preheat oven to 425°. Halve peppers; remove seeds and membranes. Place peppers, cut side down, on a foil-lined baking sheet. Bake for 20 to 25 minutes or till skins are browned and bubbly. Remove from pan; place peppers in a clean brown paper bag. Close tightly to allow steam to loosen skins. Let stand 10 minutes.

Meanwhile, rinse chicken; pat dry. In a large skillet brown chicken on both sides in hot oil over medium-high heat, about 2 minutes per side. Add tomatoes, onion, and garlic. Sprinkle with basil, oregano, salt, and pepper. Reduce heat to medium-low. Cover and cook about 8 minutes or till chicken is tender and no longer pink.

Remove skins from peppers. Cut peppers into thin bite-size strips. Add to tomato mixture in skillet. Cover and heat through. If desired, sprinkle with Parmesan or Romano cheese. Makes 4 servings.

Per serving: 210 calories, 24 g protein, 14 g carbohydrate, 7 g total fat (1 g saturated), 59 mg cholesterol, 329 mg sodium, 572 mg potassium

If you are watching your fat grams, skin the chicken making sure to remove the small nibs of fat beneath the surface of the skin.

catalonian chicken

4 medium chicken breast halves or legs (drumstick-thigh piece) (about 1½ pounds total)

1 clove garlic, minced

2 tablespoons cooking oil

1 cup chicken broth

1 medium yellow, green, or red sweet pepper, cut into thin strips

2 medium tomatoes, cut into wedges

½ teaspoon salt

¼ teaspoon crushed red pepper

1 2¼-ounce can sliced pitted ripe olives, drained

2 tablespoons cornstarch

½ cup dry red wine

2 tablespoons snipped fresh parsley

3 cups hot cooked couscous

Skin chicken, if desired. Rinse chicken; pat dry. In a 12-inch skillet cook chicken with garlic in hot oil about 10 minutes or till chicken is lightly browned, turning to brown evenly. Drain off excess fat.

Add chicken broth, pepper strips, tomatoes, salt, and crushed red pepper. Bring mixture to boiling; reduce heat. Simmer, covered, for 35 minutes or till chicken is tender and no longer pink. Remove chicken and vegetables from skillet; cover and keep warm. Skim off fat from pan drippings. Stir olives into juices in skillet. Stir cornstarch into wine; stir into pan juices. Cook and stir till thickened and bubbly. Stir in parsley; cook and stir 2 minutes more. Pour sauce over chicken and vegetables. Serve with couscous. Makes 4 servings.

Per serving: 456 calories, 35 g protein, 41 g carbohydrate, 15 g total fat (3 g saturated), 78 mg cholesterol, 662 mg sodium, 605 mg potassium

casablanca chicken

This is a wonderful "fix-and-forget" one-dish meal. Accompany it with a shredded green salad and warm pita bread triangles.

4 medium chicken breast halves or legs (drumstick-thigh piece) (about 1½ pounds total)

2 tablespoons cooking oil

1 cup chopped onion

2 cups chicken broth

½ cup water

½ cup chopped pitted dates

½ cup light raisins

2 tablespoons lemon juice

1 teaspoon ground turmeric

½ teaspoon salt

½ teaspoon ground cinnamon

1 cup couscous

⅓ cup slivered almonds, toasted (optional)

2 tablespoons snipped parsley (optional)

Rinse chicken; pat dry. In a 12-inch skillet cook chicken in hot oil about 10 minutes or till lightly browned, turning to brown evenly. Remove chicken; set aside. Add onion to skillet; cook till tender. Drain off excess fat. Add broth, water, dates, raisins, lemon juice, turmeric, salt, and cinnamon to skillet. Bring mixture to boiling. Return chicken to skillet. Reduce heat; simmer, covered, about 35 minutes or till chicken is tender and no longer pink.

Remove chicken; cover and keep warm. Stir couscous into mixture in skillet; bring to boiling. Cover and remove from heat. Let stand 5 minutes. Serve chicken with couscous mixture. Sprinkle with almonds and parsley, if desired. Makes 4 servings.

Per serving: 549 calories, 38 g protein, 74 g carbohydrate, 12 g total fat (3 g saturated), 79 mg cholesterol, 730 mg sodium, 804 mg potassium

braised chicken with plantains

4 medium chicken breast halves or legs (drumstick-
   thigh piece) (about 1¾ pounds total)
2 tablespoons cooking oil
2 large ripe plantains, peeled and cut into chunks
1 cup chopped onion
2 cloves garlic, minced
1 14½-ounce can tomatoes, cut up
1 teaspoon sugar
1 teaspoon chili powder
½ teaspoon salt
½ teaspoon ground cumin
¼ teaspoon pepper
1 tablespoon cornstarch
¼ cup chicken broth
   Hot cooked rice (optional)

Skin chicken, if desired. Rinse chicken; pat dry. In a
12-inch skillet cook chicken in hot oil about 10 minutes
or till lightly browned, turning to brown evenly. Remove
chicken; set aside.

Add plantains, onion, and garlic to skillet; cook for
5 minutes. Return chicken to skillet; stir in *undrained*
tomatoes, sugar, chili powder, salt, cumin, and pepper.
Bring to boiling; reduce heat. Simmer, covered, for 30 to
35 minutes or till chicken is tender and no longer pink.

Remove chicken and plantains to serving dish.
Combine cornstarch and chicken broth; add to pan juices.
Cook and stir till thickened and bubbly. Cook and stir 2
minutes more. Serve chicken, plantains, and sauce with
hot cooked rice, if desired. Makes 4 servings.

Per serving: 438 calories, 35 g protein, 41 g carbohydrate, 16 g total fat (4 g saturated),
91 mg cholesterol, 571 mg sodium, 1,041 mg potassium

When you are shopping for plantains, note that ripe ones are mostly yellow in color; unripe plantains will have a green hue.

basque-style chicken

4 large chicken breast halves or legs (drumstick-
    thigh piece) (about 2 pounds total)

1 tablespoon cooking oil

1 tablespoon margarine or butter

8 ounces fresh mushrooms, quartered

2 cups red, green, or yellow sweet pepper strips

1 medium onion, sliced

1 clove garlic, minced

1 14½-ounce can Italian-style stewed tomatoes

½ cup dry white wine

1½ teaspoons dried basil, crushed

1 bay leaf

2 tablespoons cornstarch

1 cup loose-pack frozen peas

2 cups hot cooked rice

When thickening sauces with cornstarch, be sure to combine it with cold water first so it dissolves. Your result will be a smooth sauce.

Skin chicken; rinse and pat dry. In a 12-inch skillet cook chicken in hot oil and margarine about 10 minutes or till chicken is lightly browned, turning to brown evenly. Add mushrooms, pepper, onion, and garlic to skillet; cook 3 minutes. Drain off excess fat.

Stir in *undrained* tomatoes, wine, basil, bay leaf, 1 teaspoon *salt,* and ¼ teaspoon *pepper.* Bring mixture to boiling; reduce heat. Simmer, covered, about 25 to 30 minutes or till chicken is tender and no longer pink.

Transfer chicken to platter. Cover; keep warm. Discard bay leaf. Skim fat from vegetable mixture. Stir cornstarch into ¼ cup *cold water;* stir into skillet. Add peas. Cook and stir till thickened and bubbly; cook and stir 2 minutes. Spoon over chicken and rice. Makes 4 servings.

Per serving: 490 calories, 43 g protein, 46 g carbohydrate, 12 g total fat (3 g saturated), 104 mg cholesterol, 1,022 mg sodium, 1,019 mg potassium

italian chicken vino

6 chicken legs (drumstick-thigh piece) or breast halves (about 2½ pounds total)

2 tablespoons olive oil or cooking oil

1½ cups fresh mushrooms, quartered

1 cup chopped onion

⅔ cup dry white wine

½ cup chicken broth

4 ounces sliced proscuitto or fully-cooked ham, cut into ¼-inch strips

1 teaspoon dried thyme, crushed

1 teaspoon dried oregano, crushed

1 tablespoon cornstarch

½ of a 7-ounce jar roasted red sweet peppers, drained

2 tablespoons snipped fresh parsley

9 ounces spaghetti, cooked and drained

Skin chicken; rinse and pat dry. In a 12-inch skillet brown chicken in hot oil about 10 minutes, turning to brown evenly; remove from pan. In pan drippings cook mushrooms and onion for 3 minutes, stirring occasionally. Return chicken to skillet. Add wine, broth, proscuitto, thyme, oregano, ½ teaspoon *salt*, and ¼ teaspoon *pepper*. Bring mixture to boiling; reduce heat. Simmer, covered, about 30 minutes or till chicken is tender and no longer pink. Remove chicken; cover and keep warm.

Combine cornstarch and 1 tablespoon *cold water*. Add to skillet. Cook and stir till slightly thickened. Cut peppers into strips. Add to pan with parsley; cook and stir 2 minutes more. Pour atop chicken. Serve over hot cooked pasta. Makes 6 servings.

Per serving: 445 calories, 29 g protein, 41 g carbohydrate, 16 g total fat (2 g saturated), 59 mg cholesterol, 633 mg sodium, 360 mg potassium

tandoori-style chicken legs

Tandoori-style cooking refers to the East Indian method of mixing garlic with fresh ginger, curry, and a dash of hot chile for spice, and then "cooling" it down with yogurt or rice.

4 chicken legs (drumstick-thigh piece)
   (about 2 pounds total)
½ cup finely chopped onion
2 cloves garlic, minced
1 teaspoon grated fresh gingerroot
2 tablespoons cooking oil
1 to 2 teaspoons curry powder
1 teaspoon seasoned salt
⅛ teaspoon ground red pepper
1 8-ounce carton plain yogurt
2 tablespoons lemon juice

Preheat oven to 425°. Skin chicken, if desired. Rinse chicken; pat dry. Place chicken in a lightly greased shallow baking dish; set aside.

In a medium skillet cook onion, garlic, and gingerroot in hot oil for 3 minutes. Stir in curry powder, seasoned salt, and red pepper. Cook and stir 1 minute. Stir in yogurt and lemon juice just till combined; remove from heat. Brush *half* of the yogurt mixture over chicken pieces. Bake for 25 minutes.

Brush remaining yogurt mixture over chicken; bake 10 to 15 minutes more or till chicken is tender and no longer pink. Transfer chicken to serving platter. If desired, garnish with sliced cucumber, chopped tomato, and parsley or cilantro. Makes 4 servings.

Per serving: 378 calories, 32 g protein, 7 g carbohydrate, 24 g total fat (6 g saturated), 109 mg cholesterol, 450 mg sodium, 441 mg potassium

Don't overlook thighs and drumsticks for dishes like this one. They're cheaper than breasts and almost as low-cal without the skin.

peasant-style chicken skillet

1 pound chicken drumsticks

1 pound chicken thighs

1 tablespoon cooking oil

2 medium carrots, cut into ½-inch chunks

1 medium onion, cut into wedges

1 15-ounce can tomato sauce with tomato tidbits

½ cup chicken broth

1 9-ounce package frozen cut green beans

•8 ounces small red potatoes, halved or quartered

1 teaspoon dried thyme, crushed

½ teaspoon salt

½ teaspoon dried tarragon, crushed

¼ teaspoon pepper

3 cups hot cooked noodles

Skin drumsticks and thighs, if desired. Rinse chicken; pat dry. In a 12-inch skillet cook chicken in hot oil about 10 minutes or till chicken is lightly browned, turning to brown evenly. Remove chicken; set aside.

Add carrots and onion to skillet; cook 3 minutes. Drain off excess fat. Return chicken to skillet. Add tomato sauce, broth, green beans, potatoes, thyme, salt, tarragon, and pepper. Bring mixture to boiling; reduce heat. Simmer, covered, for 35 minutes or till chicken is tender and no longer pink and vegetables are tender.

Drain chicken and vegetables, reserving pan drippings. Skim off fat from pan drippings; spoon drippings over chicken, vegetables, and noodles. Makes 6 servings.

Per serving: 375 calories, 26 g protein, 40 g carbohydrate, 12 g total fat (3 g saturated), 95 mg cholesterol, 765 mg sodium, 757 mg potassium

hungarian chicken with noodles

3 tablespoons all-purpose flour

1 teaspoon seasoned salt

¼ teaspoon pepper

2½ pounds chicken thighs or breast halves

2 tablespoons cooking oil

1 16-ounce can diced tomatoes

1 cup sliced onion

1 cup dry white wine

2 to 3 tablespoons paprika

6 cups hot cooked noodles

4 teaspoons all-purpose flour

½ cup dairy sour cream

In a plastic or paper bag combine 3 tablespoons flour with seasoned salt and pepper. Skin chicken, if desired. Rinse chicken; pat dry. Add chicken, 2 or 3 pieces at a time, to the bag, shaking to coat well.

In a 12-inch skillet cook chicken in hot oil about 10 minutes or till chicken is lightly browned, turning to brown evenly. Drain fat. Add *undrained* tomatoes, onion, wine, and paprika. Bring mixture to boiling; reduce heat. Simmer, covered, for 35 minutes or till chicken is tender and no longer pink.

Line a serving platter with hot cooked noodles; transfer chicken and tomatoes to platter. Cover and keep warm. Skim fat from pan juices. Stir remaining flour into sour cream; stir into pan juices. Cook and stir till mixture is thickened and bubbly; cook and stir 2 minutes more. Spoon some sauce over chicken and noodles; pass remainder. Makes 6 servings.

Per serving: 592 calories, 34 g protein, 52 g carbohydrate, 24 g total fat (7 g saturated), 147 mg cholesterol, 441 mg sodium, 588 mg potassium

french onion-baked chicken

2 pounds chicken thighs or drumsticks

⅓ cup creamy ranch salad dressing or French salad
    dressing

¼ teaspoon bottled hot pepper sauce

1 3-ounce can french-fried onions, crumbled

½ cup crushed cornflakes

Preheat oven to 425°. Skin chicken. Rinse chicken; pat dry. In a shallow bowl stir together salad dressing and hot pepper sauce. In another bowl combine crumbled onions and crushed cornflakes.

In a 3-quart rectangular baking dish arrange chicken pieces, meaty side up, on a rack. Brush with salad dressing mixture. Sprinkle with onion mixture, pressing mixture onto chicken.

Bake, uncovered, for 35 to 40 minutes or till chicken is tender and no longer pink, covering loosely the last 10 minutes if topping is getting too brown. If desired, serve with green beans. Makes 4 servings.

You can substitute chicken breasts for the thighs or drumsticks in this recipe. Or, for a unique crispy appetizer, use chicken wings with the tips removed and the joints split. Serve them with additional ranch-style dressing for a dipper.

Per serving: 478 calories, 32 g protein, 14 g carbohydrate, 32 g total fat (5 g saturated), 108 mg cholesterol, 425 mg sodium, 336 mg potassium

chicken thighs cacciatore

- 2 pounds chicken thighs or breast halves
- 1 tablespoon cooking oil
- 1½ cups sliced fresh mushrooms
- 1 cup sliced onion
- 1 cup green or red sweet pepper cut into 1½-inch squares
- 2 cloves garlic, minced
- 1 14½-ounce can Italian-style stewed tomatoes
- 1 8-ounce can tomato sauce
- ¼ cup dry red wine
- 1 teaspoon dried Italian seasoning, crushed
- ½ teaspoon salt
- ¼ teaspoon pepper
- 3 cups hot cooked pasta

Skin chicken. Rinse chicken; pat dry. In a 12-inch skillet cook chicken in hot oil about 10 minutes or till chicken is lightly browned, turning to brown evenly. Drain excess fat.

Add mushrooms, onion, sweet pepper, and garlic to skillet along with *undrained* tomatoes, tomato sauce, wine, Italian seasoning, salt, and pepper. Bring to boiling; reduce heat. Simmer, covered, for 20 minutes. Remove cover and simmer 15 minutes more or till chicken is tender and no longer pink. Serve with hot cooked pasta. Makes 4 servings.

Italian seasoning is a convenient combination of basil, oregano, red pepper, rosemary, and often garlic powder.

Per serving: 501 calories, 41 g protein, 49 g carbohydrate, 15 g total fat (4 g saturated), 149 mg cholesterol, 1,098 mg sodium, 1,054 mg potassium

chicken soup

1 pound chicken thighs
2 14½-ounce cans chicken broth
½ cup water
2 stalks celery
1 onion, quartered
¼ to ½ teaspoon pepper
1 bay leaf
1½ cups bias-sliced carrots
½ cup bow tie pasta or medium noodles
1 teaspoon dried basil, crushed

Skin chicken. Rinse chicken. Place chicken in a Dutch oven; add broth and water. Cut tops off celery; slice stalks and set aside. Add celery tops, onion, pepper, and bay leaf to Dutch oven. Bring mixture to boiling; reduce heat. Cover and simmer 25 minutes or till chicken is tender and no longer pink.

Remove chicken from pan, reserving broth; strain broth, discarding mixture in sieve. Cool chicken slightly. Remove meat from bones and discard bones; chop meat and set aside. Skim fat from broth; add sliced carrots, celery, pasta, and basil. Bring mixture to boiling; reduce heat. Simmer, covered, for 10 to 15 minutes or till vegetables and pasta are tender. Stir in chicken; heat through. Makes 4 servings.

This old-fashioned chicken soup tastes just like Mom's. Next time, try unstuffed tortellini in the soup.

Per serving: 226 calories, 21 g protein, 14 g carbohydrate, 9 g total fat (3 g saturated), 59 mg cholesterol, 770 mg sodium, 572 mg potassium

chicken macquechoux

8 chicken thighs or 4 large chicken breast halves
   (about 2 pounds total)

1 tablespoon cooking oil

1 tablespoon margarine or butter

1 cup chopped green or red sweet pepper

1 10-ounce package frozen whole kernel corn

¼ cup chicken broth

1 tablespoon snipped fresh chives

½ teaspoon seasoned salt

½ teaspoon dried thyme, crushed

½ teaspoon dried basil, crushed

½ teaspoon ground black pepper

⅛ teaspoon ground red pepper

2 large tomatoes, cored and chopped (2 cups)

2 cups hot cooked rice

Skin chicken. Rinse chicken; pat dry. In a large skillet cook chicken in hot oil and margarine or butter about 10 minutes or till chicken is lightly browned, turning to brown evenly. Add sweet pepper, corn, broth, chives, seasoned salt, thyme, basil, and black and red pepper. Bring to boiling; reduce heat. Simmer, covered, for 25 to 30 minutes or till chicken is tender and no longer pink. Uncover and simmer 5 minutes to reduce liquid slightly. Stir in tomatoes; heat through. Serve over hot cooked rice. Makes 4 servings.

Macquechoux (mahk-SHOO) is a Cajun word that means "a smothered dish made with fresh corn."

Per serving: 509 calories, 35 g protein, 43 g carbohydrate, 23 g total fat (5 g saturated), 103 mg cholesterol, 349 mg sodium, 687 mg potassium

Creole cooks pair chicken with all sorts of seafood and fish in their jambalayas.

chicken and shrimp jambalaya

1 pound chicken drumsticks or thighs, skinned
2 tablespoons cooking oil
2 cups chopped red and/or green sweet pepper
1 cup coarsely chopped onion
2 cloves garlic, minced
1 6- or 6¾-ounce package Spanish rice mix
1 16-ounce can diced tomatoes
1½ cups water
¼ teaspoon bottled hot pepper sauce
¼ teaspoon ground black pepper
⅛ teaspoon ground red pepper
4 ounces fresh or frozen peeled and deveined shrimp
    (thawed, if frozen)

Skin chicken. Rinse chicken; pat dry. In a 12-inch skillet cook chicken in hot oil about 10 minutes or till chicken is lightly browned, turning to brown evenly. Remove chicken from skillet. In drippings cook sweet pepper, onion, and garlic for 3 minutes. Add rice from rice mix; cook and stir 2 minutes more or till golden.

Carefully add seasoning packet from rice mix, *undrained* tomatoes, water, hot pepper sauce, ground black pepper, and ground red pepper; stir to combine. Arrange chicken on top. Heat mixture to boiling; reduce heat. Cover and simmer 25 minutes or till liquid is nearly absorbed. Add shrimp; cook 3 to 5 minutes more or till chicken is tender and no longer pink and the shrimp turn pink. Makes 4 or 5 servings.

Per serving: 466 calories, 24 g protein, 55 g carbohydrate, 15 g total fat (3 g saturated), 95 mg cholesterol, 1,425 mg sodium, 328 mg potassium

buttermilk chicken

This old Southern recipe takes advantage of the distinctive flavor of buttermilk. There is no substitute!

2½ to 3 pounds meaty chicken pieces
    (breasts, thighs, and drumsticks)
2 tablespoons cooking oil
1 cup chopped onion
1 15-ounce can tomato sauce
½ teaspoon salt
½ teaspoon dried dillweed
¼ teaspoon pepper
¼ teaspoon bottled hot pepper sauce
½ cup chicken broth
¼ cup all-purpose flour
1 cup buttermilk
3 tablespoons snipped fresh parsley
3 cups hot cooked noodles or rice

Rinse chicken; pat dry. In a 12-inch skillet cook chicken in hot oil about 10 minutes or till chicken is lightly browned, turning to brown evenly. Drain off excess fat.

Add onion, tomato sauce, salt, dillweed, pepper, and pepper sauce. Stir together the chicken broth and flour; add to the skillet. Bring to boiling; reduce heat. Simmer, covered, for 30 to 35 minutes or till chicken is tender and no longer pink. Remove chicken to serving dish; cover and keep warm.

Stir the buttermilk into liquid in skillet; heat through. Stir in parsley. Pour sauce over chicken. Serve with noodles or rice. Makes 6 servings.

Per serving: 424 calories, 36 g protein, 36 g carbohydrate, 15 g total fat (4 g saturated), 117 mg cholesterol, 622 mg sodium, 724 mg potassium

If you want real Texas flavor when serving this dish, accompany it with warmed flour tortillas and pass the bottled hot pepper sauce.

texas-style pollo

2 pounds meaty chicken pieces (breasts, thighs, and drumsticks)

2 tablespoons cooking oil

1 cup chopped onion

4 cloves garlic, minced

1 16-ounce can diced tomatoes

1¼ cups chicken broth

1 4-ounce can diced green chili peppers, drained

2 tablespoons snipped cilantro or parsley

1 teaspoon ground cumin

½ teaspoon salt

¼ teaspoon pepper

⅔ cup long grain rice

1 15-ounce can pinto beans, rinsed and drained

Skin chicken, if desired. Rinse chicken; pat dry. In a 12-inch skillet cook chicken in hot oil about 10 minutes or till chicken is lightly browned, turning to brown evenly. Remove chicken from skillet. In drippings cook onion and garlic for 3 minutes. Drain off excess fat.

Return chicken to skillet. Add *undrained* tomatoes, broth, chili peppers, cilantro or parsley, cumin, salt, and pepper. Bring to boiling; reduce heat. Simmer, covered, for 10 minutes. Add uncooked rice and simmer, covered, 20 minutes more or till chicken is tender and no longer pink and rice is tender.

Stir in pinto beans; heat through. If desired, garnish with additional cilantro or parsley. Makes 6 servings.

Per serving: 368 calories, 30 g protein, 34 g carbohydrate, 12 g total fat (3 g saturated), 73 mg cholesterol, 878 mg sodium, 702 mg potassium

tarragon chicken with fennel

2½ to 3 pounds meaty chicken pieces (breasts, thighs, and drumsticks)

 1 tablespoon olive oil or cooking oil

 ¼ teaspoon lemon-pepper seasoning or pepper

 ½ cup dry white wine

 ½ cup chicken broth

 2 tablespoons chopped fresh tarragon or 1½ teaspoons dried tarragon, crushed

 2 cloves garlic, minced

 1 large fennel bulb

 ⅓ cup half-and-half, light cream, or milk

 2 tablespoons all-purpose flour

Rinse chicken; pat dry. In a large skillet cook chicken in hot oil about 10 minutes or till lightly browned, turning to brown evenly. Drain off excess fat. Season chicken with lemon-pepper seasoning and ¼ teaspoon *salt.* Add wine, broth, tarragon, and garlic; bring to boiling. Reduce heat; simmer, covered, 20 minutes.

Meanwhile, trim off woody stalks of fennel to within ½ inch of the bulb, reserving leaves. Quarter fennel; core and cut into thin slices. Add to chicken; cover and simmer 15 to 20 minutes more or till chicken is tender and no longer pink and fennel is tender.

Transfer chicken and fennel to serving platter. Skim fat from pan drippings. Measure *1 cup* pan juices (add *water,* if necessary). Whisk cream into flour; stir into pan juices. Cook and stir till thickened and bubbly; cook and stir 1 minute more. Spoon some sauce over chicken; pass remaining sauce. Makes 6 servings.

Per serving: 275 calories, 24 g protein, 5 g carbohydrate, 13 g total fat (4 g saturated), 91 mg cholesterol, 297 mg sodium, 390 mg potassium

skillet chicken with peas and pearl onions

2½ to 3 pounds meaty chicken pieces (breasts, thighs, and drumsticks)

1 tablespoon cooking oil

2 medium carrots, cut into ½-inch pieces

⅔ cup chicken broth

1 teaspoon paprika

1 teaspoon salt

¼ teaspoon pepper

1 10-ounce package frozen peas with pearl onions

½ cup half-and-half or light cream

1 tablespoon all-purpose flour

3 cups hot cooked noodles

Skin chicken, if desired. Rinse chicken; pat dry. In a large skillet cook chicken in hot oil about 10 minutes or till chicken is lightly browned, turning to brown evenly.

Drain off excess fat. Add carrots, broth, paprika, salt, and pepper to skillet. Bring mixture to boiling; reduce heat. Simmer, covered, for 20 minutes. Add peas and pearl onions; cook 15 minutes more or till chicken is tender and no longer pink.

Remove chicken from pan; transfer to platter and keep warm. Skim fat from pan drippings. Stir cream into flour; stir mixture into juices in skillet. Cook and stir till mixture is thickened and bubbly; cook and stir 1 minute more. Pass creamed peas and onion sauce with chicken and serve over noodles. Makes 6 servings.

Per serving: 400 calories, 34 g protein, 28 g carbohydrate, 16 g total fat (5 g saturated), 120 mg cholesterol, 386 mg sodium, 393 mg potassium

chicken with fruit pilaf

2½ to 3 pounds meaty chicken pieces (breasts, thighs, and drumsticks)

4 tablespoons margarine or butter

4 tablespoons lemon juice

½ teaspoon salt

½ teaspoon dried basil, crushed

⅛ teaspoon pepper

1 cup long grain rice

2 cups chicken broth

½ cup snipped dried apricots

½ cup snipped dried pitted prunes or dates

½ cup finely chopped celery

¼ cup sliced green onions

½ teaspoon ground allspice

2 tablespoons toasted pine nuts or slivered almonds

Apricots and prunes give this Moroccan-style pilaf an exotic flavor and add a nice moistness to the rice.

Preheat oven to 425°. Rinse chicken; pat dry. Arrange chicken in a shallow roasting pan. Melt *2 tablespoons* of the margarine; brush over chicken. Drizzle with *3 tablespoons* of the lemon juice; sprinkle with salt, basil, and pepper. Bake for 35 to 40 minutes or till chicken is tender and no longer pink.

Meanwhile, cook rice in broth according to package directions. In a large skillet melt remaining margarine or butter. Add apricots, prunes, celery, and onion; cook and stir 5 minutes or till tender. Stir in remaining lemon juice and allspice; season to taste with *salt* and *pepper*. Add cooked rice and nuts; heat through. Keep warm. Serve chicken with rice pilaf. Makes 6 servings.

Per serving: 485 calories, 34 g protein, 42 g carbohydrate, 21 g total fat (5 g saturated), 87 mg cholesterol, 623 mg sodium, 649 mg potassium

spicy fried chicken

2½ to 3 pounds meaty chicken pieces (breasts, thighs, and drumsticks)
1 slightly beaten egg
¼ cup milk
1 cup packaged biscuit mix
1 1¼-ounce package taco seasoning mix
   Cooking oil for frying

Skin chicken, if desired. Rinse chicken. In a large saucepan cover chicken with lightly salted water. Bring to boiling; reduce heat. Cover and simmer for 20 minutes or till chicken is just done and no longer pink. Drain. Pat chicken pieces dry with paper towels.

Meanwhile, in a shallow bowl combine the egg and milk; set aside. In another shallow bowl combine the biscuit mix and taco seasoning. In a 12-inch skillet heat 1 inch of cooking oil to 365°.

Dip chicken pieces into the egg mixture, one at a time. Coat with dry mixture. Fry pieces for 3 to 5 minutes or till golden, turning once. Carefully remove; drain well on paper towels. If desired, serve with corn and garnish with avocado slices. Makes 6 servings.

You can keep pieces of just-fried chicken hot on a heated platter in a 250° oven while you're frying up the rest.

Per serving: 408 calories, 32 g protein, 15 g carbohydrate, 25 g total fat (5 g saturated), 123 mg cholesterol, 921 mg sodium, 252 mg potassium

kentucky whiskey chicken

2½ to 3 pounds meaty chicken pieces (breasts, thighs,
   and drumsticks)
1 tablespoon cooking oil
½ teaspoon poultry seasoning
2 medium onions, cut into wedges
½ cup chicken broth
¼ cup whiskey
2 cups fresh mushrooms, halved or quartered
½ cup half-and-half, light cream, or milk
2 tablespoons all-purpose flour
3 cups hot cooked rice or noodles

Skin chicken, if desired. Rinse chicken; pat dry. In a
large skillet cook chicken in hot oil about 10 minutes or
till lightly browned, turning to brown evenly. Sprinkle
with poultry seasoning and ½ teaspoon *salt*. Remove
chicken; set aside. Add onions to skillet; cook 3 minutes.
Drain off excess fat. Return chicken to skillet; carefully
add broth and whiskey. Bring to boiling; reduce heat.
Cover and simmer 20 minutes. Add mushrooms; cover
and simmer 15 minutes more or till chicken is tender and
no longer pink.

Transfer chicken and vegetables to a platter; keep
warm. Skim fat from pan juices; measure ¾ *cup* of the pan
juices and return to skillet. Stir cream into flour till
smooth; stir into pan juices. Cook and stir till mixture is
thickened and bubbly. Cook and stir 1 minute more.
Spoon some of the sauce over chicken; pass remaining
sauce. Serve with rice or noodles. Garnish with thyme,
if desired. Makes 6 servings.

Per serving: 430 calories, 33 g protein, 35 g carbohydrate, 14 g total fat (5 g saturated),
94 mg cholesterol, 330 mg sodium, 422 mg potassium

greek-style chicken with orzo

2½ to 3 pounds meaty chicken pieces (breasts, thighs, and drumsticks)
2 cloves garlic, minced
1 tablespoon olive oil or cooking oil
¼ teaspoon lemon-pepper seasoning or pepper
1 16-ounce can diced tomatoes
1 small onion, cut into wedges
1½ cups chicken broth
1 tablespoon lemon juice
1 teaspoon dried oregano, crushed
½ teaspoon dried rosemary, crushed
½ teaspoon ground cumin
1½ cups orzo (rosamarina) or other small pasta (such as elbow macaroni or small shells)
½ cup sliced Greek olives or pitted ripe olives
3 tablespoons crumbled feta cheese

Skin chicken, if desired. Rinse chicken; pat dry. In a 12-inch skillet cook chicken with garlic in hot oil about 10 minutes or till lightly browned, turning to brown evenly. Sprinkle with lemon-pepper seasoning. Drain off excess fat. Stir in tomatoes, onion, broth, lemon juice, oregano, rosemary, and cumin. Bring to boiling; reduce heat. Simmer, covered, for 20 minutes.

Stir in orzo; cover and cook 15 minutes more or till orzo and chicken are tender and chicken is no longer pink. Stir in olives; heat through. Serve chicken over orzo mixture. Sprinkle with feta cheese. Makes 6 servings.

Per serving: 451 calories, 37 g protein, 39 g carbohydrate, 16 g total fat (5 g saturated), 94 mg cholesterol, 573 mg sodium, 491 mg potassium

chicken with brussels sprouts

¼ cup all-purpose flour

1 teaspoon paprika

2½ to 3 pounds meaty chicken pieces (breasts, thighs, and drumsticks)

1 tablespoon cooking oil

1½ cups sliced fresh mushrooms

½ cup chopped onion

1 14½-ounce can chicken broth

½ cup water

½ teaspoon dried basil, crushed

½ teaspoon dried thyme, crushed

2 cups fresh or loose-pack frozen brussels sprouts, halved

½ cup half-and-half or light cream

2 tablespoons all-purpose flour

  Hot cooked noodles (optional)

To halve frozen brussels sprouts, thaw them slightly by rinsing in warm water then slice lengthwise.

In a plastic bag combine ¼ cup flour, the paprika, ¼ teaspoon *salt,* and ¼ teaspoon *pepper.* Skin chicken, if desired. Add a few pieces of chicken at a time to bag, shaking to coat well. In a 12-inch skillet cook chicken in hot oil about 10 minutes or till lightly browned. Drain off fat. Add mushrooms, onion, broth, water, basil, and thyme. Bring to boiling; reduce heat. Cover and simmer for 35 minutes or till chicken is no longer pink. Halve sprouts; add sprouts during last 12 minutes of cooking. Remove chicken and sprouts. Skim fat from pan juices. Combine cream and 2 tablespoons flour. Stir into pan juices. Cook and stir till bubbly; cook and stir 1 minute more. Spoon some sauce over chicken; pass remaining sauce. Serve with hot cooked noodles, if desired. Serves 6.

Per serving: 319 calories, 32 g protein, 13 g carbohydrate, 15 g total fat (5 g saturated), 94 mg cholesterol, 401 mg sodium, 527 mg potassium

Tip: To skim the fat from pan drippings, wrap an ice cube in a square of cheesecloth and drag through drippings. The fat will cling to the ice.

chicken with leeks, bacon, and shallots

2 to 2½ pounds meaty chicken pieces (breasts, thighs, and drumsticks)

4 or 5 slices bacon, chopped (4 ounces)

2 medium leeks, sliced (⅔ cup)

4 shallots, peeled and sliced

¾ cup chicken broth

½ teaspoon poultry seasoning

¼ teaspoon pepper

⅓ cup dry white wine

1 tablespoon cornstarch

2 tablespoons snipped fresh parsley

Hot cooked rice or pasta (optional)

Skin chicken, if desired. In a large skillet cook bacon till crisp. Drain, reserving *2 tablespoons* drippings in pan; set bacon aside. Cook chicken in bacon drippings over medium heat about 10 minutes or till lightly browned, turning to brown evenly and adding leeks and shallots the last 5 minutes of cooking. Drain off excess fat.

Add broth, poultry seasoning, and pepper. Bring to boiling; reduce heat. Simmer, covered, about 30 minutes or until chicken is tender and no longer pink. Remove chicken; keep warm. Skim fat from drippings. Measure drippings; add enough additional broth to make *¾ cup.* Return to skillet. Stir together wine and cornstarch; stir into pan drippings. Cook and stir till thickened and bubbly; cook and stir 2 minutes. Stir in bacon and parsley. Serve with cooked rice or pasta, if desired. Serves 4.

Per serving: 377 calories, 38 g protein, 13 g carbohydrate, 17 g total fat (5 g saturated), 110 mg cholesterol, 379 mg sodium, 500 mg potassium

chicken with black-eyed peas

2½ to 3 pounds meaty chicken pieces (breasts, thighs, and drumsticks)

4 or 5 slices bacon, chopped (4 ounces)

1 cup chopped onion

1 cup sliced celery

1 cup diced carrots

2 cloves garlic, minced

1 cup chicken broth

1 teaspoon seasoned salt

¼ teaspoon pepper

¼ teaspoon ground allspice

1 bay leaf

1 15-ounce can black-eyed peas, drained

Skin chicken, if desired. Rinse chicken; pat dry. In a large skillet cook bacon till done, but not crisp. Drain the bacon, reserving *2 tablespoons* drippings in skillet. Set bacon aside.

Cook chicken in bacon drippings over medium heat about 10 minutes or till chicken is lightly browned, turning to brown evenly. Remove chicken. Add onion, celery, carrots, and garlic to pan; cook and stir till vegetables are tender. Drain off excess fat.

Return chicken and bacon to pan. Add broth, seasoned salt, pepper, allspice, and bay leaf. Bring to boiling; reduce heat. Simmer, covered, for 35 minutes or till chicken is tender and no longer pink. Stir in black-eyed peas; heat through. Discard bay leaf. Serve vegetables over chicken. Makes 6 servings.

Per serving: 331 calories, 35 g protein, 15 g carbohydrate, 14 g total fat (4 g saturated), 91 mg cholesterol, 806 mg sodium, 643 mg potassium

The Cajuns serve black-eyed peas on New Year's Day; they are said to bring good luck to everyone in the coming year.

chicken pancho villa

4 medium chicken breast halves or legs (drumstick-thigh piece) (about 1½ pounds total)

2 tablespoons cooking oil

1 15-ounce can tomato puree

1 cup water

1 1¼-ounce package taco seasoning mix

1 tablespoon lime or lemon juice
Several dashes bottled hot pepper sauce

2 cups quick-cooking rice

2 tablespoons snipped fresh cilantro

Rinse chicken; pat dry. In a 12-inch skillet cook chicken in hot oil about 10 minutes or till lightly browned, turning to brown evenly. Drain off excess fat.

Add tomato puree, water, taco seasoning mix, lime or lemon juice, and hot pepper sauce. Bring to boiling; reduce heat. Simmer, covered, for 35 minutes or till chicken is tender and no longer pink.

Remove chicken to serving platter; cover and keep warm. Bring tomato mixture to boiling. Add quick-cooking rice and cilantro. Remove from heat. Cover and let stand 5 minutes. Add additional *water,* if necessary, to moisten rice. Serve rice with chicken. Makes 4 servings.

Cut up any remaining chicken into thin strips; use them with flour tortillas to make soft tacos, quesadillas, or burritos the next day. Serve with salsa and slices of avocado.

Per serving: 440 calories, 35 g protein, 54 g carbohydrate, 11 g total fat (2 g saturated), 78 mg cholesterol, 1,388 mg sodium, 718 mg potassium

chicken bavarian

2½ to 3 pounds meaty chicken pieces (breasts, thighs, and drumsticks)

1 tablespoon cooking oil

1 12-ounce can dark beer

1½ cups sliced onion

½ cup chicken broth

2 tablespoons cider vinegar

1 tablespoon brown sugar

1 clove garlic, minced

1 teaspoon dried thyme, crushed

½ teaspoon salt

½ teaspoon caraway seed

¼ teaspoon pepper

1 10-ounce package frozen tiny whole carrots

¼ cup cold water

2 tablespoons all-purpose flour

2 tablespoons snipped fresh parsley

For an authentic Bavarian menu, serve spaetzle alongside the chicken. Spaetzle are tiny dumplings you can buy dried; cook them like pasta.

Skin chicken, if desired. Rinse chicken; pat dry. In a 12-inch skillet cook chicken in hot oil about 10 minutes or till lightly browned, turning to brown evenly.

Drain off excess fat. Add beer, onion, chicken broth, vinegar, brown sugar, garlic, thyme, salt, caraway seed, and pepper. Bring mixture to boiling; add carrots. Reduce heat; simmer, covered, for 35 to 40 minutes or till chicken is tender and no longer pink.

Transfer chicken and carrots to a warm platter. Combine water and flour; stir into pan drippings. Cook and stir till mixture is thickened and bubbly; cook and stir 1 minute more. Stir in parsley. Pass sauce with chicken. Makes 6 servings.

Per serving: 306 calories, 30 g protein, 16 g carbohydrate, 12 g total fat (3 g saturated), 86 mg cholesterol, 353 mg sodium, 417 mg potassium

Sage Sauce: Melt 2 tablespoons margarine; stir in 2 tablespoons all-purpose flour, ¼ teaspoon ground sage, ¼ teaspoon salt, and ⅛ teaspoon pepper. Add 1½ cups light cream, half-and-half, or milk all at once. Cook and stir over medium heat till mixture is thickened and bubbly. Cook and stir 1 minute more.

chicken baked with sage biscuits

2½ to 3 pounds meaty chicken pieces
1 tablespoon cooking oil
1½ teaspoons paprika
1 teaspoon salt
¼ teaspoon lemon-pepper seasoning
1⅓ cups all-purpose flour
2 teaspoons baking powder
1½ teaspoons sugar
¼ teaspoon ground sage
¼ teaspoon cream of tartar
¼ teaspoon baking soda
⅓ cup shortening, margarine, or butter
⅔ cup buttermilk
Sage Sauce (see box at left)

Preheat oven to 425°. Rinse chicken; pat dry. Arrange chicken in a 15x10x1-inch baking pan. Brush with oil. Stir together paprika, 1 teaspoon salt, and lemon-pepper seasoning; sprinkle over chicken. Bake for 35 minutes.

For biscuits, in a bowl stir together flour, baking powder, sugar, sage, cream of tartar, baking soda, and ⅛ teaspoon *salt.* Cut in shortening till mixture resembles coarse crumbs. Make a well in center; add buttermilk all at once. Stir till dough clings together.

Increase oven temperature to 450°. Drop dough beside chicken. Bake 12 to 15 minutes or till biscuits are golden and a toothpick inserted in biscuit comes out clean.

Meanwhile, prepare Sage Sauce. Transfer biscuits and chicken to a serving platter; spoon some of the sauce over. Pass remaining sauce. Makes 5 or 6 servings.

Per serving: 672 calories, 40 g protein, 33 g carbohydrate, 41 g total fat (13 g saturated), 128 mg cholesterol, 917 mg sodium, 456 mg potassium

chicken and pea pods with wild rice

2½ to 3 pounds meaty chicken pieces (breasts, thighs, and drumsticks)

¼ teaspoon pepper

2 tablespoons cooking oil

1 cup sliced onion

1 clove garlic, minced

1 tablespoon cooking oil

2 cups water

1 6¼- or 6¾-ounce package quick-cooking long grain and wild rice mix

1 6-ounce package frozen pea pods

Skin chicken, if desired. Rinse chicken; pat dry. Sprinkle chicken with pepper. In a large skillet cook chicken in 2 tablespoons hot oil about 10 minutes or till lightly browned, turning to brown evenly. Reduce heat to low; cover. Cook for 25 minutes, turning once. Uncover; cook for 5 minutes more or till chicken is tender and no longer pink. Drain on paper towels.

Meanwhile, in a medium skillet cook onion and garlic in 1 tablespoon oil till tender but not brown. Carefully add water, rice, and seasoning packet from rice mix. Bring to boiling; reduce heat and simmer, covered, for 5 minutes or till liquid is absorbed. Stir in pea pods; heat through. Serve with chicken. Makes 6 servings.

Per serving: 366 calories, 32 g protein, 27 g carbohydrate, 14 g total fat (3 g saturated), 86 mg cholesterol, 581 mg sodium, 307 mg potassium

baked chicken with ambrosia sauce

2½ to 3 pounds meaty chicken pieces (breasts, thighs, and drumsticks)
½ cup thinly sliced red onion
1 tablespoon margarine or butter
2 teaspoons cornstarch
¼ cup orange or grapefruit juice
2 teaspoons sugar
1 teaspoon finely shredded orange peel
1 medium grapefruit, peeled and sectioned
2 oranges, peeled and sectioned
1 tablespoon snipped fresh parsley
2 tablespoons coconut

Preheat oven to 425°. Rinse chicken; pat dry. Arrange chicken, skin side down, in a lightly greased 13x9x2-inch baking pan. Sprinkle with ¼ teaspoon *salt* and ¼ teaspoon *pepper*. Bake for 20 minutes. Turn skin side up. Bake 20 minutes or till chicken is tender and no longer pink.

Meanwhile, in a medium saucepan cook onion in margarine about 5 minutes or till tender. Stir in cornstarch. Add fruit juice, sugar, orange peel, and ½ cup *water*. Cook and stir till thickened and bubbly; cook and stir 2 minutes more. Fold in grapefruit sections, orange sections, and parsley; heat through. Season to taste with *salt* and *pepper*. Remove chicken to platter. Spoon some sauce atop and sprinkle with coconut. Pass remaining sauce. Makes 6 servings.

Per serving: 280 calories, 29 g protein, 11 g carbohydrate, 13 g total fat (4 g saturated), 86 mg cholesterol, 189 mg sodium, 354 mg potassium

oven-fried coconut chicken

½ cup flaked coconut

¼ cup fine dry seasoned bread crumbs

2½ to 3 pounds meaty chicken pieces (breasts, thighs, and drumsticks)

¼ cup margarine or butter, melted

Preheat oven to 375°. In a shallow bowl stir together coconut and bread crumbs; set aside.

Rinse chicken; pat dry. Brush chicken with melted margarine. Roll chicken pieces in coconut mixture to coat on all sides. Place in a 15x10x1-inch or a 13x9x2-inch baking pan, arranging chicken pieces, skin side up, so pieces don't touch. Drizzle any remaining melted margarine over chicken.

Bake for 45 to 50 minutes or till chicken is tender and no longer pink. Do not turn. If desired, garnish with lettuce and orange sections. Makes 6 servings.

Did you know that chicken supplies as much high-quality protein as beef and other red meats, but with less fat (especially if skin is removed before cooking) and fewer calories? It also costs less per pound than red meat.

Per serving: 328 calories, 29 g protein, 6 g carbohydrate, 20 g total fat (6 g saturated), 86 mg cholesterol, 290 mg sodium, 238 mg potassium

Tip: If you are using dried mushrooms, substitute 8 dried mushrooms for the fresh, and soak them in warm water to cover for 30 minutes.

roasted chicken with shiitake mushroom sauce

2½ to 3 pounds meaty chicken pieces (breasts, thighs, and drumsticks)
1 tablespoon olive oil or cooking oil
½ teaspoon salt
½ teaspoon ground sage
¼ teaspoon pepper
  Chicken broth
2 tablespoons margarine or butter
1 cup fresh shiitake mushrooms, or brown or button mushrooms
1 cup sliced onion
2 tablespoons all-purpose flour
½ cup dry white wine
3 cups hot cooked rice or pasta

Preheat oven to 425°. Rinse chicken; pat dry. Arrange chicken in a lightly greased roasting pan. Brush with oil; sprinkle with salt, sage, and pepper. Bake for 35 to 45 minutes or until chicken is tender and no longer pink.

Transfer chicken to a serving platter; cover and keep warm. Skim fat from pan drippings; add broth to drippings to measure *1 cup.* In a skillet melt margarine or butter. Add mushrooms and onion and cook for 5 minutes or till tender. Stir flour into mixture. Add pan drippings and wine all at once. Cook and stir till mixture is thickened and bubbly; cook and stir 1 minute more. Season with *salt* and *pepper.* Pass sauce with chicken. Serve with rice or pasta. Makes 6 servings.

Per serving: 414 calories, 32 g protein, 28 g carbohydrate, 17 g total fat (4 g saturated), 87 mg cholesterol, 430 mg sodium, 376 mg potassium

cornbread-coated chicken with sweet potatoes

Keep a freezer bag stashed in your freezer to hold chicken necks, backs, wing tips and giblets; use later for chicken soup stock

2 to 2½ pounds meaty chicken pieces (breasts, thighs, and drumsticks)

1½ pounds sweet potatoes

¼ cup margarine or butter, melted

¼ teaspoon seasoned salt

Dash pepper

1 cup cornbread stuffing mix

2 tablespoons finely chopped green onion

1 teaspoon dried basil or oregano, crushed

¼ teaspoon garlic powder

Preheat oven to 425°. Skin chicken, if desired. Rinse chicken; pat dry. Peel potatoes; cut into ¾- to 1-inch thick slices. Arrange potato slices at one end of a lightly greased 15x10x1-inch baking pan. Brush about *1 tablespoon* of the melted margarine over potatoes. Sprinkle seasoned salt and pepper over potatoes.

In a shallow bowl combine stuffing mix, green onion, basil or oregano, and garlic powder. Brush chicken pieces with remaining melted margarine; roll in coating mixture. Place pieces, skin side up, at other end of pan. Drizzle any remaining margarine atop. Bake, uncovered, about 30 to 35 minutes or till potatoes are tender and chicken is tender and no longer pink. Cover loosely with foil the last 10 to 15 minutes if necessary to prevent overbrowning. Makes 4 servings.

Per serving: 579 calories, 38 g protein, 49 g carbohydrate, 25 g total fat (6 g saturated), 104 mg cholesterol, 558 mg sodium, 728 mg potassium

saucy chicken with potatoes

2½ to 3 pounds meaty chicken pieces (breasts, thighs, and drumsticks)
1 tablespoon cooking oil
1 medium onion, sliced
1 cup chicken broth
2 tablespoons white wine vinegar
1 teaspoon seasoned salt
1 teaspoon dried dillweed
¼ teaspoon whole black peppercorns
1 pound whole tiny new potatoes
1 tablespoon cornstarch
⅔ cup dairy sour cream

Skin chicken, if desired. Rinse chicken; pat dry. In a large skillet cook chicken in hot oil about 10 minutes or till chicken is lightly browned, turning to brown evenly. Remove chicken; set aside. Add onion to skillet; cook till tender. Drain off excess fat. Return chicken to skillet. Add broth, vinegar, seasoned salt, dillweed, and whole peppercorns. Bring to boiling; reduce heat. Simmer, covered, for 35 minutes or till chicken is no longer pink.

Meanwhile, cut potatoes into halves or quarters; cook in boiling salted water to cover for 10 to 15 minutes or till tender. Remove chicken to platter; cover and keep warm. Skim fat from pan juices. Stir cornstarch into sour cream; stir into skillet. Cook and stir till mixture is thickened and bubbly; cook and stir 2 minutes more.

Drain potatoes; arrange on platter with chicken. Spoon sauce over chicken and potatoes; garnish with fresh dill, if desired. Makes 6 servings.

Per serving: 380 calories, 31 g protein, 21 g carbohydrate, 19 g total fat (7 g saturated), 98 mg cholesterol, 437 mg sodium, 638 mg potassium

chicken with papaya salsa

- 6 chicken quarters (4½ to 5 pounds total)
- 1 tablespoon olive oil or cooking oil
- 1 tablespoon lime or lemon juice
- 1¼ cups chopped, peeled papaya (1 medium)
- ¼ cup sliced green onion
- 1 4½-ounce can diced green chili peppers, drained
- 1 to 2 tablespoons snipped fresh cilantro
- 1 tablespoon grated fresh gingerroot
- 1 tablespoon lime or lemon juice
- 1 clove garlic, minced

Preheat oven to 425°. Rinse chicken; pat dry. Place chicken on a rack in a roasting pan. Brush with oil and 1 tablespoon lime or lemon juice; sprinkle with *salt* and *pepper*. Bake for 45 to 50 minutes or till chicken is tender and no longer pink.

Meanwhile, for salsa, in a medium bowl combine papaya, onion, chili peppers, cilantro, gingerroot, 1 tablespoon lime or lemon juice, and garlic; cover and chill. Transfer chicken to serving platter. Pass salsa with chicken. If desired, garnish with additional cilantro. Makes 6 servings.

When you are using papaya for a recipe, scoop out the seeds and reserve them. You can add them to a creamy or poppyseed-type salad dressing for an interesting touch.

Per serving: 361 calories, 37 g protein, 4 g carbohydrate, 21 g total fat (5 g saturated), 118 mg cholesterol, 252 mg sodium, 393 mg potassium

chicken au poivre

2½ to 3 pounds meaty chicken pieces (breasts, thighs,
     and drumsticks)
1 tablespoon olive oil or cooking oil
1 teaspoon coarsely ground pepper
½ teaspoon salt
3 tablespoons all-purpose flour
     Chicken broth or water
¼ cup marsala or dry sherry

Preheat oven to 425°. Rinse chicken; pat dry. Brush chicken with oil; sprinkle pepper and salt over chicken. Rub seasonings over chicken. Arrange chicken in a 13x9x2-inch baking pan. Bake for 35 to 40 minutes or till chicken is tender and no longer pink.

Transfer chicken to a serving platter; cover and keep warm. Pour pan drippings into a measuring cup, scraping the browned bits into the cup. Skim and reserve fat from drippings. Place *2 tablespoons* of the fat in a medium saucepan. Stir in flour. Add enough broth or water to remaining drippings to measure *1¼ cups*. Stir broth mixture and wine all at once into flour mixture. Cook and stir over medium heat till thickened and bubbly. Cook and stir 1 minute more; season to taste with *salt* and *pepper*. Pass sauce with chicken. Makes 6 servings.

The safest way to thaw chicken is to leave it loosely wrapped in the fridge, never at room temperature. For faster thawing, immerse tightly wrapped chicken in cold water.

Per serving: 268 calories, 29 g protein, 4 g carbohydrate, 13 g total fat (3 g saturated), 87 mg cholesterol, 384 mg sodium, 257 mg potassium

chicken and shrimp paella

1½ pounds meaty chicken pieces (breasts, thighs, and drumsticks)
1 tablespoon cooking oil
1 medium red or green sweet pepper, thinly sliced in bite-size strips
1 cup sliced onion
1 14½-ounce can chicken broth or 1¾ cups water
¼ cup dry white wine
1 6-ounce package regular saffron-flavored rice mix
1 cup loose-pack frozen peas
8 ounces fresh or frozen large shrimp in shells

Rinse chicken; pat dry. In a Dutch oven or large skillet cook chicken over medium-high heat in hot oil about 10 minutes or till lightly browned, turning to brown evenly. Remove chicken; set aside.

Add pepper and onion to skillet; cook 4 to 5 minutes or just till onion is crisp-tender. Drain off excess fat.

Return chicken to skillet with broth and wine. Bring mixture to boiling; stir in rice mix. Reduce heat; simmer, covered, for 25 to 30 minutes or till chicken and rice are tender and chicken is no longer pink.

Meanwhile, thaw shrimp, if frozen; peel and devein. Stir shrimp and peas into skillet; cover and cook 3 to 5 minutes more or till shrimp turn pink. Makes 4 servings.

This dish works well cooked in the skillet, or you may want to invest in a real paella pan—a round pan with short handles on both sides.

Per serving: 489 calories, 41 g protein, 44 g carbohydrate, 14 g total fat (4 g saturated), 154 mg cholesterol, 793 mg sodium, 554 mg potassium

baked chicken with peaches

1 2½- to 3-pound broiler-fryer chicken, quartered
1 tablespoon lemon juice
½ teaspoon salt
⅛ teaspoon pepper
1 29-ounce can peach halves in syrup
1 tablespoon grated fresh gingerroot
⅛ teaspoon ground allspice
2 teaspoons cornstarch
1 tablespoon cold water
2 cups hot cooked rice

Preheat oven to 425°. Skin chicken, if desired. Rinse chicken; pat dry. Arrange chicken pieces in a lightly greased baking dish. Brush chicken with lemon juice. Sprinkle with the salt and pepper. Bake, uncovered, for 20 minutes.

Drain peaches, reserving syrup. Arrange peach halves around chicken. Combine gingerroot, allspice, and peach syrup. Pour over chicken. Cover; bake 20 to 25 minutes more or till chicken is tender and no longer pink.

Remove chicken and peach halves to platter; cover and keep warm. For sauce, skim fat from pan juices. Measure *1 cup* of juices and place in a small saucepan. Combine cornstarch and cold water. Stir into pan juices. Cook and stir till thickened and bubbly. Cook and stir 2 minutes more. Season to taste with *salt* and *pepper*. Serve chicken and peaches with rice; pass sauce. Makes 4 servings.

Per serving: 559 calories, 34 g protein, 71 g carbohydrate, 16 g total fat (4 g saturated), 99 mg cholesterol, 373 mg sodium, 491 mg potassium

cajun chicken with dumplings

2½ to 3 pounds meaty chicken pieces (breasts, thighs, and drumsticks)

3 tablespoons cooking oil

1 cup chopped onion

2 cups chicken broth or water

1 cup dry white wine

1 to 2 teaspoons Cajun seasoning

⅓ cup all-purpose flour

⅓ cup cornmeal

1 tablespoon snipped fresh parsley

1 teaspoon baking powder

¼ cup milk

1 cup loose-pack frozen whole kernel corn

1 10-ounce package frozen cut okra

Skin chicken, if desired. Rinse chicken; pat dry. In a 12-inch skillet cook chicken in *1 tablespoon* of the oil about 10 minutes or till lightly browned, turning to brown evenly. (Remove chicken; set aside.) Drain off fat.

Return chicken to skillet with onion, broth, wine, Cajun seasoning, ¼ teaspoon *salt,* and ¼ teaspoon *pepper.* Bring to boiling; reduce heat. Simmer, covered, for 30 minutes. Meanwhile, for dumplings, in a medium bowl stir together flour, cornmeal, parsley, and baking powder. Stir in milk and remaining oil just till moistened; fold in *⅓ cup* of the corn. Stir remaining corn and the okra into skillet; bring to boiling. Drop dumpling dough in 6 mounds atop bubbling liquid. Cover; cook 10 to 12 minutes more or till a toothpick inserted in a dumpling comes out clean. Makes 6 servings.

Per serving: 378 calories, 33 g protein, 23 g carbohydrate, 14 g total fat (4 g saturated), 87 mg cholesterol, 468 mg sodium, 582 mg potassium

Sweet potatoes taste great in this recipe! For fun, next time try Yukon gold potatoes, yellow Finnish potatoes which have a buttery taste, or purple russet potatoes.

chicken-topped bakers

4 large sweet potatoes (7 to 8 ounces each)
1 cup chopped broccoli or green pepper
½ cup finely chopped carrots or mushrooms
½ cup loose-pack frozen whole kernel corn
1 tablespoon cooking oil
1 cup shredded cooked chicken
3 tablespoons creamy ranch salad dressing
1 cup shredded cheddar, Monterey Jack, or
   Swiss cheese (4 ounces)
1 tablespoon grated Parmesan or Romano cheese

Preheat oven to 425°. Scrub sweet potatoes; halve lengthwise. Place potatoes, cut side down, on a lightly greased baking sheet. Bake the potatoes for 35 to 45 minutes or till tender.

Meanwhile, in a medium skillet cook broccoli, carrots, and corn in hot oil for 5 to 7 minutes or till vegetables are tender. Drain, if necessary. Stir in chicken and salad dressing; heat through. Remove from heat. Cover and keep warm.

When potatoes are done, turn potatoes cut side up. Fluff potatoes with a fork, if desired. Spoon hot chicken mixture over cut sides of potatoes; sprinkle with cheddar and Parmesan cheeses. Return to oven for 5 minutes or till cheese is melted. Makes 4 servings.

Per serving: 452 calories, 23 g protein, 45 g carbohydrate, 21 g total fat (8 g saturated), 68 mg cholesterol, 344 mg sodium, 814 mg potassium

swiss, chicken and broccoli quiche

- ½ of a 15-ounce package folded refrigerated unbaked piecrust (1 crust)
- 1 cup loose-pack frozen cut broccoli
- 3 slightly beaten eggs
- 1¼ cups half-and-half, light cream, or milk
- ¾ cup chopped cooked chicken
- 1 cup shredded Swiss, Monterey Jack, or cheddar cheese (4 ounces)
- ½ teaspoon salt
- ¼ teaspoon pepper
- ¼ teaspoon ground nutmeg

Preheat oven to 450°. Unfold pastry into a 9-inch pie plate. Flute edges; do not prick pastry. Place a double thickness of foil on top of the pastry in pie plate. Bake for 8 minutes. Remove foil and bake 4 to 5 minutes more or till crust is set and dry. Reduce oven temperature to 325°. Set crust aside.

Meanwhile, run cold water over broccoli to separate; drain. In a medium bowl stir together eggs and cream. Stir in chicken, broccoli, cheese, salt, pepper, and nutmeg. Place partially-baked crust on oven rack; pour egg mixture into crust. Bake about 40 minutes or till a knife inserted halfway between center and edge comes out clean. Let stand 5 minutes before cutting. Makes 6 to 8 servings.

If you need cooked chicken for a recipe, poach skinned and boned chicken breast halves by simmering for 12 to 14 minutes.

Per serving: 377 calories, 17 g protein, 20 g carbohydrate, 25 g total fat (8 g saturated), 169 mg cholesterol, 440 mg sodium, 220 mg potassium

cornish hens with basil vegetables

2 1¼- to 1½-pound Cornish game hens, split

3 cups desired loose-pack frozen vegetables

½ cup dry white wine or chicken broth

½ cup water

1 teaspoon dried basil, crushed

½ teaspoon dried dillweed

½ teaspoon salt

¼ teaspoon pepper

Preheat oven to 425°. Rinse Cornish hens; pat dry. Arrange hens, cut side down, in a shallow roasting pan. Sprinkle vegetables around hens. Pour wine or broth and water over vegetables. In a small bowl combine basil, dillweed, salt, and pepper; sprinkle mixture over the hens and vegetables.

Bake for 40 to 50 minutes or till hens are tender and no longer pink, brushing frequently with pan juices. Transfer hens and vegetables to platter. Makes 4 servings.

When serving poultry, be sure to serve it immediately after cooking. Don't let it stand at room temperature longer than 1 hour or bacteria will form—especially in warm weather. Refrigerate leftovers as soon as possible.

Per serving: 357 calories, 32 g protein, 11 g carbohydrate, 19 g total fat (4 g saturated), 100 mg cholesterol, 373 mg sodium, 180 mg potassium

turkey stuffed eggplant

- 2 small eggplants (2 pounds total)
- 2 tablespoons olive oil or cooking oil
- 8 ounces ground raw turkey or chicken or ground turkey sausage
- ¾ cup chopped red or green sweet pepper
- ½ cup chopped zucchini
- ½ cup chopped onion
- 1 medium tomato, chopped
- ½ teaspoon salt
- ½ teaspoon dried basil, crushed
- ½ teaspoon dried oregano, crushed
- ¼ teaspoon pepper
- 1 cup herb-seasoned croutons
- 1½ cups shredded Monterey Jack or mozzarella cheese

Preheat oven to 400°. Trim stems from eggplants; cut in half lengthwise. Brush cut sides with *1 tablespoon* of the oil; place halves, cut-side down, on an ungreased baking sheet. Bake for 15 minutes. When cool enough to handle, spoon out centers of eggplant halves, leaving a ½-inch-thick shell. Chop pulp.

Meanwhile, in a large skillet cook turkey or chicken, pepper, zucchini, and onion in remaining oil till turkey is no longer pink and vegetables are tender. Remove from heat. Drain well. Stir in chopped eggplant, tomato, salt, basil, oregano, and pepper. Place eggplant shells in a greased 2-quart rectangular baking dish. Fill shells with turkey mixture. Spoon any extra into the baking dish. Top with croutons and cheese. Bake for 15 to 20 minutes or till heated through. Makes 4 servings.

Per serving: 368 calories, 21 g protein, 23 g carbohydrate, 22 g total fat (10 g saturated), 59 mg cholesterol, 622 mg sodium, 746 mg potassium

Pepper Sauce: *In a blender container puree one 7-ounce jar roasted red sweet peppers, drained; set aside. In a saucepan melt 2 tablespoons margarine; stir in 2 tablespoons all-purpose flour and ¼ teaspoon salt. Add 1½ cups milk all at once. Stir in ½ cup mayonnaise or salad dressing. Cook and stir till mixture thickens; cook and stir 1 minute more. Stir in pureed peppers and 1 table-spoon lemon juice till combined. Heat through.*

turkey manicotti with pepper sauce

8   manicotti pasta shells
　　 Pepper Sauce (see box at left)
8   ounces ground raw turkey or chicken
1   4-ounce can mushroom stems and pieces, drained
½   cup chopped carrot
½   cup chopped onion
2   cloves garlic, minced
1   tablespoon cooking oil
½   of a 15-ounce container ricotta cheese (1 cup)
1   cup shredded mozzarella cheese (4 ounces)
¼   cup grated Parmesan or Romano cheese
¼   teaspoon salt

Preheat oven to 400°. Cook manicotti following package directions. Prepare Red Pepper Sauce; keep warm.

In a large skillet cook turkey, mushrooms, carrot, onion, and garlic in hot oil till vegetables are tender and turkey is no longer pink. Drain off excess fat. Cover and keep warm. In a mixing bowl stir together the ricotta, ⅔ *cup* of the mozzarella, the Parmesan cheese, and salt. Stir in turkey mixture till combined; set aside.

Drain manicotti shells; pat dry with paper towels. Spoon turkey mixture into shells. Arrange filled shells in a lightly greased 2-quart rectangular baking dish. Pour Pepper Sauce over manicotti; sprinkle with remaining ⅓ cup mozzarella. Bake, covered, for 20 minutes or till heated through. Makes 4 servings.

Per serving: 731 calories, 33 g protein, 45 g carbohydrate, 47 g total fat (14 g saturated), 84 mg cholesterol, 1,020 mg sodium, 553 mg potassium

turkey-stuffed squash

2 medium acorn squash (about 1 pound each)

12 ounces ground raw turkey or chicken

1 cup chopped fresh mushrooms

1 cup finely chopped red or green sweet pepper

1 clove garlic, minced

⅓ cup shredded Monterey Jack or Swiss cheese (1½ ounces)

1 3-ounce package cream cheese, softened

¼ cup fine dry seasoned bread crumbs

1 tablespoon margarine or butter, melted

Preheat oven to 350°. Halve squash; remove seeds. Place squash, cut side down, in a shallow baking dish. Bake for 30 minutes. Meanwhile, in a large skillet cook turkey, mushrooms, pepper, and garlic till turkey is browned and vegetables are tender; drain well. Stir in shredded cheese and cream cheese. Turn squash cut side up. Spoon turkey mixture into squash. Bake, covered, 20 minutes more or till squash is tender. Stir together bread crumbs and melted margarine; sprinkle over turkey filling. Bake, uncovered, 3 minutes more. Serves 4.

You can purchase all white or all dark meat ground turkey or chicken or grind your own. Buy your favorite parts, skin, cut into 1-inch pieces, and process in a food processor.

Per serving: 361 calories, 19 g protein, 29 g carbohydrate, 20 g total fat (9 g saturated), 65 mg cholesterol, 386 mg sodium, 819 mg potassium

chicken with polenta

1 5- to 6-pound roasting chicken
2 tablespoons olive oil or cooking oil
2 cloves garlic, minced
1 teaspoon dried basil, crushed
1 teaspoon dried oregano, crushed
   Polenta
1 tablespoon grated Parmesan or Romano cheese
2 14½-ounce cans pasta-style chunky tomatoes

Preheat oven to 325°. Prepare chicken for roasting (see page 300). Brush with oil; spread garlic over bird. Rub herbs and ½ teaspoon *salt* onto bird. Roast, uncovered, for 1¾ to 2½ hours or till chicken is no longer pink and meat thermometer registers 180° to 185°. Baste occasionally with pan juices. Meanwhile, prepare Polenta. Remove chicken from oven; cover and keep warm. Increase oven temperature to 375°. Bake Polenta for 15 to 20 minutes or till hot. Sprinkle cheese atop. Meanwhile, bring tomatoes to boiling. Reduce heat; simmer, uncovered, for 10 to 15 minutes. Serve with chicken and Polenta. Makes 12 servings.

Polenta: In a large saucepan bring 5½ cups *chicken broth* to boiling. In a bowl stir together 2 cups *cornmeal*, 2 cups cold *water*, and ½ teaspoon *salt*. If desired, stir in one 4-ounce can diced *green chili peppers,* drained. Slowly add cornmeal mixture to broth, stirring constantly. Cook and stir till mixture boils. Reduce heat; simmer 15 to 20 minutes more or till very thick, stirring occasionally. Spread mixture in two 9-inch pie plates or a 13x9x2-inch baking pan. Cover; chill about 45 minutes till firm.

Per serving: 358 calories, 25 g protein, 23 g carbohydrate, 18 g total fat (4 g saturated), 59 mg cholesterol, 775 mg sodium, 474 mg potassium

This dish has an interesting, uneven texture, with a crust resembling the surface of the moon—but it's a lot more delicious!

popover pizza casserole

1 pound ground raw chicken or turkey
1 cup chopped onion
1 cup chopped green pepper
1 15-ounce can pizza sauce
1 4½-ounce can whole mushrooms, drained
1 teaspoon dried Italian seasoning, crushed
½ teaspoon fennel seed, crushed
¼ teaspoon crushed red pepper
1 cup milk
1 tablespoon cooking oil
2 eggs
1 cup all-purpose flour
6 ounces thinly sliced mozzarella cheese
¼ cup grated Parmesan cheese

Preheat oven to 400°. In a large skillet cook chicken or turkey, onion, and green pepper till meat is brown and vegetables are tender. Drain. Stir in pizza sauce, mushrooms, Italian seasoning, fennel, and crushed red pepper. Bring to boiling. Reduce heat and simmer, covered, for 10 minutes, stirring occasionally.

Meanwhile, for topping, in a small bowl combine milk, oil, and eggs. Add flour; beat with a rotary beater or wire whisk till smooth.

Grease the sides of a 3-quart baking dish; spoon meat mixture into dish. Arrange cheese slices over hot meat mixture. Pour topping over cheese, covering completely. Sprinkle with Parmesan cheese. Bake for 25 to 30 minutes or till puffed and golden brown. Cut into wedges or squares to serve. Makes 8 servings.

Per serving: 276 calories, 20 g protein, 22 g carbohydrate, 12 g total fat (5 g saturated), 97 mg cholesterol, 594 mg sodium, 457 mg potassium

pot-roasted chicken

2½ to 3 pounds meaty chicken pieces (breasts, thighs, and drumsticks)

2 tablespoons cooking oil

3 medium carrots, cut into ½-inch slices

1 medium onion, sliced

1 medium rutabaga or turnip, peeled and cubed (2 cups)

1 cup chicken broth

1 teaspoon dried basil, crushed

1 teaspoon poultry seasoning

1 bay leaf

1 16-ounce can tomatoes, cut up

⅓ cup dry white wine, apple juice, or chicken broth

3 tablespoons cornstarch

Don't overlook the virtues of adding turnips or rutabagas to stews like this one. They're high in fiber, with just 32 calories per serving.

Skin chicken, if desired. Rinse chicken; pat dry. In a Dutch oven cook chicken in hot oil 10 minutes or till lightly browned, turning to brown evenly. Drain off fat.

Add carrots, onion, rutabaga, broth, basil, poultry seasoning, bay leaf, ¼ teaspoon *salt,* and ¼ teaspoon *pepper.* Bring mixture to boiling. Reduce heat. Cover and simmer 20 minutes or till vegetables are tender. Add *undrained* tomatoes and wine. Cover and simmer 5 to 10 minutes more or till chicken is tender and no longer pink. Remove chicken to platter; keep warm. Skim fat; discard bay leaf. Stir cornstarch into ¼ cup *water;* stir into Dutch oven. Cook and stir till thickened and bubbly; cook and stir 2 minutes more. Season to taste with *salt* and *pepper.* Pour vegetable mixture over chicken. Serve with mashed potatoes, if desired. Makes 6 servings.

Per serving: 328 calories, 31 g protein, 19 g carbohydrate, 13 g total fat (3 g saturated), 86 mg cholesterol, 457 mg sodium, 764 mg potassium

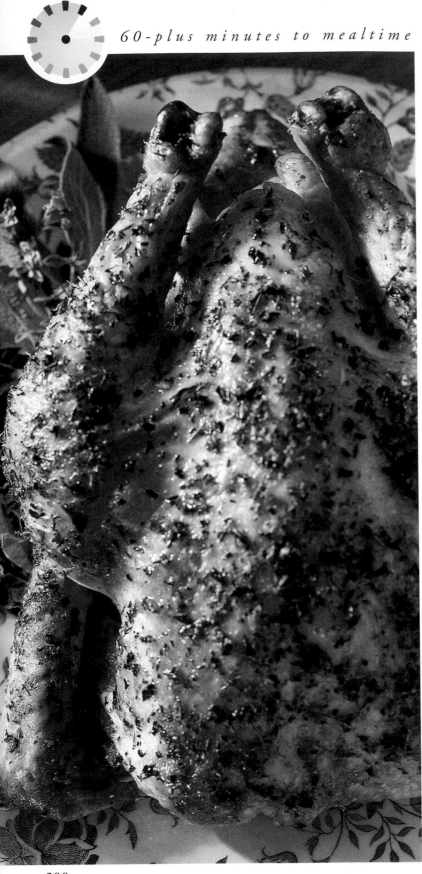

herb-roasted chicken

1 2½- to 3-pound whole broiler-fryer chicken
2 tablespoons margarine or butter, melted
2 cloves garlic, minced
1 teaspoon dried basil, crushed
½ teaspoon salt
½ teaspoon ground sage
½ teaspoon dried thyme, crushed
¼ teaspoon lemon-pepper seasoning or pepper

Preheat oven to 375°. Prepare chicken for roasting (see page 300). Brush chicken with melted margarine; spread garlic over bird. In a small bowl stir together basil, salt, sage, thyme, and lemon-pepper seasoning; rub onto bird.

If desired, insert a meat thermometer into center of an inside thigh muscle. Do not allow thermometer to touch bone. Roast, uncovered, for 1¼ to 1½ hours or till drumsticks move easily in their sockets, chicken is no longer pink, and meat thermometer registers 180° to 185°. Cover bird and allow to stand 10 minutes before carving. Makes 6 servings.

Per serving: 215 calories, 21 g protein, 1 g carbohydrate, 14 g total fat (4 g saturated), 66 mg cholesterol, 329 mg sodium, 178 mg potassium

roast chicken with seafood stuffing

1 5- to 6-pound roasting chicken
1 tablespoon olive oil or cooking oil
   Seafood Stuffing

Preheat oven to 325°. Prepare chicken for roasting (see page 300). Brush with oil; sprinkle with *salt* and *pepper*. Insert meat thermometer. Roast for 1¾ to 2½ hours or till chicken is no longer pink and meat thermometer registers 180° to 185°. Baste occasionally with pan juices.

Meanwhile, prepare Seafood Stuffing. Bake in oven with chicken for the last 45 minutes of roasting. Transfer chicken to serving platter. Cover; let stand 10 minutes before carving. Skim fat from pan juices; pass juices with stuffing and chicken. Makes 10 to 12 servings.

Seafood Stuffing: In large saucepan melt 2 table-spoons *margarine or butter.* Add 1 cup chopped *onion;* cook and stir 3 minutes. Peel, devein, and chop 1 pound medium *shrimp.* Cut 8 ounces fresh or frozen *scallops* into ½-inch chunks. Add shrimp, scallops, and 2 tablespoons *dry sherry* to onion in saucepan; cook, stirring occasionally, till shrimp are pink and scallops are opaque. Stir in 2 table-spoons snipped fresh *parsley;* 1 teaspoon dried *thyme,* crushed; ¼ teaspoon *salt;* ¼ teaspoon *pepper;* and dash crushed *red pepper.*

In a large bowl toss together 3 cups dry *bread cubes* and ¼ cup grated *Parmesan cheese.* Add 1 slightly beaten *egg,* 1 tablespoon *lemon juice,* and the shrimp mixture; toss well. Spoon stuffing into a 1½-quart casserole. Cover. Bake as directed above.

You can double the stuffing mixture for a 12- to 16-pound turkey, or halve the recipe for a 3-pound chicken.

Per serving: 382 calories, 35 g protein, 7 g carbohydrate, 23 g total fat (6 g saturated), 152 mg cholesterol, 397 mg sodium, 327 mg potassium

stuffed chicken italian-style

1 5- to 6-pound roasting chicken
⅔ cup Italian salad dressing
   Stuffing

Rinse chicken; pat dry. Brush inside of chicken with some of the salad dressing; place in a deep non-metal bowl. Pour remaining dressing over bird. Cover; chill 2 to 6 hours, turning bird occasionally. Preheat oven to 325°. Prepare Stuffing. Drain chicken from marinade; reserve marinade. Pat chicken dry. Sprinkle cavity with salt, if desired. Spoon stuffing loosely into the neck cavity; skewer neck skin to back. Lightly spoon Stuffing into the body cavity. (Place any remaining Stuffing in a small casserole; heat, covered, alongside chicken during last 30 minutes of roasting.) Tie legs to tail. Twist wing tips under back. Place bird, breast side up, on rack in a shallow roasting pan. Roast for 1¾ to 2½ hours or till chicken is no longer pink and meat thermometer registers 180° to 185°. Baste occasionally with marinade, except the last 5 minutes of roasting. Cover chicken; let stand 10 minutes before carving. Makes 10 to 12 servings.

Stuffing: In a large skillet cook 1 cup chopped *zucchini or yellow summer squash,* 1 cup chopped *red onion,* and 2 cloves *garlic,* minced, in 2 tablespoons *olive oil* till vegetables are tender. Drain off fat. Stir in 1 cup chopped, peeled *tomatoes* and 2 tablespoons snipped *fresh basil* or 2 teaspoons *dried* basil, crushed. Remove from heat. Toss together 3 cups seasoned croutons and ½ cup sliced pitted *ripe olives.* Add vegetable mixture; toss. Moisten with *water or chicken broth* if mixture seems dry.

Per serving: 353 calories, 26 g protein, 10 g carbohydrate, 23 g total fat (5 g saturated), 70 mg cholesterol, 271 mg sodium, 271 mg potassium

swiss chicken strata

8 slices white bread, halved diagonally

1 cup shredded gruyère or Swiss cheese (4 ounces)

1½ cups chopped cooked chicken or turkey (8 ounces)

½ cup chopped red or green sweet pepper

⅓ cup finely chopped onion

4 eggs

2 cups milk

1 tablespoon prepared mustard

½ teaspoon pepper

¼ teaspoon paprika

⅓ cup shredded Gruyère or Swiss cheese
   (about 1½ ounces)

In a greased 2-quart rectangular baking dish layer *eight* of the bread slice halves, 1 cup shredded cheese, chicken, sweet pepper, and onion; top with remaining bread slice halves.

In a medium bowl beat eggs; whisk in milk, mustard, pepper, and paprika till combined. Pour mixture over bread layer, being careful to moisten all the bread. Sprinkle with remaining cheese. Cover; chill in the refrigerator for 2 to 24 hours.

Preheat oven to 325°. Bake, uncovered, about 45 minutes or till set and lightly browned. Let stand 10 minutes before cutting into servings. Makes 8 servings.

Per serving: 276 calories, 21 g protein, 17 g carbohydrate, 13 g total fat (6 g saturated), 158 mg cholesterol, 305 mg sodium, 264 mg potassium

Tip: Roast or simmer two chickens instead of one. Then, cut the extra meat into bite-size pieces or strips and freeze for later use in casseroles like this one.

chicken croquettes with orange sauce

2 tablespoons margarine or butter
½ cup finely chopped onion
½ cup finely chopped green sweet pepper
2 cloves garlic, minced
2 tablespoons all-purpose flour
1½ cups finely chopped cooked chicken or turkey
1 teaspoon dried basil, crushed
½ cup milk
1 slightly beaten egg
2 cups cornflakes, crushed
　Orange Sauce

In a large skillet melt margarine; cook onion, green pepper, and garlic for 5 minutes. Stir in flour, chicken, basil, ½ teaspoon *salt,* and ⅛ teaspoon *pepper.*

Add milk. Cook and stir till mixture is thickened and bubbly; cook and stir 1 minute more. Remove from heat. Cover and chill mixture for at least 1 hour.

Preheat oven to 350°. Shape chilled mixture into eight 2½- to 3-inch balls. Dip balls in egg, then roll in crushed cornflakes to coat on all sides. Flatten croquettes slightly; place in a lightly greased baking pan.

Bake, uncovered, for 25 to 30 minutes, or till golden brown. Serve with Orange Sauce, if desired. Serves 4.

Orange Sauce: In a small saucepan stir together 1 cup *chicken broth,* ½ cup *orange juice,* 2 tablespoons *cornstarch,* and 2 tablespoons *orange marmalade.* Bring to boiling; reduce heat. Cook 2 minutes till mixture thickens. Makes 1½ cups sauce.

Per serving: 346 calories, 22 g protein, 32 g carbohydrate, 14 g total fat (4 g saturated), 99 mg cholesterol, 743 mg sodium, 367 mg potassium

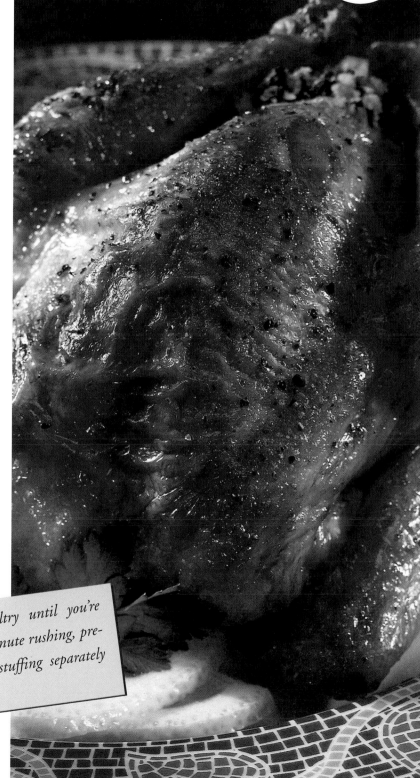

spinach-stuffed cornish hens

1 slightly beaten egg

1 10-ounce package frozen chopped spinach, cooked and well-drained

¾ cup ricotta cheese

¾ cup fine dry seasoned bread crumbs

1 teaspoon dried basil, crushed

½ teaspoon dried rosemary, crushed

4 1¼- to 1½-pound Cornish game hens

1 tablespoon olive oil or cooking oil

½ teaspoon salt

¼ teaspoon lemon-pepper seasoning or pepper

Preheat oven to 375°. In a medium bowl stir together egg, spinach, and ricotta cheese. Add bread crumbs, basil, and rosemary; stir till well combined.

Rinse hens; pat dry. Season cavities lightly with *salt.* Lightly stuff hens with spinach mixture. Pull neck skin, if present, to back of each hen. Twist wing tips under back, holding skin in place. Tie legs to tail.

Place hens, breast side up, on a rack in a shallow roasting pan. Brush with oil; sprinkle with the ½ teaspoon salt and lemon-pepper seasoning. Cover loosely with foil. Roast 30 minutes. Uncover; roast 1 to 1¼ hours more or till tender and no longer pink, basting occasionally with pan juices. Makes 4 servings.

Remember, NEVER stuff poultry until you're ready to roast it. To save last-minute rushing, prepare and chill the bird and stuffing separately ahead of time.

Per serving: 781 calories, 71 g protein, 21 g carbohydrate, 47 g total fat (11 g saturated), 267 mg cholesterol, 1,155 mg sodium, 253 mg potassium

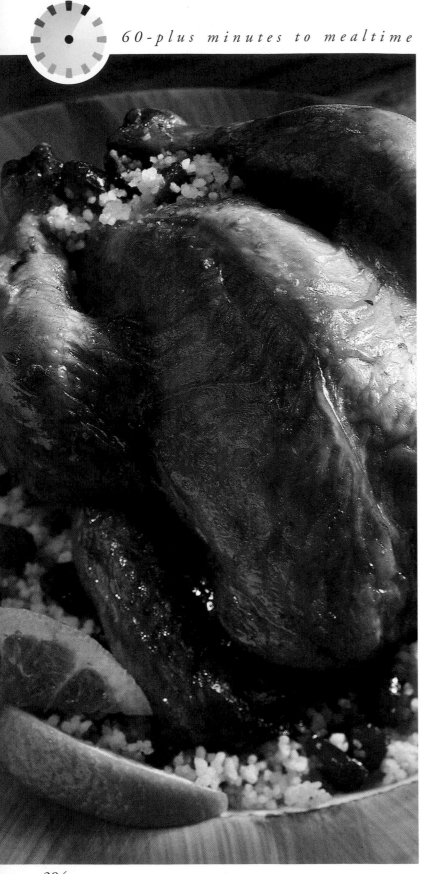

game hens with cranberry couscous

¾ cup chicken broth

1 teaspoon finely shredded orange peel

⅓ cup orange juice

¾ cup couscous

½ cup dried cranberries or currants

¼ teaspoon ground ginger

4 1¼- to 1½-pound Cornish game hens

1 tablespoon olive oil or cooking oil

1 clove garlic, minced

Preheat oven to 375°. In a small saucepan combine chicken broth and orange juice (set peel aside); bring to boiling. Stir in couscous; cover and remove from heat. Let stand 5 minutes. Stir in orange peel, dried cranberries, and ginger; set aside.

Rinse hens; pat dry. Season cavities lightly with *salt*. Lightly stuff hens with couscous mixture. Pull neck skin, if present, to back of each hen. Twist wing tips under back, holding skin in place. Tie legs to tail.

Place hens, breast side up, on a rack in a shallow roasting pan. Brush with oil; spread garlic over birds. Cover loosely with foil. Roast for 30 minutes. Uncover; roast for 1 to 1¼ hours more or till tender and no longer pink. If desired, garnish the game hens with orange wedges. Makes 4 servings.

To reduce the fat content, you can skin Cornish hens just as you would chicken. Cover as directed during roasting and they will still be moist.

Per serving: 799 calories, 66 g protein, 41 g carbohydrate, 41 g total fat (9 g saturated), 200 mg cholesterol, 301 mg sodium, 152 mg potassium

turkey lasagna

1 pound ground turkey sausage or turkey Italian sausage

1 30-ounce jar spaghetti sauce

½ of a 6-ounce can tomato paste

1 slightly beaten egg

1 15-ounce carton ricotta cheese (about 2 cups)

½ cup grated Parmesan or Romano cheese

12 lasagna noodles, cooked and drained

3 cups shredded mozzarella cheese (12 ounces)

In a large skillet cook turkey sausage about 10 minutes or till brown, stirring to break up meat. Drain. Stir in spaghetti sauce and tomato paste. Heat through. Remove from heat. Set aside. Preheat oven to 375°.

In a medium bowl stir together egg, ricotta cheese, and ¼ *cup* of the Parmesan cheese. In a greased 3-quart rectangular baking dish arrange *four* of the noodles. Spread *half* of the ricotta cheese mixture over noodles and top with *one-third* of the meat sauce. Sprinkle with *one-third* of the mozzarella cheese.

Repeat layers once. Add remaining noodles and meat sauce over all; sprinkle with remaining mozzarella and Parmesan cheeses. Cover loosely; bake for 30 minutes. Uncover; bake 5 to 10 minutes more or till hot in the center. Let stand 10 minutes before cutting. Makes 8 servings.

If you like vegetables in your lasagna, you can add a layer of thinly-sliced zucchini or yellow summer squash; arrange on top of the first layer of mozzarella.

Per serving: 491 calories, 33 g protein, 34 g carbohydrate, 24 g total fat (10 g saturated), 118 mg cholesterol, 1,005 mg sodium, 798 mg potassium

chutney-glazed turkey breast

1 1¾- to 2-pound bone-in turkey breast portion
1 tablespoon olive oil or cooking oil
¼ teaspoon salt
⅛ teaspoon pepper
½ cup whole cranberry sauce
½ cup snipped chutney
1 teaspoon finely shredded orange peel

Preheat oven to 325°. Rinse turkey; pat dry. Skin, if desired. Place turkey, skin side up, on a rack in a shallow roasting pan. Brush with oil; sprinkle with salt and pepper. If using a meat thermometer, insert it in the thickest part of the breast, not touching bone. Roast, uncovered, for 1¼ to 1½ hours or till nearly done (150°).

Meanwhile, for glaze, in a small saucepan stir together cranberry sauce, chutney, and orange peel; heat through. Spoon some of the glaze over turkey. Roast 15 to 20 minutes more, or till juices of turkey run clear and meat thermometer registers 170°.

Transfer turkey breast to cutting board; let stand 5 to 10 minutes before carving. Serve remaining glaze with turkey. Makes 6 servings.

To carve a turkey breast, start at the outside of the breast half and slice downward, keeping slices thin. Continue slicing, moving slightly higher up on the breast with each slice.

Per serving: 276 calories, 24 g protein, 22 g carbohydrate, 9 g total fat (2 g saturated), 64 mg cholesterol, 154 mg sodium, 271 mg potassium

roast turkey with pasta

1 8- to 12-pound turkey
2 tablespoons Italian salad dressing
2 cloves garlic, minced
2 tablespoons snipped fresh parsley
    Pasta and Vegetables

Preheat oven to 325°. Prepare turkey for roasting (see page 300). Place turkey, breast side up, on a rack in a shallow roasting pan. Brush with salad dressing; spread garlic over bird. Sprinkle parsley, ¼ teaspoon *salt,* and ⅛ teaspoon *pepper* over bird. Insert a meat thermometer into center of an inside thigh muscle. Do not allow thermo-meter to touch bone. Roast, uncovered, for 3 to 4 hours till meat thermometer registers 180° to 185°, basting occasionally with pan juices. Meanwhile, prepare Pasta and Vegetables; bake, covered, during the last 40 to 45 minutes of roasting time. Cover bird; allow to stand 15 minutes before carving. Makes 12 servings.

Pasta and Vegetables: In a large pan of boiling salted water cook 1⅓ cups uncooked *pasta* (orzo, tiny bow ties, or small shells) according to package directions; drain. In a large skillet cook 1½ cups chopped *carrot* and ¾ cup sliced *green onion* in 2 tablespoons *margarine* over medium heat until carrots are crisp-tender. Remove from heat. Stir in 2 cups loose-pack frozen *whole-kernel corn;* one 4-ounce jar sliced *pimiento,* drained; ½ cup *Italian salad dressing;* and ¼ cup snipped *parsley.* Season to taste with *salt* and *pepper.* In a large bowl toss together drained pasta, vegetable mixture, and 1 slightly beaten *egg.* Place in a lightly greased 2-quart casserole.

Per serving: 387 calories, 31 g protein, 20 g carbohydrate, 20 g total fat (4 g saturated), 119 mg cholesterol, 329 mg sodium, 432 mg potassium

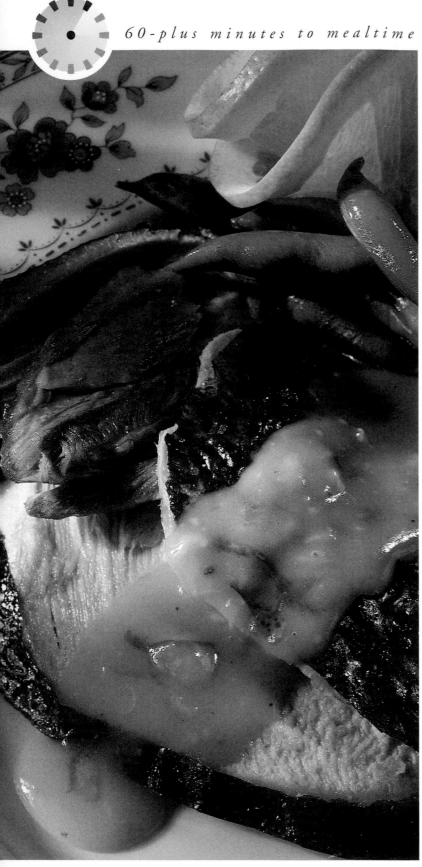

turkey à la orange with citrus sauce

1 8- to 12-pound turkey
2 teaspoons finely shredded orange peel
1 cup orange juice
2 tablespoons olive oil or cooking oil
1 clove garlic, minced
   Citrus Sauce

Preheat oven to 325°. Prepare turkey for roasting (see page 300). Place turkey, breast side up, on a rack in a shallow roasting pan. In a small bowl stir together the orange peel, orange juice, oil, and garlic. Brush some of the mixture over bird. Insert a meat thermometer into center of an inside thigh muscle. Do not allow thermometer to touch bone. Roast, uncovered, for 3 to 4 hours or till meat thermometer registers 180° to 185°, brushing with orange juice mixture every 30 minutes after the first 1½ hours. If necessary, cover loosely with foil to prevent overbrowning. Cover bird; allow to stand 15 minutes before carving. Reserve pan juices; skim fat, reserving ¼ cup. Prepare Citrus Sauce and serve with turkey. Makes 12 servings.

Citrus Sauce: In a medium saucepan combine ¼ cup *reserved fat* from pan juices and ¼ cup *all-purpose flour*. Add *chicken broth* or *water* to *reserved pan juices* to measure 2 cups; add to flour mixture. Cook and stir till thickened and bubbly. Stir in 3 tablespoons *orange marmalade,* 1 teaspoon finely shredded *lemon peel,* and 1 tablespoon *lemon juice.* Cook and stir 1 minute more. Season to taste with *salt* and *pepper.*

Per serving: 262 calories, 29 g protein, 8 g carbohydrate, 12 g total fat (3 g saturated), 95 mg cholesterol, 242 mg sodium, 355 mg potassium

barbecue turkey sandwiches

2 turkey drumsticks (4 to 6 pounds total)
1 tablespoon cooking oil
½ teaspoon salt
¼ teaspoon pepper
⅔ cup bottled hickory smoke-flavored barbecue sauce
¼ cup finely chopped green onion
2 tablespoons honey
2 teaspoons Dijon-style mustard
4 Kaiser rolls, split

Preheat oven to 325°. Rinse turkey; pat dry. Arrange drumsticks in a roasting pan. Brush with oil; sprinkle with salt and pepper. Bake, uncovered, for 30 minutes.

Meanwhile, in a small bowl stir together barbecue sauce, onion, honey, and mustard till combined. Brush mixture over turkey legs. Roast 45 to 60 minutes more or till turkey is tender and no longer pink, brushing frequently with barbecue sauce mixture. Remove turkey legs from pan. Slice meat and serve on rolls with additional barbecue sauce, if desired. Makes 4 servings.

Turkey drumsticks are often an overlooked part of the bird. Actually, they offer the turkey's most succulent dark meat. One turkey leg will provide two servings of meat. To serve, cut thin slices parallel to the bone.

Per serving: 625 calories, 49 g protein, 50 g carbohydrate, 24 g total fat (6 g saturated), 139 mg cholesterol, 1,276 mg sodium, 506 mg potassium

roasting poultry

To prepare a bird for roasting, follow the steps below. Since birds vary in size, shape, and tenderness, use the times as general guides.

- Rinse whole bird well on outside as well as inside body and neck cavities. Pat dry. Rub salt inside the body cavity, if desired.

- For an unstuffed bird, place quartered onions and celery in body cavity, if desired. Pull the neck skin to the back and fasten with a skewer. If a band of skin crosses the tail, tuck the drumsticks under the band. If there is no band, tie the drumsticks to the tail. Twist the wing tips under the back.

For a stuffed bird, do not stuff until just before cooking. To stuff, spoon some stuffing loosely into the neck cavity; fasten neck skin as for an unstuffed bird. Lightly spoon stuffing into the body cavity. Secure the drumsticks and wings as directed above.

- Place the bird, breast side up, on a rack in a shallow roasting pan. Brush the bird with cooking oil. (When cooking a domestic duckling or goose, prick the skin well all over and omit the cooking oil.) If desired, for large birds, insert a meat thermometer into the center of one of the inside thigh muscles. The bulb should not touch the bone.

- Cover Cornish game hens, quail, squab, and turkey with foil, leaving an air space between the bird and the foil. Press the foil lightly at the ends of the drumsticks and the neck. Leave all other types of poultry uncovered.

- Roast in an uncovered pan. Baste occasionally with pan drippings. When the bird is two-thirds done, cut the band of skin or string between the drumsticks. Uncover the bird for last 45 minutes of cooking (leave quail covered for entire cooking time).

Continue roasting until the meat thermometer registers 180° to 185°, or till drumsticks move easily in their sockets and juices run clear. (In a whole or half turkey breast, thermometer should register 170°.) Remove bird from the oven and cover it with foil. Let large birds stand for 15 to 20 minutes before carving.

Type of Bird	Weight	Oven Temp.	Roasting Time
Capon	5 to 7 pounds	325°	1¾ to 2½ hours
Chicken, whole*	2½ to 3 pounds	375°	1 to 1¼ hours
	3½ to 4 pounds	375°	1¼ to 1¾ hours
	4½ to 5 pounds	375°	1½ to 2 hours
	5 to 6 pounds	325°	1¾ to 2½ hours
Cornish game hen	1 to 1½ pounds	375°	1 to 1¼ hours
Duckling, domestic	3 to 5 pounds	375°	1¾ to 2¼ hours
Goose, domestic	7 to 8 pounds	350°	2 to 2½ hours
	8 to 10 pounds	350°	2½ to 3 hours
	10 to 12 pounds	350°	3 to 3½ hours
Pheasant	2 to 3 pounds	350°	1½ to 1¾ hours
Quail	4 to 6 ounces	375°	30 to 50 minutes
Squab	12 to 14 ounces	375°	45 to 60 minutes
Turkey, boneless, whole	2½ to 3½ pounds	325°	2 to 2½ hours
	4 to 6 pounds	325°	2½ to 3½ hours
Turkey, unstuffed**	6 to 8 pounds	325°	3 to 3½ hours
	8 to 12 pounds	325°	3 to 4 hours
	12 to 16 pounds	325°	4 to 5 hours
	16 to 20 pounds	325°	4½ to 5 hours
	20 to 24 pounds	325°	5 to 6 hours
Turkey breast, whole	4 to 6 pounds	325°	1½ to 2¼ hours
	6 to 8 pounds	325°	2¼ to 3¼ hours
Turkey drumstick	1 to 1½ pounds	325°	1¼ to 1¾ hours
Turkey thigh	1½ to 1¾ pounds	325°	1½ to 1¾ hours

* Choose broiler-fryer or roasting chickens.

** Stuffed birds generally require 30 to 45 minutes more roasting time than unstuffed birds.

broiling poultry

Remove skin from poultry, if desired. Rinse and pat dry with paper towels. If desired, sprinkle with salt and pepper.

Remove the broiler pan and preheat the broiler for 5 to 10 minutes. Arrange the poultry on the unheated rack of the broiler pan with the bone side up. If desired, brush with cooking oil. Place the pan under the broiler so the surface of the poultry is 4 to 5 inches from the heat. (Chicken and Cornish game hen halves should be 5 to 6 inches from the heat.) Turn the pieces over when browned on one side, usually after half of the broiling time. Chicken halves and meaty pieces should be turned after 20 minutes. Brush again with oil. The poultry is done when the meat is no longer pink and the juices run clear. Brush with a sauce the last 5 minutes of cooking, if desired.

Type of Bird	Weight	Broiling Time
Chicken, broiler-fryer, half	1¼ to 1½ pounds	28 to 32 minutes
Chicken breast, skinned and boned	4 to 5 ounces	12 to 15 minutes
Chicken breast halves, thighs, and drumsticks	2 to 2½ pounds total	25 to 35 minutes
Chicken kabobs (boneless breast, cut into 2 x ½-inch strips and threaded loosely onto skewers)	1 pound	8 to 10 minutes
Cornish game hen half	½ to ¾ pound	30 to 40 minutes
Turkey breast steak or slice	2 ounces	6 to 8 minutes
Turkey breast tenderloin steak	4 to 6 ounces	8 to 10 minutes
Turkey patties (ground raw turkey)	¾ inch thick	10 to 12 minutes

direct-grilling poultry

Remove the skin from the poultry, if desired. Rinse poultry and pat dry with paper towels. Test for desired temperature of the coals. Place poultry on the grill rack, bone side up, directly over the preheated coals. (For ground turkey patties, use a grill basket.) Grill, uncovered, for the time given or till tender and no longer pink. (Note: White meat will cook slightly faster.) Turn poultry over after half of the grilling time. During last 10 minutes, brush often with a sauce, if desired.

Type of Bird	Weight/Size	Coal Temperature	Direct-Grilling Time
Chicken, broiler-fryer, half	1¼ to 1½ pounds	Medium	40 to 50 minutes
Chicken breast, skinned and boned	4 to 5 ounces	Medium-hot	15 to 18 minutes
Chicken breast halves, thighs, and drumsticks	2 to 2½ pounds total	Medium	35 to 45 minutes
Chicken kabobs (boneless breasts, cut into 2 x ½-inch strips and threaded loosely onto skewers)	1 pound	Medium-hot	8 to 10 minutes
Cornish game hen half	½ to ¾ pound	Medium-hot	45 to 50 minutes
Turkey breast tenderloin steak	4 to 6 ounces	Medium	12 to 15 minutes
Turkey drumstick	½ to 1½ pounds	Medium	¾ to 1¼ hours
Turkey hindquarter	2 to 4 pounds	Medium	1¼ to 1½ hours
Turkey patties (ground raw turkey)	¾ inch thick	Medium-hot	15 to 18 minutes
Turkey thigh	1 to 1½ pounds	Medium	50 to 60 minutes

indirect-grilling poultry

In a grill with a cover arrange medium-hot coals around a drip pan, then test for medium heat above the pan. Place unstuffed poultry, breast side up, on the grill rack directly over the drip pan, not over the coals. Lower the grill hood. Grill for the time given or till done, adding coals as necessary. (Note: Birds vary in size, shape, and tenderness. Use these times as general guides.)

To test for doneness, cut into the thickest part of the meat near a bone; juices should run clear and meat should not be pink. Or, grasp the end of the drumstick with a paper towel. It should move up and down and twist easily in the socket. For turkeys and larger chickens, insert a meat thermometer into the center of the inside thigh muscle, not touching bone; thermometer should register 180° to 185°. In a whole or half turkey breast, thermometer should register 170°.

Type of Bird	Weight	Indriect-Grilling Time
Chicken, whole*	2½ to 3 pounds	1 to 1¼ hours
	3½ to 4 pounds	1¼ to 1¾ hours
	4½ to 5 pounds	1¾ to 2 hours
	5 to 6 pounds	2 to 2½ hours
Cornish game hen	1 to 1½ pounds	1 to 1¼ hours
Pheasant	2 to 3 pounds	1 to 1½ hours
Quail	4 to 6 ounces	about ½ hour
Squab	12 to 14 ounces	¾ to 1 hour
Turkey, unstuffed	6 to 8 pounds	1¾ to 2¼ hours
	8 to 12 pounds	2½ to 3½ hours
	12 to 16 pounds	3 to 4 hours
Turkey, boneless, whole	2½ to 3½ pounds	1¾ to 2¼ hours
	4 to 6 pounds	2½ to 3½ hours
Turkey breast, whole	4 to 6 pounds	1¾ to 2¼ hours
	6 to 8 pounds	2½ to 3½ hours

*Choose broiler-fryer or roasting chickens.

o - q

r - s

chicken parts

metric cooking hints

By making a few conversions, cooks in Australia, Canada, and the United Kingdom can use the recipes in Better Homes and Gardens® *Minutes to Mealtime Chicken and Turkey Recipes* with confidence. The charts on this page provide a guide for converting measurements from the U.S. customary system, which is used throughout this book, to the imperial and metric systems. There also is a conversion table for oven temperatures to accommodate the differences in oven calibrations.

Volume and Weight: Americans traditionally use cup measures for liquid and solid ingredients. The chart (top right) shows the approximate imperial and metric equivalents. If you are accustomed to weighing solid ingredients, here are some helpful approximate equivalents.

■ 1 cup butter, caster sugar, or rice = 8 ounces = about 250 grams

■ 1 cup flour = 4 ounces = about 125 grams

■ 1 cup icing sugar = 5 ounces = about 150 grams

Spoon measures are used for smaller amounts of ingredients although the size of the tablespoon varies slightly among countries. However, for practical purposes and for recipes in this book, a straight substitution is all that's necessary.

Measurements made using cups or spoons should always be level, unless stated otherwise.

Product Differences: Most of the ingredients called for in the recipes in this book are available in English-speaking countries. However, some are known by different names. Here are some common American ingredients and their possible counterparts:

■ Sugar is granulated or caster sugar.

■ Powdered sugar is icing sugar.

■ All-purpose flour is plain household flour or white flour. When self-rising flour is used in place of all-purpose flour in a recipe that calls for leavening, omit the leavening agent (baking soda or baking powder) and salt.

■ Light corn syrup is golden syrup.

■ Cornstarch is cornflour.

■ Baking soda is bicarbonate of soda.

■ Vanilla is vanilla essence.

useful equivalents

⅛ teaspoon = 0.5 ml	⅔ cup = 5 fluid ounces = 150 ml
¼ teaspoon = 1 ml	¾ cup = 6 fluid ounces = 175 ml
½ teaspoon = 2 ml	1 cup = 8 fluid ounces = 250 ml
1 teaspoon = 5 ml	2 cups = 1 pint
¼ cup = 2 fluid ounces = 50 ml	2 pints = 1 litre
⅓ cup = 3 fluid ounces = 75 ml	½ inch =1 centimetre
½ cup = 4 fluid ounces = 125 ml	1 inch = 2 centimetres

baking pan sizes

American	Metric
8x1½-inch round baking pan	20x4-centimetre sandwich or cake tin
9x1½-inch round baking pan	23x3.5-centimetre sandwich or cake tin
11x7x1½-inch baking pan	28x18x4-centimetre baking pan
13x9x2-inch baking pan	32.5x23x5-centimetre baking pan
2-quart rectangular baking dish	30x19x5-centimetre baking pan
15x10x2-inch baking pan	38x25.5x2.5-centimetre baking pan (Swiss roll tin)
9-inch pie plate	22x4- or 23x4-centimetre pie plate
7- or 8-inch springform pan	18- or 20-centimetre springform or loose-bottom cake tin
9x5x3-inch loaf pan	23x13x6-centimetre or 2-pound narrow loaf pan or paté tin
1½-quart casserole	1.5-litre casserole
2-quart casserole	2-litre casserole

oven temperature equivalents

Farenheit Setting	Celsius Setting*	Gas Setting
300°F	150°C	Gas Mark 2
325°F	160°C	Gas Mark 3
350°F	180°C	Gas Mark 4
375°F	190°C	Gas Mark 5
400°F	200°C	Gas Mark 6
425°F	220°C	Gas Mark 7
450°F	230°C	Gas Mark 8
Broil		Grill

Electric and gas ovens may be calibrated using Celsius. However, increase the Celsius setting 10 to 20 degrees when cooking above 160°C with an electric oven. For convection or forced-air ovens (gas or electric), lower the temperature setting 10°C when cooking at all heat levels.